Silent war

Manchester University Press

Melland Schill Studies in International Law

General editors *Iain Scobbie and Jean D'Aspremont*

Founded as a memorial to Edward Melland Schill, a promising scholar killed during the First World War, the Melland Schill Lectures (1961–74) were established by the University of Manchester following a bequest by Edward's sister, Olive B. Schill, to promote the understanding of international law and implicitly lessen the possibilities for future conflict. Dedicated to promoting women's employment rights and access to education, Olive's work is commemorated in both the Melland Schill series and the Women in International Law Network at the University of Manchester.

The Melland Schill lecture series featured a distinguished series of speakers on a range of controversial topics, including Quincy Wright on the role of international law in the elimination of war, Judge Sir Robert Jennings on the acquisition of territory, and Sir Ian Sinclair on the Vienna Convention on the Law of Treaties.

In the 1970s, Gillian White, the first woman appointed as a Professor of Law in mainland Britain, transformed the lectures into a monograph series, published by Manchester University Press. Many of the works previously published under the name 'Melland Schill monographs' have become standard references in the field, including: A.P.V. Rogers' *Law on the battlefield*, which is currently in its third edition, and Hilary Charlesworth and Christine Chinkin's *The boundaries of international law*, which offered the first book-length treatment of the application of feminist theories to international law.

Closely linked to the Melland Schill Classics and Melland Schill Perspectives series, Melland Schill Studies in International Law has become a home for exceptional academic work from around the world.

To buy or to find out more about the books currently available in this series, please go to: https://manchesteruniversitypress.co.uk/series/melland-schill-studies-in-international-law/

Silent war

Remote warfare and the politics of silence

Elisabeth Schweiger

MANCHESTER UNIVERSITY PRESS

Published by Manchester University Press
Oxford Road, Manchester, M13 9PL

www.manchesteruniversitypress.co.uk

British Library Cataloguing-in-Publication Data
A catalogue record for this book is available from the British Library

ISBN 978 1 5261 6953 2 hardback

First published 2026

Typeset
by Cheshire Typesetting Ltd, Cuddington, Cheshire

To my daughter
who arrived as I wrote the second chapter,
with all my love.

Silence can be a plan
rigorously executed
the blueprint to a life
It is a presence
it has a history a form
Do not confuse it
with any kind of absence

Adrienne Rich, "Cartographies of Silence"

Contents

Acknowledgements

Olivia Rutazibwa once said that "there is no better way of desilencing each other than through collaboration in trust".[1] This means to me a form of working together, towards the same purpose and through a process that relies on community and communality. Writing is such a process.

I am grateful to my fellow travellers Susan Forde, Barbara Gruber, Thomas Martin, Alice Martini, Nina Perkowski, Renske Vos and Luba Zatsepina. Thank you for your friendship and for reminding me of the strength found in collaboration. To Birgit Poopuu, Elena Simon and Fazal Wahab for teaching me what it means to care for the world academically and to speak up with courage.

I am grateful to Sara de Jong, who has opened worlds of wisdom to me and shown me that there are always more questions to be asked. And to Xavier Guillaume, whose intellect and generosity have supported me even in moments of doubt. Thank you for always having my back.

To Sophia Dingli, Oliver Kearns and Aoife O'Leary McNeice for your careful reading of my drafts, your thoughtful challenges and intellectual companionship that has enriched this book. And to Jaap de Wilde, Harriet Gray, Jef Huysmans, Anna Leander, Nick Ritchie and Andrea Schapper for your insights and support.

To my students at the University of Stirling, whose bright questions remind me that international laws and political structures must respond to lived experiences. And to the editors at Manchester University Press, Humairaa Dudhwala and Siobhán Poole, who have patiently helped this book take shape.

I am grateful beyond words to my partner, my family and friends, whose love has been a source of inspiration and whose presence has taught me to relate to the beauty and vulnerability of our condition as living creatures. As Judith Butler suggests, it is through acknowledging our shared vulnerability that "the possibility of making different kinds of ties emerges".[2]

To all those who dare to speak up when heavy silence surrounds them, who raise questions and raise chants and music to challenge injustice disguised as truth. Even if our paths never cross, I hope these pages honour a communal purpose of knowing and resisting.

Notes

1 Olivia Rutazibwa, "The Decolonization of Our Storytelling," speech delivered at the International Baccalaureate (IB) Peterson Academic Symposium in The Hague, Netherlands, July 5–6, 2012, https://oliviarutazibwa.wordpress.com/2012/07/05/the-decolonization-of-our-storytelling/?utm_source=chatgpt.com (accessed October 30, 2025).

2 Judith Butler, *Precarious Life: The Powers of Mourning and Violence* (Verso, 2004), 25.

Introduction: Silent war

On February 2, 2020, the United States carried out an air strike in Jilib, Somalia, resulting in the death of 18-year-old Nurto Kusow Oma and injuring her two younger sisters and grandmother.[1] The incident went unreported by major Western media outlets.[2] United States Africa Command (USAFRICOM) claimed in a press release following the attack that "initial assessment concluded the airstrike killed one (1) terrorist."[3] In the following weeks, Somali news sources, social media and NGO (non-governmental organisation) coverage of the strike provided growing evidence that the strike had caused civilian harm.[4] This was eventually acknowledged by USAFRICOM itself in its third quarterly civilian casualty report[5] – still without coverage by Western media. As UN Special Rapporteur Callamard has argued, "the vast majority of targeted killings by drones are subjected to little public scrutiny at either national or international levels".[6]

This book analyses the hidden machinations of silence in sustaining imperial violence. While scholarly and public attention has often centred on overt propaganda and the explicit legal and political justifications for the use of force, this book argues that asymmetrical military force is equally sustained by a parallel architecture of silences and omissions. The book traces the multifaceted functions of silence – encompassing acquiescence, secrecy, neglect and the tacit power of presuppositions – in discourses on drone warfare and colonial police bombing. Ultimately, the book argues that silence is not merely an absence but a constitutive force within global power relations which enables imperial violence.

Silences by dominant actors, who are seen to withhold information or refuse to speak, often become the subject of intense debate. I call them *loud silences* because they are noticed, explicitly acknowledged and interpreted. In international law, for instance, silence by states can work as acquiescence that supports the formation of new customary international law.[7] Silence has been invoked as tacit consent to counterterrorism practices because the "muted reaction [...] in regard to the U.S. drone campaign"[8] confirms that "most other states seem to be willing to acquiesce in this reinterpretation of the customary law of self-defense".[9] While the expansion of parameters for the use of force has been contested in international law scholarship,[10] silence-as-acquiescence has played an important role in legitimising and normalising controversial military practices. Linking to critical scholarship in international law,[11] this book examines how acquiescence in international law operates within broader discursive structures that have a long colonial history.

Far from being a mere absence, silences play an important role in enabling military violence, such as drone warfare. Indeed, drone warfare and similar counterinsurgency practices have come to be characterised through loud silences as "secret, unaccountable, borderless wars".[12] Secrecy shields powerful actors from legal and political accountability because "the process for determining who is targeted by drones, and why, is decided by a small group of government officials who are not accountable".[13] Secrecy not only excludes the wider public but also actively constructs a subject position of exclusion – demarcating who is, and is not, privy to knowledge.[14] For those excluded from the inner circles of the targeting regime – ranging from citizens, journalists and NGOs to parliamentarians and state officials – it becomes difficult to understand and speak about the war.

Secrecy thus cultivates a zone of uncertainty about the knowability of violence, thereby destabilising the foundations upon which critique or dissent might otherwise be articulated. Knowledge about imperial violence becomes framed as the prerogative of powerful state actors, while those on the outside remain unable to fully comprehend or speak about it. At the same time, silence on the part of these "outsiders" is often interpreted not as exclusion but as acquiescence – as a lack of objections and tacit consent to such violence. Not speaking here disappoints speech expectations, such as the "need to challenge the underpinning legal interpretation of the US global war on terror in order to prevent this approach from becoming a common practice among states".[15]

This book analyses the productive role of silences in constructing and enabling "opaque, ambiguous and effectively unaccountable"[16] military practices. This is not to suggest that the political functions of silence are confined to such practices, nor that they are a phenomenon exclusive to contemporary global politics. Silence has a long history of enabling violence and oppression. For example, in the early twentieth century, British and other European colonial states employed aeroplanes for the violent oppression of uprisings in mandates and colonies in so-called "police bombing" attacks.[17] The practice was also understood as part of a secret policy and sustained through hidden logics of silence. The rationale for "police bombing" operations was rooted in implicit, orientalist portrayals, where bombing campaigns were justified as a way "of dealing with outlying districts".[18] As this book will show, there was minimal public debate of police bombing in both parliamentary and media discourses. Similar to contemporary discourses, key aspects, such as the impact of bombing campaigns on colonised populations, were consistently ignored or relegated to the background.

The importance of silence in enabling military violence is often overlooked in studies of war, which tend to focus on overt propaganda, such as patriotic speeches made by state officials, the use of national symbols or media narratives that demonise the "enemy". However, beneath the surface of overt war propaganda lies an important, often ignored, dimension of silences and omissions. The book thus contributes to scholarship in critical military studies and security studies[19] by revealing the role of silences in legitimising warfare. In the context of imperial power relations, this undercurrent of silence plays a fundamental role in enabling violence. It operates not only through top-down censorship and state control of information but also through what I term *banal silencings* – the everyday, often unnoticed, decisions of not speaking and ignoring. They link to a wider cultural condition of what Stoler refers to as "colonial aphasia" – a disabling silence that prevents the articulation of colonial violence.[20]

This is not to say that there is absolute silence. Police bombing was the subject of debate in the 1920s and 1930s, and drone warfare has sparked intense discussion in some forums, such as academic circles or NGO reporting. Various aspects of bombing campaigns, including the new technology, processes of target selection and the lack of transparency, have been critically examined. Yet, these debates rest upon a bedrock of what I call *deep silences* – unspoken assumptions, presuppositions, backgrounded aspects and excluded irrelevances. For example, underneath the discussion that "innocents" should be spared is the self-evident assumption that "bad guys" should be targeted. Silences exist within, alongside and underneath a range of utterances and articulations about imperial warfare.

The book thus offers a new conceptualisation of silence which is empirically grounded within international politics and international law. Rather than framing silence through a single function – such as exclusion, secrecy or acquiescence – this book explores the interwoven political dynamics of silence. It examines how these functions of silence depend on dominant speech expectations and assumptions. For example, what we perceive as "secrecy" is contingent upon how layers of omissions, revelations and delays are interpreted and structured. Normative speech expectations are directed at specific – often powerful – actors who are supposed to speak and are thus reaffirmed as primary epistemic authorities. Such expectations reflect what I term *regimes of (not) listening* that determine which voices – and silences – are acknowledged, and which are ignored.

While this book explores the hidden machinations of silence in enabling imperial violence and oppression, it does not suggest that silence, in and of itself, is the root of the problem, nor that an increase in speech and transparency would necessarily dismantle these structures of violence. Indeed, the liberal, logocentric impulse toward more speech and transparency can, paradoxically, reproduce the very silences that are most integral to silent wars. For example, opposing a lack of protest can unintentionally call acquiescence into being. Silence is not just the opposite of speech; rather, it is entangled with speech, constructed in relation to utterances and gaining functions with and through text. Whether silence is perceived at all, and how it is interpreted, depends on prevailing *regimes of (not) listening*, on who is expected to speak, about what topics, in what style and through which channels.

When silence is observed and called out, this can in turn reveal the assumptions and expectations of speech held within a discursive community. For example, when international law scholars invoke the silence of states in response to counterterrorism measures to argue that "the international community seems to have become more tolerant of breaches of Article 2(4)",[21] this interpretation depends on entrenched regimes of (not) listening. It presupposes specific speakers, particular forms of speech and specific sites where speech is expected (e.g. the UN Security Council). While international lawyers may expand their listening, for instance by including press releases by states or newspaper coverage of state practice, these sources, too, are often filtered through a Western lens, due to the methodological whiteness of international law.[22] Such selective regimes of (not) listening matter because silences may be invoked loudly even when there is in fact no silence. Practices such as "targeted killing" have, in numerous instances, been contested, yet those objections have been rendered inaudible by dominant interpretive frames.[23]

Silences are embedded within material and ideational structures that determine which silences become loud and which silences are normalised, which voices are heard and what is considered ir/relevant. For example, media coverage of armed conflict relies predominantly on state sources, often excluding other sources and points of view. This reliance is driven by ideational assumptions that official state sources are more trustworthy than alternative sources – even though states often misreport the casualties of military violence.[24] It also depends on material structures. Media organisations operate within profit-driven market structures and are under pressure to save investigative expense and avoid libel claims, which draws them to state sources and easily accessible news bites.[25] Silence is thus embedded within a global economy, shaped by racial capitalism and its institutionalised patterns of inclusion and exclusion that are reflected in prevalent regimes of (not) listening. In this context, silence on death and suffering is not accidental but rooted in wider systems of structural violence – what Athanasiou describes as the "chronic necropolitical economies"[26] of racial capitalism where slow processes of disenfranchisement, deprivation of resources, extraction and militarisation are central to how certain bodies and populations are produced and rendered vulnerable.[27]

Such *deep silences*, as I term them, are often not noticed because they fall outside of expected discursive norms. Yet, this does not mean that they lack communicative power. On the contrary, deep silences can have powerful discursive effects precisely because they reinforce what is deemed relevant or irrelevant. The exclusion of certain voices or topics can send a stronger signal than any explicit demotion that they *are to be* irrelevant. Thus, when the suffering and death of colonial "others" is erased in legal and political discourses about drone warfare, it not only reflects existing norms of what is to be considered irrelevant but actively reinforces these norms. When British parliamentary debates foreground concerns about the psychological toll of drone warfare on drone pilots, while ignoring the impact on victims of attacks, they implicitly communicate who is valued and "who is disposable".[28] This selective attention contributes to a distorted and sanitised understanding of military violence – one in which its devastating effects are rendered inaudible.

In contrast to prevailing approaches in the expanding field of silence studies,[29] I contend that silences which are neither acknowledged nor imbued with specific expressive meaning in discourses can nonetheless function communicatively and exert significant discursive influence. Systematic neglect can reinforce what is to be seen as irrelevant while implicit assumptions convey notions of what is to be taken for granted and beyond debate. Precisely because these notions are implied rather than explicitly stated, they are difficult to challenge.[30] For instance, discourses in the 1920s and 1930s frequently presupposed the necessity of killing so-called "rebels" and the imperative of controlling mandates and colonies. Rather than explicitly stating this imperative, it was mainly invoked implicitly. Bombing was justified on the grounds that tribal populations had been warned that "if they do not behave themselves aircraft will take action against them".[31] This presupposed that the colonial "other" had to "behave" according to British standards, implicitly positioning British civilisational norms as unquestionably superior, while casting violence and colonial control as self-evidently necessary. The resulting discourse reinforced these ideas as foundational and taken for granted, rendering them immune to scrutiny precisely because they remained unspoken.

Deep silences can be difficult to perceive because they reaffirm the underlying assumptions and expectations embedded within entrenched regimes of (not) listening. As such, they are frequently dismissed and ignored. However, disregarding these silences – despite the methodological convenience of doing so – ultimately sustains a normative status-quo orientation that privileges what is already audible, noted and acknowledged. As Rutazibwa has powerfully argued, embracing an anti-colonial ethos requires us to denaturalise the colonial omissions and historical amnesia that permeate everyday life, including seemingly innocuous symbols such as street and place names. The persistence of violence in the present, she suggests, is often concealed there, "hidden in the banality of plain sight".[32] Prevailing regimes of (not) listening are thus shaped by the erasures produced by coloniality and other intersecting structures of power – structures that have systematically drowned out alternative epistemologies and masked both the historical and ongoing manifestations of imperial violence.

Kontrapunkt

In his seminal work *Orientalism*, written prior to the advent of the War on Terror, Edward Said observed that "the parallel between European and American imperial designs on the Orient (Near and Far) is obvious".[33] Scholars have similarly drawn connections between early twentieth-century police bombing and contemporary drone warfare, particularly with respect to the geographic areas targeted and the representational logics that underpin them.[34] The US and its allies – especially through the Five Eyes intelligence network – have committed armed drone attacks both within and beyond declared conflict zones in locations such as Afghanistan, Pakistan, Iraq, Yemen and Somalia. These regions substantially overlap with those subjected to British aerial bombing in the first decades of the twentieth century, including present-day Iraq, the North-West Frontier of British India (now Afghanistan and Pakistan) and Aden (modern-day Yemen).[35] In both historical and contemporary contexts, aerial violence has been discursively framed as offering unprecedented strategic and military advantages: it is depicted as cost-effective, "riskless" for Western military personnel and capable of enabling panoptic surveillance over territories imagined as unruly, opaque and resistant to governance. New technology has played a central role in these narratives, with both bombing aeroplanes and drones construed as instruments of awe and terror designed to repress insurgencies and maintain military control.[36] Tracing these continuities – across material practices as well as the discourses and imaginaries entangled with them – demonstrates how not only the colony but also the Western imperial core "were deeply altered by the colonial process".[37]

This book centres on drone warfare and colonial police bombing, as these two instances of military violence provide a valuable lens through which to examine the role of silence in imperial practices of military violence. This dual focus is particularly important, given that "targeted killing" strikes with armed drones are often framed as unprecedented, rooted in an assumption of technological and strategic novelty.[38] Alluding to the continuities in presentations of aerial warfare, I use the concept *imperial violence* in the book for both contemporary and historical uses of violence that are embedded within imperial structures of oppression. This builds on Ania Loomba's definition of imperialism as processes of domination that originate in the metropolis and lead to control of the colonial periphery.[39] I use the term *colonialism* to denote the historical time period of direct territorial occupation and administrative control by European powers.

The conceptual framing of *imperial violence* is not intended as a simplistic equivalence between British police bombing and US/Western practices of domination, such as drone warfare. Substantial differences exist, not only in tactics and technologies but also in the frameworks through which these practices are grasped. As I will demonstrate, ethical, legal and political justifications of both practices differed considerably. For example, justifications of police bombing tended to be articulated through the rule of sparing innocent bystanders by giving inhabitants prior warning of strikes. In contrast, drone strikes are more frequently legitimised through discourses of precision bombing and an emphasis of adherence to procedures of international humanitarian law. I do not mean to suggest that it would be helpful to conflate the distinctive context, cultural grammar and implications of both practices. Yet, as Loomba has argued, imperial methods, practices, ideas and discourses have varied over time, locality and cultural positions even while "they produced comparable (and sometimes uncannily similar) relations of inequity and domination the world over".[40]

This book does not primarily focus on the practice of police bombing or drone warfare in their own right. Rather, I explore the role that silences have played in legitimising both practices, and what this reveals about the broader, political functions of silence in shaping and facilitating military violence and oppression. The analysis of colonial police bombing discourses is employed here as a *Kontrapunkt* – a counterpoint – that sharpens our understanding of silence in contemporary security narratives. Engaging with colonial discourses allows us to attune to the deep, often obscured silences that undergird, permeate and entangle present-day discussions of warfare. For example, the racialised registers through which the killing of "rebels" was justified in colonial discourses were audibly implied and may, due to historical distance, appear less naturalised today than the self-evident assumptions underpinning the perceived legitimacy of killing "terrorists" in the twenty-first century. By using police bombing as a *Kontrapunkt*, this study seeks to refine our sensitivity to the echoes of deep silences in current discourses, the tacit assumptions, exclusions and silencings that provide the epistemic and normative foundations for military violence.

Both colonial-era police bombing and contemporary drone warfare have frequently been justified as benign, police-like forms of violence conducted with advanced and ostensibly precise technologies. Critical voices, both historically and in the present, have consequently drawn attention to the inherent brutality, asymmetrical distance and affective impact – what might be called the *awe-fulness* – of such campaigns. Yet, presenting such practices as exceptional risks obscuring the broader, structural embedding of violence within liberal political orders. As Howell argues, "martial relations inhere in liberal politics as they are enacted on those who are racialized, Indigenous, disabled, queer or otherwise constituted as a threat to civil order".[41] The everyday operation of coloniality, and its intersections with other structures of domination such as patriarchy and class, routinely enact and legitimise violence. In this context, focusing analytical attention solely on seemingly exceptional acts – such as aerial bombing – may, as Manchanda cautions, "actually help in escalating and not merely obscuring the violence faced by subjects outside the ambit of militarization thus conceived".[42]

However, as I demonstrate in this book, even discussions around those seemingly exceptional and attention-seeking acts of violence are permeated with silences. This book's focus on "drone warfare" and "police bombing" is therefore not intended to suggest that these practices represent radical departures from liberal norms and practices – even if that presumption might be a reason why they have attracted attention. Rather, it is to highlight that even attention to such acts remains constrained by prevailing regimes of (not) listening, constituted through everyday political practices of omission, erasure, backgrounding and neglect. These silences are not marginal but central to the production and reproduction of imperial violence.

At a practical, methodological level, the focus on drone warfare and police bombing allows for the integration of a diverse array of sources spanning multiple domains. For instance, British parliamentary discussions on drone warfare cover debates on NATO, Middle Eastern security, data protection, defence policy and the 2021 Overseas Operations Act. Drone warfare features prominently across various discursive arenas, including mainstream media, popular culture, parliamentary discourses, NGO reporting and deliberations within international bodies such as the UN Human Rights Council or the UN Security Council. Investigating utterances and silences across these domains – and tracing their development over time – enables the identification of wider patterns through which silence facilitates violence and oppression. However, this approach necessarily entails some trade-offs. It risks glossing over specific contextual details, linguistic nuances and disciplinary distinctions. The analysis offered in this book therefore entails a degree of abstraction and generalisation, undertaken in order to map the broader discursive architecture of silence within imperial narratives of military violence.

Although the discourses examined in this study draw from a wide range of sources, they largely emerge from dominant, white, Western discursive arenas. Focusing on such platforms – and even employing the term "Western" to categorise them – carries the risk of reconstituting these actors and epistemologies as central nodes of power, thereby amplifying the prominence of already dominant voices. As Mignolo contends, there is a necessity of "shrinking the wide spectrum of Western overconfidence to its own size".[43] By focusing on silence within these dominant discourses, this book seeks to foreground what remains unheard, who is rendered inaudible and which knowledges are dismissed as irrelevant within discourses often misrepresented as universal. In critically investigating the assumptions and expectations through which silences are produced and reproduced, I follow Spivak's suggestion of inquiring into why the West cannot – or will not – listen.[44] Thus, this engagement with hegemonic regimes of (not) listening is conceived not as a naïve reproduction of power but as a critical act of reconstitution. Following Mignolo, the aim is to transform "the assumptions and presuppositions – not just the contents – that currently validate Western political economy, political theory, and the opinions transmitted by the corporate media to the public at large".[45]

In mapping both loud and deep silences within global power structures and investigating their political and legal function in sustaining violence and oppression, I do not intend to suggest that this is a linear story of domination. Silences themselves are inherently fragmented, ambiguous and entangled with speech, text and context. They are, moreover, fundamentally predicated on regimes of (not) listening and because of that can reveal the assumptions and expectations through which we hear. It is in this relational dynamic that I locate the critical potential of silence: while not everyone can – or is permitted to – speak, we are all, inevitably, listeners. As I demonstrate in Chapter 6, resistance to imperial warfare often emerges through creative practices of de-silencing, reinterpreting loud silences, disrupting and subverting linguistic registers and transforming speech expectations. Such acts of listening otherwise constitute crucial interventions in hegemonic discourses and may reconfigure the terms through which violence is rendered intelligible.

Structure of the book

In order to engage with the critical potential of silence, the book develops a new conceptual framework for understanding silence, situating silence as embedded within regimes of (not) listening. Rather than treating silence as the mere antithesis of speech, Chapter 1 introduces the conceptualisation of silence as constituted through messy layers of omissions, disclosures, delays and backgrounding. These layers are entangled with text and fundamentally dependent on listening practices. The very perception of silence, as well as its interpretation, hinges on what is (not) attended to, which can vary considerably depending on the discursive community. This also means that the ways in which silence is invoked can illuminate the underlying assumptions and expectations within specific discursive communities.

I argue that an analysis of silence calls for sustained attention to the power relations and material capabilities that shape who is heard, what is excluded and how meaning is produced across professional and discursive fields, such as media, academia or policy. What I refer to as the *global economy of silence* captures how silence circulates and acquires value within these interlocking material and ideational structures. Capitalist market relations, coloniality and other, intersecting power structures shape the processes through which silence is constructed and gains meaning in discourses on military violence. Importantly, this process is neither homogeneous nor solely the result of deliberate censorship or intentional suppression. Rather, silences are continually produced and sustained through countless everyday acts of not speaking and not listening – acts that are deeply embedded in discursive hegemonies and practices of banal silencing.

To aid in the analysis, the book introduces the concepts of *loud* and *deep silences*, not as rigid categories but as heuristic devices. Loud silences refer to silences which are acknowledged and made meaningful within a given discourse, such as secrecy, diplomacy or tacit consent. Their very existence, their recognition, interpretation and framing – such as being read as lack of protest and acquiescence – are shaped by prevailing regimes of (not) listening. Deep silences remain unrecognised because there are no speech expectations, because certain voices or topics are deemed utterly irrelevant, unintelligible or unworthy of attention. Yet these deep silences are not inert; they perform critical communicative functions by reinforcing what is to be considered irrelevant, inconsequential, outside the bounds of legitimate discourse, or to be taken for granted and beyond debate.

Chapter 2 explores the deep silences constituted by unspoken assumptions and presuppositions within discourses of imperial warfare. Drawing on work in linguistics and philosophy of language, I investigate the discursive function of presuppositions and implications to invoke points as self-evident and beyond debate. Through an analysis of British parliamentary debates, press coverage and popular cultural representations of police bombing from the 1910s to the 1930s, I trace how discussions around the efficiency and ethics of aerial policing were underpinned by an unchallenged assumption: that "guilty" tribes could and should be subjected to lethal force. These debates were saturated with implicit, orientalist logics of the peoples and areas "controlled" by British military force.

The chapter argues that these historical assumptions have important synergies with contemporary discourses on drone warfare. Today, similar presuppositions underpin the legitimisation of "targeted killing". The notion that "terrorists" should be killed is rarely explicitly stated or contested and is instead presented as a taken-for-granted assumption which is entangled in orientalist imaginaries of the "other" and the implied virtue of the Western "self". It is important that these notions are invoked through implicit assumptions, rather than explicit arguments, embedding them into the background of discourses and rendering them more difficult to contest. The very unspoken-ness of these assumptions lends them notions of self-evidence. They are invoked as beyond debate, as fundamental, common-sense understandings of the world which do not need to be said out loud.

While this analysis draws attention to historical continuities between deep silences in discourses on police bombing and drone warfare, it also recognises important differences. There are significant changes regarding the rules for how bombing is to be conducted "humanely". In the context of police bombing practices, the morality of bombing was claimed through advance warning of bombing raids to allow tribes to "behave" and make amends, to surrender or to let the innocent retreat. In contrast, drone warfare emphasises precision and legality, claiming to spare innocent lives through advanced targeting technologies and legal procedures. Yet, beneath these differences lies a remarkably consistent bedrock of unspoken assumptions which is not questioned and serves to naturalise military violence as beyond fundamental debate.

Chapter 3 examines the broader patterns of deep silences that underpin discourses surrounding warfare and explores their entanglement with processes of exclusion and silencing. Through an analysis of British parliamentary and US congressional debates and media coverage, I examine how certain elements are systematically backgrounded, ignored or neglected. For instance, in US congressional debates, significant attention has been devoted to the hypothetical use of armed drones against American citizens within the US, while the routine deployment of armed drones abroad receives very little scrutiny. This asymmetry reveals and reinforces racialised registers of whose lives are grievable, who is considered killable and which spaces are deemed politically and morally significant. Such deep silences are not new, but are rooted in a longer history of colonial erasure. Similar patterns can be observed in interwar debates on police bombing which were predominantly framed through concerns about its implications for the "Empire at its heart", rather than its impact on colonised populations.

I conceptualise these absences as "silencings" – a term that moves beyond agency-centric notions of deliberate war propaganda or top-down state censorship. While undeniably embedded in power relations, these deep silences also emerge through routine, banal acts of not speaking and not listening. They reflect what Stoler calls colonial aphasia – a widespread inability or unwillingness to articulate or register colonial forms of suffering and violence.[46] Not necessarily linked into causal chains of state control, these deep silences are not mere absences but are actively performative. Not speaking about something can denote more effectively than any words could, that this issue is – and is to be considered – irrelevant and unimportant. By systematically omitting the chaos, terror, suffering and death created by Western military violence, these deep silences enable the sanitisation of warfare. Armed violence becomes reimagined as rational, controlled, riskless and clean – distanced from its material consequences. The predominant framing of warfare as a form of "high-tech policing" thus relies fundamentally on what is excluded, suppressed or rendered inaudible within dominant narratives.

Chapter 4 analyses the role of secrecy in shaping the conduct and perception of warfare. Secrecy is frequently framed as a protective mechanism that obstructs public oversight and impedes accountability for state-sanctioned violence. Within debates on drone warfare, it has been widely identified as a central barrier – hindering public understanding of military operations and limiting the ability to hold state actors accountable. This protective function of secrecy has tangible, material consequences, such as obstructing compensation or access to medical care for victims of so-called "targeting errors". More broadly, it legitimises military violence by concealing its most controversial or damaging aspects from public scrutiny. As a result, international lawyers and human rights advocates have often called on governments to reveal more information and ensure greater transparency.

However, this chapter argues that equating transparency with accountability, and assuming it to be a liberal panacea against violence and suffering, is overly reductive. Secrecy is not a static or monolithic entity; it is composed of multiple layers and operates through a dynamic interplay of concealment and disclosure. It manifests in a range of discursive practices, including denials, classified documents, selective revelations and delays. These practices do not merely obscure information but actively shape its meaning and function within power structures. Indeed, even as a wealth of data on drone strikes is produced by NGOs, activists, journalists and scholars, the US government and its transnational intelligence networks continue to be positioned as the primary, authoritative sources of knowledge whom we rely on to know about the war. Calls for greater disclosure therefore often reinforce the epistemic authority of the state, sustaining the very power relations that make secrecy effective. The expectation that the state should speak – should reveal – reproduces the idea that only certain actors are capable of producing legitimate knowledge about warfare.

The chapter contends that secrecy does not merely shield; it actively constitutes the war. It creates and performs hierarchies of access, producing relations of inclusion and exclusion that become part of the spectacle of state power. Opposing secrecy in order to find out about the war overlooks how secrecy defines and sustains the war. In a performative logic, secrecy endows those "in the know" with authority, while casting others as epistemically marginal – unable to speak with credibility or certainty. In the case of drone warfare, it creates a powerful core of top-secret agents on the one hand, and a broad periphery of actors on the other hand, who are framed as unable to know and speak about the war. At the same time, the absence of speech is not neutral; silence may be read as support, indifference or tacit approval. Thus, secrecy functions not only as a barrier to knowledge but also as a mechanism through which war is defined, legitimised and sustained.

Chapter 5 engages with the political work of silence-as-acquiescence, highlighting its role in legitimising military violence by presenting it as aligned with democratic support. The chapter traces the historical and theoretical underpinnings of acquiescence in liberal politics, from contract theories to the foundational narratives of the international system, where silence is taken as indicative of consent. This framing is grounded in liberal assumptions about individual agency which closely link "agency" with "voice". Within this framing silence becomes imbued with meaning that provides legitimacy to decision-making processes. This, however, overlooks the power relations that condition who is able to speak, be heard and be recognised as a political subject.

Like secrecy, acquiescence relies on a particular interpretation of silence and on processes of not listening through which silence itself comes to be perceived. These processes are steeped in power relations which have excluded actors from having a voice. For example, during colonialism, non-European societies were not recognised as sovereign states and were denied a legal voice to protest against invasion, expropriation or occupation. These asymmetries in the capacity to speak and be recognised continue to shape contemporary discourses around drone warfare where regimes of (not) listening determine who can be understood as a valid knowledge producer, where speech expectations are directed and which sources are – and are not – taken into account. The chapter deconstructs invocations of silence to drone warfare as acquiescence in international law. It critically interrogates the assumptions behind such interpretations, particularly where the structural conditions for speaking and being heard are absent. Even in the context of steep power relations that hinder the ability of actors to speak, silence is often construed as acquiescence, thereby providing a veneer of democratic legitimacy.

This dynamic is underwritten by liberal political imaginaries which presume individual agency and associate agency with voice. As a result, acquiescence can function to democratically legitimise political decisions that have not in fact been accepted by everyone or even by most. It offers the appearance of popular support for top-down decision making, even when that support is illusory, manufactured or presumed. By abstracting silence from its political and relational context, it becomes approached as a thing and conflated with a lack of protest – when protest was expected. Silence is thus often read as tacit consent to violent practices and has played important functions in legalising, legitimising and normalising imperial warfare, despite the asymmetric conditions for speaking and being heard.

Chapter 6 turns to the question of how silent warfare – a term that encapsulates the interlinking functions of silence in enabling imperial wars – might be resisted. Drawing on examples from grassroots movements, civil rights organisations, investigative journalism, activists and NGOs, the chapter explores creative strategies of resistance. This focus is crucial because more conventional forms of opposition – such as breaking silence, demanding official speech or representing the silenced – can inadvertently recreate the silences they seek to challenge. More speech does not necessarily translate into ethical or political transformation. For example, when public protest centres only on civilian casualties, it may implicitly reaffirm the assumption that terrorists can or even should be killed. Similarly, when demands are made for state actors to disclose information, these appeals risk reinforcing the epistemic authority of state actors as the primary arbiters of truth whom we rely on in order to know about the war. Likewise, representing silenced individuals risks further essentialising them and silencing their agency as passive victims that need to be spoken for.

Understanding silence as a layered and relational phenomenon – embedded within regimes of (not) listening – opens space for a more nuanced and transformative politics. It shows that there are fractures and ambiguities in hegemonic discursive constellations which are openings for subversion and reconfiguration. I suggest taking the critical potential of silence seriously, not only as an opportunity to more fundamentally question dominant discourses but also as a creative space to reimagine what it means to listen, and to whom. Resistance can take the form of consciously shifting out of dominant linguistic frames, making audible what is typically muffled by deep silences and reinterpreting silence itself beyond its taken-for-granted modalities. For example, silence on strikes by military and political elites might be reframed not as secrecy but as institutional incapacity and incompetence.

Importantly, silence is not solely a tool of domination, enabling oppression and violent relations of power but can also be mobilised in resistance. Moving beyond liberal paradigms of representation that conflate agency with voice, silence can be a powerful form of protest and subversion – particularly within discursive registers that limit, control and dictate ways of speaking. In such contexts, silence can function as a centrifugal force pushing back against imposed participation and legibility. Resisting audibility and participation, especially in the face of demands from dominant institutions, can itself be a form of dissent. This may include exit-based strategies, such as voting abstentions, political disengagement or "voting with the feet". The discursive effects of silence are also at play when silence is used in performative ways, for example in silent vigils. These forms of protest invoke layers of meaning and affective responses beyond the capacity of language. Quiet and non-verbal resistance challenge the boundaries of the sayable and invite alternative modes of understanding. Revealing and disrupting the limitations of dominant discursive regimes, they gesture towards a politics beyond what is currently sayable.

Notes

All URLs were last accessed on October 30, 2025.

1 Amnesty International, *Somalia: Zero Accountability as Civilian Deaths Mount from US Air Strikes*, 2020, www.amnesty.org/en/latest/news/2020/04/somalia-zero-accountability-as-civilian-deaths-mount-from-us-air-strikes/

2 Searching through LexisNexis for British newspaper reporting as well as the *New York Times*, *Fox News* and the *Washington Post* in the three weeks following the strikes through search terms of ‘Somalia’ AND ‘Drone’.

3 US Africa Command, “Press Release on Twitter, 2nd February 2020,” 2020, https://tinyurl.com/bd5kxjph

4 Airwars, Assessment USSOM274-C, February 2, 2020 https://airwars.org/civilian-casualties/ussom274-c-february-2-2020/

5 US Africa Command, “Civilian Casualty Assessment Quarterly Report; 3rd Quarter, FY2020,” 2020, www.africom.mil/what-we-do/airstrikes/civilian-harm-report/us-africa-command-civilian-casualty-assessment-quarterly-report-3rd-quarter-fy2020

6 UN Doc A/HRC/44/38, *Report of the Special Rapporteur on Extra-judicial, Summary or Arbitrary Executions*, 2020.

7 Paulina Starski, “Silence within the Process of Normative Change and Evolution of the Prohibition on the Use of Force: Normative Volatility and Legislative Responsibility,” *Journal on the Use of Force and International Law* 4, no. 1 (2017): 14–65; Maurice Mendelson, “The Subjective Element in Customary International Law,” *British Yearbook of International Law* 66, no. 1 (1996): 185; Sophia Kopela, “The Legal Value of Silence as State Conduct in the Jurisprudence of International Tribunals,” *Australian Year Book of International Law* 29 (2010): 87–134.

8 Avery Plaw and Joao Franco Reis, “The Contemporary Practice of Self-Defense: Evolving Toward the Use of Preemptive or Preventive Force?,” in *Preventive Force: Drones, Targeted Killing, and the Transformation of Contemporary Warfare*, ed. Kerstin Fisk and Jennifer M. Ramos (New York University Press, 2016), 243.

9 Plaw and Reis, “The Contemporary Practice of Self-Defense,” 246.

10 Mary Ellen O’Connell, “Remarks: The Resort to Drones Under International Law,” *Denver Journal of International Law & Policy* 39 (2010): 585; Antony Anghie, “The War on Terror and Iraq in Historical Perspective,” *Osgoode Hall Law Journal* 43 (2005): 45; Andrea

Birdsall, "Drone Warfare in Counterterrorism and Normative Change: US Policy and the Politics of International Law," *Global Society*, 2018, 1–22; Susanne Krasmann, "Targeted Killing and Its Law: On a Mutually Constitutive Relationship," *Leiden Journal of International Law* 25, no. 3 (2012): 665–82, https://doi.org/10.1017/S0922156512000337; Oliver Kessler and Wouter Werner, "Extrajudicial Killing as Risk Management," *Security Dialogue* 39, nos. 2–3 (2008): 289–308.

11 B. S. Chimni, "Customary International Law: A Third World Perspective," *American Journal of International Law* 112, no. 1 (2018): 1–46, https://doi.org/10.1017/ajil.2018.12; Martti Koskenniemi, "The Fate of Public International Law: Between Technique and Politics," *The Modern Law Review* 70, no. 1 (2007): 1–30; Antony Anghie, "Colonialism and the Birth of International Institutions: Sovereignty, Economy, and the Mandate System of the League of Nations," *New York University Journal of International Law and Politics* 34 (2001): 513; Anghie, "The War on Terror and Iraq in Historical Perspective"; Tanja Aalberts, "Rethinking the Principle of (Sovereign) Equality as a Standard of Civilisation," *Millennium-Journal of International Studies* 42, no. 3 (2014): 767–89; Makau W. Mutua, "Critical Race Theory and International Law: The View of an Insider-Outsider." *Villanova Law Review* 45, no. 5 (2000); Obiora Chinedu Okafor, "Newness, Imperialism, and International Legal Reform in Our Time: A TWAIL Perspective," *Osgoode Hall Law Journal* 43 (2005): 171.

12 ECCHR, *Litigating Drone Strikes: Challenging the Global Network of Remote Killing* (European Center for Constitutional and Human Rights, 2017), www.ecchr.eu/en/publication/litigating-drone-strikes-challenging-the-global-network-of-remote-killing/

13 WILPF, *The Humanitarian Impact of Drones* (Women's International League for Peace and Freedom, 2017), https://article36.org/wp-content/uploads/2017/10/Humanitarian-impact-of-drones.pdf

14 William Walters, "Everyday Secrecy: Oral History and the Social Life of a Top-Secret Weapons Research Establishment during the Cold War," *Security Dialogue* 51, no. 1 (2020): 60–76, https://doi.org/10.1177/0967010619887850

15 ECCHR, *Litigating Drone Strikes*.

16 APPG, *All Party Parliamentary Group on Drones Inquiry Report: The UK's Use of Armed Drones: Working with Partners*, 2018, www.bsg.ox.ac.uk/sites/default/files/2018-07/INH_PG_Drones_AllInOne_v25.pdf

17 Priya Satia, *Spies in Arabia: The Great War and the Cultural Foundations of Britain's Covert Empire in the Middle East* (Oxford University Press, 2008).

18 UK House of Commons, *HC Debates*, June 13, 1933, Vol. 279, Foreign Office, Cc29–146, 1933.

19 Victoria M. Basham, "Liberal Militarism as Insecurity, Desire and Ambivalence: Gender, Race and the Everyday Geopolitics of War," *Security Dialogue* 49, nos. 1–2 (2018): 32–43, https://doi.org/10.1177/0967010617744977; Afxentis Afxentiou, "A History of Drones: Moral(e) Bombing and State Terrorism," *Critical Studies on Terrorism* 11, no. 2 (2018); Alice Martini, "Making Women Terrorists into 'Jihadi Brides': An Analysis of Media Narratives on Women Joining ISIS," *Critical Studies on Terrorism* 11, no. 3 (2018): 458–77, https://doi.org/10.1080/17539153.2018.1448204; Morgane Desoutter, "War, Social Media and Gender: An Analysis of the Use of TikTok by Ukrainian Soldiers," *Critical Military Studies* 0, no. 0 (2025): 1–27, https://doi.org/10.1080/23337486.2025.2472100; Linda Åhäll, "The Dance of Militarisation: A Feminist Security Studies Take on 'the Political,'" *Critical Studies on Security* 4, no. 2 (2016): 154–68, https://doi.org/10.1080/21624887.2016.1153933

20 Ann Laura Stoler, "Colonial Archives and the Arts of Governance," *Archival Science* 2, no. 1 (2002): 87–109, https://doi.org/10.1007/BF02435632

21 Andrew Garwood-Gowers, "Israel's Airstrike on Syria's Al-Kibar Facility: A Test Case for the Doctrine of Pre-Emptive Self-Defence?," *Journal of Conflict and Security Law*, 16.2 (2011), 263–91, 289.

22 Chimni, "Customary International Law," 21; for the concept "methodological whiteness" see Gurminder K. Bhambra, "Brexit, Trump, and 'Methodological Whiteness': On the Misrecognition of Race and Class," *The British Journal of Sociology* 68, no. S1 (2017): S214–32, https://doi.org/10.1111/1468-4446.12317; see also Elisabeth Schweiger, "Listen Closely: What Silence Can Tell Us about Legal Knowledge Production," *London Review of International Law* 6, no. 3 (2018): 391–411.

23 Elisabeth Schweiger, "'Targeted Killing' and the Lack of Acquiescence," *Leiden Journal of International Law* 32, no. 4 (2019): 741–57, https://doi.org/10.1017/S0922156519000475; Schweiger, "Listen Closely."

24 Muhammad Idrees Ahmad, "The Magical Realism of Body Counts: How Media Credulity and Flawed Statistics Sustain a Controversial Policy," *Journalism* 17, no. 1 (2016): 18–34, https://doi.org/10.1177/1464884915593237

25 Edward S. Herman and Noam Chomsky, *Manufacturing Consent: The Political Economy of the Mass Media* (Pantheon Books, 2002), 21.

26 Athena Athanasiou, "(Im)Possible Breathing: On Courage and Criticality in the Ghostly Historical Present," *Redescriptions: Political Thought, Conceptual History and Feminist Theory* 23, no. 2 (2020): 94–95, https://doi.org/10.33134/rds.337
27 Athanasiou, "(Im)Possible Breathing," 94–95.
28 Achille Mbembe, "Necropolitics," *Public Culture* 15, no. 1 (2003): 27, https://doi.org/10.1215/08992363-15-1-11
29 Melani Schröter, *Silence and Concealment in Political Discourse*, Discourse Approaches to Politics, Society and Culture (DAPSAC), v. 48 (John Benjamins Publishing Company, 2013); Mónica Brito Vieira et al., "The Nature of Silence and Its Democratic Possibilities," *Contemporary Political Theory* 18, no. 3 (2019): 424–47, https://doi.org/10.1057/s41296-019-00330-2; Sophia Dingli and Thomas N. Cooke, eds, *Political Silence: Meanings, Functions and Ambiguity*, Interventions (Routledge, 2019); Dennis Kurzon, "Towards a Typology of Silence," *Journal of Pragmatics* 39, no. 10 (2007): 1673–88; Melani Schröter and Charlotte Taylor, *Exploring Silence and Absence in Discourse: Empirical Approaches* (Springer, 2017).
30 Marina Sbisà, "Presupposition and Implicature: Varieties of Implicit Meaning in Explicitation Practices," *Journal of Pragmatics* 182 (September 2021): 176–88, https://doi.org/10.1016/j.pragma.2021.05.027
31 UK House of Commons, *HC Debates*, March 14, 1933, Vol. 275, Supply, Cc1795–896, 1933.
32 Olivia U. Rutazibwa, "Hidden in Plain Sight: Coloniality, Capitalism and Race/Ism as Far as the Eye Can See," *Millennium* 48, no. 2 (2020): 231.
33 Edward W. Said, *Orientalism: Western Conceptions of the Orient*, Reprinted with a new afterword, Penguin History (Penguin Books, 1995), 295.
34 Priya Satia, "Drones: A History from the British Middle East," *Humanity: An International Journal of Human Rights, Humanitarianism, and Development* 5, no. 1 (2014): 1–31, https://doi.org/10.1353/hum.2014.0002
35 Satia, "Drones," 2.
36 Afxentiou, "A History of Drones: Moral(e) Bombing and State Terrorism."
37 Ania Loomba, *Colonialism/Postcolonialism* (Routledge, 2005), 22.
38 Elisabeth Schweiger, "The Lure of Novelty: 'Targeted Killing' and Its Older Terminological Siblings," *International Political Sociology*, ahead of print, 2019, https://doi.org/10.1093/ips/olz006

39 Loomba, *Colonialism/Postcolonialism*, 12.
40 Loomba, *Colonialism/Postcolonialism*, 19.
41 Alison Howell, "Forget 'Militarization': Race, Disability and the 'Martial Politics' of the Police and of the University," *International Feminist Journal of Politics* 20, no. 2 (2018): 118, https://doi.org/10.1080/14616742.2018.1447310
42 Nivi Manchanda, "The Janus-Faced Nature of Militarization," *Critical Military Studies*, January 13, 2022, 3, https://doi.org/10.1080/23337486.2021.2022852
43 Walter D. Mignolo, *The Politics of Decolonial Investigations* (Duke University Press, 2021), 3, https://doi.org/10.2307/j.ctv1smjncs
44 Gayatri Chakravorty Spivak, "Can the Subaltern Speak?," in *Marxism and the Interpretation of Culture*, ed. Nelson Cary and Lawrence Grossberg (University of Illinois Press, 1988); see also J. Maggio, "'Can the Subaltern Be Heard?': Political Theory, Translation, Representation, and Gayatri Chakravorty Spivak," *Alternatives: Global, Local, Political* 32, no. 4 (2007): 419–43.
45 Mignolo, *The Politics of Decolonial Investigations*, 4.
46 Stoler, "Colonial Archives and the Arts of Governance."

1

Regimes of not listening

In Western thought, agency is commonly conceived as inextricably linked to having a voice, to speaking. Foundational Western understandings of social and political life often presume that the starting point for agency is speech. This assumption has deep roots in the cultural and theological traditions of the West, most notably in Judeo-Christian cosmologies, where the mythological foundations of life itself are created through divine utterance. Such a conception of creation through speech is not universally shared. In many non-Judaic cosmologies, creation emerges through silent, elemental forces; through natural cycles of growth, light and blood which *quietly* create the world as we know it without resource to verbal articulations.[1] This logocentric bias – centring speech as the primary medium of meaning and agency – is deeply embedded in Western epistemologies and shapes scientific discourses. The metaphor of the "Big Bang" for an event that did not actually make any noise illustrates the pervasive association of origin with sound.[2]

Recognising the centrality of speech in liberal Western thinking is important when interrogating the functions of silence in political discourses. Although the modalities of speech expectations have changed over time – as seen in the heightened emphasis on transparency in contemporary discussions as compared to the early twentieth century – the centrality of speech as an agentic expression of will has been a constant within liberal Western thought. This enduring logocentrism helps explain the unease through which silence tends to be approached as a lack which needs to be categorised, imbued with meaning or dismissed as irrelevant or uncanny, a "death that threatens the power to make meaning".[3]

Silence is often seen as a philosophical conundrum that challenges our ontological grasp of communication. Much scholarly attention has been devoted to developing typologies, attempting to categorise when silence is communicative and when it is merely an absence, irrelevance or form of exclusion. In contrast, this chapter proposes a conceptualisation of silence as constructed through messy layers embedded within *regimes of (not) listening*, suggesting that it cannot be objectively categorised as either communicative or non-communicative. Instead, I introduce the distinction between what I call *loud* and *deep* silences. Loud silences are those that are noted and accorded meaning, whereas deep silences remain unheard within a particular community, due to the absence of speech expectations. Speech expectations might be absent because an issue is deemed irrelevant, an actor's voice is considered inconsequential, a taboo exists around a topic or an issue is universally regarded as self-evident. Despite their imperceptibility, deep silences have important communicative functions as they limit, influence and overlap with other discursive modes.

The perception of silence hinges on our listening practices. Silence might thus be invoked and have expressive functions, even when it can be demonstrated that there is no actual silence, when utterances exist but not in the expected place. The interpretation as well as the very perception of silence is a matter of positionality, a matter of what is (not) listened to, which can vary greatly depending on the discursive community. This variability leads to interpretive struggles regarding the existence and meaning of silence, as evidenced by instances where oppressed silence has been invoked by right-wing figures such as US President Donald Trump accusing social media sites of silencing his views, and contested by others.[4] The invocation of silence can thus reveal the assumptions and expectations within particular discursive communities. For research on silence, it is perhaps as crucial to examine the assumptions through which silence is perceived and interpreted as it is to map and categorise silences themselves.

Understanding silence as embedded within regimes of (not) listening moves us beyond a binary framework in which silence is conceived simply as the negation or absence of speech. Instead, I propose approaching silence as a continuum of layers that encompass redactions, backgrounded aspects, delays, partial omissions, ambiguities etc. Rather than standing in opposition to speech, I argue that silence operates through discourse in messy layers which are constituted with and through text. Silences, whether they emerge and are acknowledged or remain unheard, are intrinsic to discursive formations. They are shaped by articulations and interpretations, and in turn influence the boundaries of what is sayable.

The conditions under which particular voices and topics become audible – or remain inaudible – are deeply entrenched in power relations and material infrastructures that govern discursive fields, from media and academia to popular culture and domestic and international politics. I refer to this network of institutional and material forces as the *global economy of silence* – a system that regulates what is (not) heard and where loud silence gains value or "currency". In the context of imperial warfare, it is particularly important to scrutinise how coloniality and neoliberal capitalist structures shape the conditions under which silence is produced and acquires meaning. This is not a uniform or monolithic process of domination, nor is it necessarily the outcome of deliberate censorship or top-down control. Silences also emerge from countless everyday acts of not speaking or failing to listen. These practices are intimately linked to discursive hegemonies and routine, banal forms of silencing.

Conceptualising silence in this way offers critical potential for analysis. It shifts the focus away from already dominant voices and topics, directing attention instead to what remains unsaid, unheard or deemed unsayable. Silence, more so than similar concepts such as absence or invisibility, compels us to interrogate our own ways of (not) listening. Precisely because of its intangibility, silence invites critical inquiry into how meaning is shaped beyond a binary present/absent dichotomy. Silence gains meaning through processes of (not) listening. And within these processes lies a form of agency. While not all of us speak, we are all implicated as listeners in shaping what comes to be heard. This book, too, emerges from a particular location within these dynamics of (not) listening. Writing within a Western university, in English and through academic conventions I have internalised, I am acutely aware of the epistemic limitations of my position. There are countless sources I have not accessed, perspectives I have not encountered and voices I have not heard.

This chapter begins by outlining key parameters through which the communicative potential of silence has been conceptualised in existing scholarship. Building on these foundations, I develop my own conceptual framework of silence that distinguishes between *loud* and *deep silences*. I then explore how both forms of silence are constructed through processes of (not) listening, emphasising that silences work in layers interspersed with text which are not clear cut but messy and contested. In the third section I introduce the concept of *regimes of listening* situated within what I term a *global economy of silence*. This framework aims to illuminate the wider material and ideational structures – within and across professional fields – through which certain voices are excluded and silences rendered meaningful. The chapter concludes with a critical reflection on the methodological choices underpinning this project and the limitations inherent in my own position as listener, recognising my complicity in the very regimes I seek to analyse.

Silence that speaks

In John Cage's famous composition *4′ 33″*, the performer takes the stage but does not play a single note for four minutes and thirty-three seconds. During the original 1952 performance in New York, the pianist set up the sheet music, closed the lid of the piano and set a timer for the duration of this silence, signalling the transition between movements by opening and closing the lid.[5] For the entire performance, Cage subverted audience expectations of the highly codified context of the concert hall, where musicians are supposed to produce sound. The piece provoked confusion, irritation and debate on whether it can be called a piece of music at all.[6] What *4′ 33″* reveals – and deliberately unsettles – are the contextual assumptions underpinning the performance space. It is precisely these assumptions that render the pianist's silence perceptible, meaningful and provocative.

This example is helpful for conceptualising "eloquent silence", or silence that speaks. As existing scholarship has emphasised, the communicative function of silence is dependent on the expectations of the listeners. While silence technically exists whenever a potential speaker refrains from speaking, it gains expressive communicative significance only when it is registered as such by others.[7] For silence to be perceived and become *loud silence*, there must be an underlying expectation of speech, an expectation which varies considerably, depending on the context. The impact of *4′ 33″* depends heavily on its performance within the formal setting of a concert hall, where conventional signals like opening sheet music trigger the expectation of sound in the audience.[8] In a less codified setting – like a piano at the train station – the same act might go unnoticed, failing to elicit the necessary expectations by the listeners.

Scholarship on silence has proposed criteria which differentiate communicative silence from what is classed as non-communicative silence, which might be due to irrelevance or oversight. These parameters are grounded in the expectations of the listeners or interlocutors. Silence is commonly understood as communicative when it forms the second move in an adjacent pair, a reaction that follows an initial question or action.[9] For example, the failure to respond to an e-mail is interpreted as meaningful only if the recipient is presumed to have received the initial message. As I will show, the importance of the first move becomes salient in international law discussions, where the question of whether silence constitutes acquiescence – for example in the case of targeted killing strikes – hinges on whether such practices are recognised as legally relevant, public and openly known.[10]

For silence to be understood as communicative, the omission also needs to be seen as relevant within that discursive context.[11] As Schröter illustrates, the public significance of what remains unsaid can shift over time. For example, a politician's divorce fifty years ago might have required public explanation, otherwise the unsaid would have provoked a political scandal. Today, a divorce would likely be seen as irrelevant, and silence not registered as a relevant omission.[12] Communicative silence is also frequently understood as an intentional act, distinguishing it from silence imposed by external circumstances which have prevented actors from speaking.[13] The perception of deliberateness hinges on assumptions that the silent actor had both the possibility and the capacity to speak.[14]

This focus on intentionality as a way of establishing whether silence can be understood as communicative pervades many discussions about silence, for example in international law debates on whether a particular silence can be understood as deliberate or whether it is due to a "mere failure to mention a matter".[15]

I suggest using the term *expressive silence* to refer to a type of *loud silence* that is interpreted as an intentional expression of meaning. I adopt this term in order to highlight that other silences are also communicative. What I call *oppressed silences* – those recognised as arising from oppression – can become acknowledged and function as another type of *loud silence*, gaining powerful symbolic resonance. Such silences have played an important role in struggles against marginalisation, such as anti-racist and feminist political struggles, where invoking oppressed silence has helped expose and de-naturalise deep silences and structures of exclusion. However, the recognition of these silences depends on the assumptions and expectations within a specific discursive community. I use the term "discursive community" very lightly here, to describe any social, political or professional community that shares discursive assumptions and norms of interaction.

If there are no speech expectations within a discursive community, silence will not be noted; it will be understood as a self-evident absence, an irrelevant, accidental or benign omission. These silences have often been understood as non-communicative in scholarship on silence. As political theorist Monica Brito-Vieira put it: "Only when this behaviour [being silent] is recognized as a significant action by others, communicative silence emerges in the sense that further (communicative and other) actions respond to it."[16] Yet, silences which are not recognised by others can still have important communicative and other effects. What I term *deep silences* shape the boundaries of what can be said; they can indicate and reproduce what is to be considered irrelevant and can convey what is taken for granted and beyond debate (Figure 1.1).

Whether silence becomes recognised and is ascribed expressive meaning, or is not noted and stays deep silence, is subject to interpretation – and therefore to political contestation. This book does not primarily aim to determine whether any silence should be seen as expressive or not. Rather, I am interested in the very process

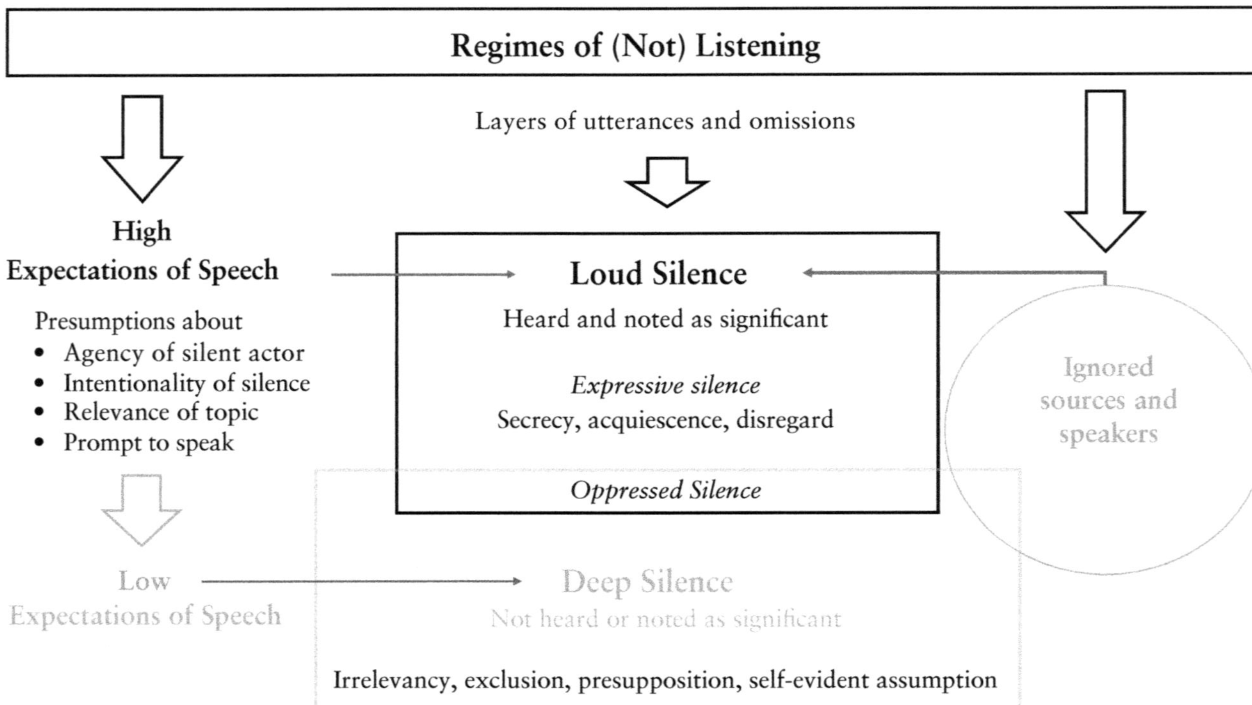

Figure 1.1 Regimes of (not) listening

of drawing these lines, a process embedded within speech expectations of regimes of (not) listening. These expectations are not static; they evolve over time. In international law, for example, scholars have argued that the significance of both protest and lack of protest by states has intensified in light of the proliferation of communication technologies, the increased availability of information on state acts[17] and "the wide-ranging opportunities that states now enjoy to express their opinion on the behaviour of other states".[18] Similarly, within domestic politics the prominence of speech expectations might also be linked to the development of communication technologies and their potential to broaden the spaces for public expression. However, this expansion is paradoxical, since the sheer amount of information available can diminish the audibility of individual voices. The possibilities for being heard are mediated by new technological infrastructures – such as algorithmically created echo-chambers – that reinforce entrenched patterns of dominant regimes of not listening.

The recognition and invocation of silence can reveal the underlying speech expectations and assumptions within a discursive community. They reveal what is deemed relevant, who is recognised as a legitimate, speaking actor and what topics are expected to be addressed. In the context of drone warfare, for example, silence by states being heard and invoked in international law reflects struggles around whether drone warfare itself is and should be considered legally relevant.[19] It reveals Western-centric expectations of speech which are directed at particular platforms – such as the UN Security Council – and particular actors, such as EU member states.[20] Any contestation over the presence and meaning of silence simultaneously reflects political struggles around a particular representation of this context.

These assumptions through which silence is heard often go unquestioned, particularly when silence is already approached through a predefined interpretive modality, such as silence-as-secrecy. I use hyphens here deliberately to highlight how such silences are frequently conflated with the particular expressive function they are presumed to have. This tendency also creeps into academia, where subfields concentrate on particular modes of silence – security studies scholars focus on silence-as-secrecy, international law scholars on acquiescence and critical scholars on oppressed and deep silence. Such framings of silence often rely on assumptions about intentionality and thus risk reinforcing stereotypical understandings of agency. Loud, expressive silence – such as secrecy or acquiescence – is typically taken as the purview of state actors and other powerful elites, whose silence is understood as a deliberate and relevant withholding of speech. In contrast, silence resulting from silencing, oppression or powerlessness tends to be analysed only in relation to peripheral actors whose silence is conflated with voicelessness – or is not noticed at all. These interpretive frameworks fail to capture the complexity of silence and may inadvertently reproduce structures of power. By focusing narrowly on the presumed function of silence, scholarship frequently overlooks the foundational assumptions and speech expectations that determine whether silence is even noticed. In so doing, it fails to interrogate the regimes of listening – and not listening – within which silence is embedded.

Not listening

Silence is not something that is encountered "out there" independently of us. Instead, silence is perceived through and within processes of (not) listening in which we ourselves are embedded. I propose understanding silence as constructed through messy layers of omissions that are interwoven with utterances and interpreted through prevailing regimes of (not) listening. As part of our discursive world, they are inseparable from dynamics of silencing and exclusion. Rather than starting from an "agentic" framework that prioritises the presumed intentionality of a given act of silence, I propose shifting analytical attention to such listening structures within which silence is heard and gains meaning.

In this view, silence is not merely the binary opposite of speech but is interwoven with text. The act of recognising, invoking and interpreting silence occurs through layers of utterances, perceived omissions of text and their interpretative context. As I will show in Chapter 4, secrecy around drone warfare exemplifies this process. It is constructed through layers of silence and speech, a conglomerate encompassing delays of information, redactions within documents, omissions, ambiguities, part-disclosures and explicit refusals to reveal. These silences are not free-floating absences; they are situated within and articulated through text and they acquire significance precisely within this intertextual and interpretive frame.

Whether silence is heard and perceived at all – and how it is subsequently interpreted – is shaped by a wider discursive context that reproduces underlying assumptions and expectations. What we are able to hear – and even what we can conceive might have been said – is conditioned by what Block De Behar terms our "horizon of expectations".[21] Both utterances and loud silences rest on a bedrock of deep silences that remain unacknowledged within or across discursive communities – and some of which may lie entirely beyond our (current) epistemic grasp. These deep silences include entrenched taboos, systematically silenced topics, voices dismissed as irrelevant, topics perceived to be self-evident and ideas impossible to articulate.[22]

Deep silences are pervasive and unsettling, not least because they challenge dominant Western conceptions of agency as rational, autonomous and reliant on individual expressions of will.[23] This worldview struggles to accommodate the idea of deep silences, tending instead to approach silence as either a deliberate expression of will or an outcome of exclusion. Yet expressions of meaning and silencing structures are entangled, overlapping and reconstituting. As I demonstrate throughout the book, *loud silences* – such as those interpreted as expressions of acquiescence – often emerge from and are sustained by silencing processes that constrain actors' ability to speak and be heard.

This is not merely a matter of misclassifying a given instance of silence; rather, it reflects the limitations of a binary epistemology that demands we classify silence as either deliberate or imposed. Because there are incongruities within and between listening communities, silence can be understood to be caused by exclusion *while at the same time* functioning as an intentional expression of will. Recognising this complexity is vital because such dissonant silences are insidious in creating and upholding hegemonic regimes. For example, critical international law scholarship has demonstrated how, throughout imperial history, non-European societies were denied legal recognition as speaking subjects even while their silence was invoked as acquiescence.[24]

Feminist and anti-racist scholarship has illuminated the subtle mechanisms through which certain voices and topics are excluded – not necessarily through overt censorship but in insipid ways, such as ridicule, belittlement or the refusal to take certain actors seriously.[25] More than that, our discourses exhibit epistemological biases that privilege particular forms of speaking while excluding others. This is particularly pertinent in light of the enduring effects of coloniality in Western-centric global knowledge production. As Maggio observes, "the subaltern can speak as long as they speak in a 'language' that is already recognised by the dominant culture of the West".[26] The audibility and authority of any given utterance is shaped by intersectional signifiers – such as race, gender, class – that are not only inscribed onto bodies and professional status but also manifest through learned styles of speaking and habitual modes of expression. As Alcoff has argued, "a speaker's location (which I take here to refer to their social location, or social identity) has an epistemically significant impact on that speaker's claims and can serve either to authorize or disauthorize one's speech".[27]

When we ask what is listened to, this requires attention not only to formal restrictions of discourse, such as censorship, but also to more indirect and diffuse forms of silencing. These include the presumed authority of a speaker, the marketability of certain issues that "sell" and the mechanisms through which particular topics are backgrounded or dismissed. Silencing, then, is not merely a matter of power politics and centralised suppression of speech but is performed through *banal silencings*, a multitude of everyday forms of not speaking and not listening. It operates through implicit norms and assumptions held by scholars, journalists, legal professionals and other actors who sustain dominant discursive frameworks. Such collective silences are produced and reinforced through innumerable everyday decisions not to speak and not to listen. They are upheld through formal sanctions – such as legal punishment of campaigners or whistleblowers – and through subtler forms of social discipline, including demotions in workplaces, disapproval in social settings or the deafening silence in response to transgressing the boundaries of what can be said. These silences are further upheld through self-censorship and the internalisation of discursive boundaries, determining what might (not) be said, what is ir/relevant, what should be listened to. Collective silences possess a paradoxical character: they are powerful while at the same time being fragile, precisely because they rely on broad social participation. Once disrupted – such as we witnessed during the #MeToo movement – it can become easier to speak up again.

At this juncture it is worth complicating the commonly held assumption that silencing – as the exclusion of certain topics or voices – is inherently oppressive and normatively undesirable. Depending on one's standpoint, silencing structures may filter out redundant information, reinforce shared understandings of self-evident truths or maintain tactful and protective silences. Perceptions of silences are shaped by one's positionality and assumptions. Silencing can offer forms of epistemic and social protection that empower marginalised communities, for example when sexist or racist comments are sanctioned as politically incorrect or when uptake is refused to hate speech. The protective value of such silencing often becomes apparent only when it is disrupted, such as in the case of Donald Trump's overtly racist and misogynistic social media campaign that tactically invoked "political incorrectness"[28] to break these norms. Silences thus reflect and produce the implicit rules of a particular discursive community. These rules are not always detrimental to marginalised groups; in some cases they offer protection and can be mobilised as a form of subversion and resistance – as I will explore further in Chapter 6. However, in many cases prevailing listening regimes reproduce dominant power relations which retain status-quo privileges and hegemonic understandings of the world. As postcolonial feminist scholars have pointed out, "ultimately, at the exclusion of the majority of this planet, it is the White male experience in a handful of countries in the West that has shaped not just what, but also how and why we learn the world".[29]

Taking silencing structures seriously requires us to ask not only who can speak and what is spoken about within particular discourses but also what is (not) listened to. At a basic level, this involves interrogating who has access to influential platforms – such as being granted the floor at the UN Security Council or being cited in mainstream media – and how such access is regulated by implicit hierarchies. For example, it is often assumed that state authorities are the most reliable knowledge producers on military violence, sidelining alternative perspectives. Even when marginalised voices are formally included in a particular discourse, power relations influence their practical ability to speak and to be taken seriously. As I will explore in Chapter 5, representatives of Global South states may have the formal right to influence international law formation, but in practice their contributions are frequently constrained – by political pressure from powerful states, by epistemic exclusion and the methodological whiteness of international law.[30] Thus, in addition to overt and formal silencing structures, we need to attend to more implicit forms which render certain topics irrelevant, redirect speech expectations away from certain issues or fail to recognise alternative forms of expression as valid knowledge production. These more insidious silences often go unnoticed and are methodologically difficult to trace, a point I will discuss further below.

There is a tendency to frame silence through the lens of agency and intentionality. Even when engaging with forms of exclusion and *deep silence*, analytical attention often centres on the presumed agency of a silencing actor – typically envisioned as a powerful, oppressive actor deliberately suppressing utterances. This framing foregrounds direct censorship and coerced oppression, often associated with authoritarian regimes.[31] In this approach silencing is often imagined to take place predominantly in the "illiberal" non-West.[32] Less direct forms of silencing and oppression in the context of Western, neoliberal politics frequently escape scrutiny. These forms are reproduced not solely through direct state censorship but through the subtle workings of what Michael Freeden has aptly described as "non-agentic social devices and practices that are not aimed at repressing individual freedom of expression and action but that nonetheless impede speech and intelligibility, bringing about silence in a non-conspirational manner".[33] While overt state censorship and control over media and public discourses may be less prevalent in many Western contexts, powerful silencing structures persist. These are shaped by the enduring legacies of coloniality, by concentrated wealth and economic power and by institutional hierarchies which together constitute what I refer to as the global *economy of silence*. To take silence seriously requires more than identifying instances of silence; it necessitates critical attention to the political and economic structures under which speech is possible, audible and meaningful. Without such analysis, normative status-quo perspectives will be naturalised and left unchallenged. As Alcoff has aptly noted, "Who is speaking, who is spoken of, and who listens is a result, as well as an act, of political struggle. Simply put, the discursive context is a political arena."[34]

A global economy of silence

Conceptualising silence within the framework of a global economy foregrounds the material and institutional power structures that shape prevalent *regimes of not listening*. Power, in this context, is not reducible to measurable assets such as wealth, economic resources or military capacity. Rather, following Foucault, I approach power as a relational and dispersed force that is everywhere: the "multiplicity of force relations immanent in the sphere in which they operate and which constitute their own organization".[35] Drawing on critical theory and postcolonial scholarship, I understand power as both reflected in and reproduced by the institutional and economic structures of colonial capitalism.

The term *global economy of silence* is thus employed to draw attention to the material and institutional structures in which silence is embedded. These power relations shape the discourses, institutional norms and professional practices that delimit who and what is listened to. Across professional fields – such as media, academia, policy making, international law – power relations shape communicative boundaries, determining what is amplified and what is rendered inaudible or irrelevant. Borrowing from Bourdieu, professional fields constitute distinct yet interrelated social spaces within which professionals are restricted – and restrict themselves – in what they talk and write about, without losing credibility and professional standing.[36] These field dynamics are not isolated but are shaped by broader global power relations, including neoliberal market structures and the enduring legacies of coloniality which influence the boundaries of what is heard and can be said.

Quijoana's concept of coloniality is particularly useful here, as it describes how racialised hierarchies continue to structure institutions, modes of production and social relations. Coloniality, in this sense, is not a historical remnant but a persistent logic constructing the periphery and the capitalist colonial world power.[37] As the main axis around which society is organised, capitalism is inherently linked to coloniality, not just as an economic system but also through social relations and a particular type of knowledge production which is linked to ideas of modernity and rationality.[38] The silencing effects of coloniality are apparent in the context of "police bombing" practices in the 1920s and 1930s, where non-European peoples were denied the status of sovereign statehood and, as such, excluded from speaking as international subjects. As I will explore in Chapter 3, this was also reflected in the structuring of relevance. Bombing operations in the outlying regions of the Empire were largely absent from parliamentary debates unless they directly touched upon the interests of the white European bourgeoisie. Such silences are not incidental, but reflect a broader economy of attention shaped by race, empire and class.

Coloniality has also influenced more indirect regimes of (not) listening – regimes in which only certain voices are recognised as valid knowledge producers and only particular discursive forms are deemed intelligible or credible. For instance, the concept of property has historically been codified through Western, capitalist understandings of private ownership and marked by Western signifiers, such as fences, maps or patents. These epistemic frameworks continue to shape contemporary knowledge production in global analysis, where Western theories and conceptual categories – such as those around statehood and good governance – are taken as self-evident, neutral and universal rather than culturally situated constructs.[39] As Mignolo argues: "No living organism at this point in time is immune to coloniality, no less the changing cast of actors running the institutions that maintain coloniality under the rhetoric of modernity celebrating change, development, the cybernetic revolution, AI [artificial intelligence], and democracy as unquestionable victories."[40] Coloniality persists not only in institutional structures but in the epistemic foundations that underpin global discourses and privilege certain ways of knowing while silencing others.

Silence is not only born from the regimes of the global economy of silence; it also gains "currency" and value within them. In certain contexts, loud silences – such as secrecy – can be commodified and "sold" as signifiers of authority and power, a dynamic I will explore further in Chapter 4. Silence can produce material, social and ideational privileges. It can function as a mechanism to shield individuals or organisations from accountability. By not acknowledging certain acts and their consequences, actors may avoid political, legal or financial repercussions, such as the obligation to issue apologies, pay medical bills or provide reparations. As the literature on whistleblowing has shown, silence surrounding corruption or misconduct in institutions and corporations can yield tangible benefits for individuals who choose not to speak out – as well as the institutions or corporations that benefit from the acts and continued concealment of them.[41]

At a broader structural level, *deep silences* can create and uphold entrenched systems of privilege. Patriarchal norms, for example, are naturalised through the silencing of gender-diverse, egalitarian and matriarchal cultural histories that pre-date colonial encounters.[42] This silence naturalises patriarchy as a universal system that has always been and will always be.[43] Similarly, the systematic exclusion of non-Western intellectual traditions, scientific contributions and cultural innovations from dominant historical narratives has created a silence that presumes, naturalises and legitimises Western supremacy and violent domination.[44] Violence perpetrated by the West is itself often silenced, while attention is disproportionally directed towards violence by non-Western actors which is cast as the predominant problem for the international system – a problem understood to be innate to the Global South. As Kieh has shown, this masks how violence in the Global South is enabled by structural and subjective violence in which Western actors are deeply implicated.[45]

When I use the term *global economy of silence*, I do not suggest defining the current international system but simply referring to the material and ideational power structures within which silence is embedded and reproduced. Indeed, debates over the nature of the contemporary world order often remain state-centric and based on normative presumptions. For example, Ikenberry distinguishes between an "imperial order" where the most powerful state acts unilaterally and above international rules and a "liberal hegemonic order" where the leading state ostensibly adheres to mutually agreed norms and institutions.[46] Such distinctions do little to illuminate the material and ideational structures which influence prevalent regimes of not listening. These regimes are shaped by Eurocentrism, understood in the sense of "the cognitive perspective not of Europeans only, but of the Eurocentered world, of those educated under the hegemony of world capitalism".[47]

While not defining the contemporary world order, this book acknowledges certain structures of power that shape prevailing regimes of (not) listening. These include coloniality, Eurocentrism and neoliberal capitalism. Neoliberalism, as I employ the term, refers to "a bricolage of ideas and practices".[48] It encompasses economic policies such as deregulation and privatisation, but also ideas and principles such as individual liberty and personal responsibility – ideas through which these measures are justified. Despite rhetorical commitments to liberty, neoliberal structures have facilitated the demise of small entrepreneurial firms and the rise of oligopolistic transnational corporations.[49] Neoliberalism's logic extends into spheres traditionally seen as outside the economic domain, such as water provision, healthcare and education, all of which have shifted towards neoliberal practices, privatisation and profit maximisation.

Warfare has also been understood as imbricated in neoliberal rationalities, as evidenced by the increasing reliance on special forces and private military contractors. As postcolonial scholars have furthermore pointed out, "unending war and militarization are tactics in racial capitalism's strategies of accumulation, dispossession, and exploitation".[50] The term "racial capitalism" draws attention to the interwoven nature of racism and capitalism, revealing both as mutually reinforcing strategies within a global extractive order.[51] The discursive boundaries of what can be said are shaped by power structures, such as the entrenched influence of the military-industrial complex. Political elites often maintain close personal, financial and professional ties to defence corporations and military institutions. The arms industry and powerful unions that represent defence-sector workers function as influential veto players within Western policy making, causing difficulties for political actors to challenge prevailing security orthodoxies or advocate for policy shifts that conflict with their vested interests.[52] This is not only relevant for maintaining a narrow, tacit consent on security policies within Western state institutions but also within the public more widely, where media reporting plays an important role.

Within neoliberal market structures, media corporations have also been analysed as operating according to a market logic that prioritises profitability. In this logic, media outlets effectively commodify their audiences, selling access to audiences to other businesses for the purpose of advertising. As a result, media content is heavily influenced by sellers and buyers – groups largely composed of highly influential individuals with particular corporate and political interests.[53] Media outlets are subject to profit-oriented forces and maintain close ties to other major corporations, financial institutions and branches of the state.[54] As I will show in Chapter 3, these structures have significant implications for how armed drone attacks are (not) reported in Western media. For example, when state confirmation of drone strikes is absent or delayed, media outlets – relying on official state sources for information – may not report on them. Once the news cycle has moved on, the story may no longer be deemed commercially viable and is dropped, despite its ethical and political significance.

Academia is not outside of such power structures that shape prevalent regimes of (not) listening. The enduring legacies of coloniality, coupled with the neoliberal marketisation of academia, have further entrenched the dominance of anglophone academia as the central hub of so-called "international" research activity. This centralisation is evident in both teaching and research, with "a gradual monopolisation of the idea of 'international publishing' by a group of journals published in English in the UK or the USA".[55] The hierarchical valuation of journals is part of colonial capitalist structures where the prestige of publications gets "identified with US/UK-based journals that are indexed by one US-based firm, Thomson ISI".[56] Under increasing pressure from audits, evaluation schemes and performance reviews,[57] scholars often find limited possibilities to creatively write (and listen) outside of accepted or tolerated discursive structures.

These dynamics in academia are linked to normative, legal and institutional structures in international politics. For example, in the field of international commercial arbitration, European legal academics and corporate litigators from Wall Street law firms have monopolised the forum for handling high-profile commercial conflicts.[58] Being positioned at the core of the anglophone-centric market brings status, funding and influence that are essential for their recognition as valid experts in international policy-making forums. This Western-centrism is integral to the global economy of silence, as neoliberal capitalist structures shape what can(not) be said and what is (not) listened to. Non-governmental organisations similarly operate within these constraints. Their reliance on funding streams and social capital concentrated in the Global North "makes them peculiarly open to abuse by powerful interests".[59] This is the case for Public Interest NGOs as well as more obviously for business and industry associations (sometimes called BINGOs), which are often lumped together with public interest NGOs by global governance forums such as the World Bank.[60] While NGOs are important actors in international discourses on drone warfare, they also speak from within neoliberal coloniality, and experience pressure in what can and cannot be said.[61]

I argue that silence needs to be analysed within these material and ideational power structures. This is not to suggest that such structures *determine* what can/not be said and listened to, or that the global economy of silence should be grasped as monolithic and unidirectional. Silence holds critical potential of agency because of its ambiguous, fragmented and relational nature embedded within regimes of (not) listening that function through collective and diffused processes of not speaking and not listening. Yet, in order to engage silence as a site of resistance and foster more just and inclusive modes of listening, we need to first examine how silences emerge, where they remain submerged and the political configurations within which they are embedded. Such analysis requires critical interrogation of entrenched regimes of (not) listening and awareness of the wider global economy within which they are situated.

Not out there

The ephemeral nature of silences and their embeddedness in structures of (not) listening pose significant methodological challenges of how to trace, measure and evidence silences. In this section, I will outline several strategies I have employed for analysing silences, including the creation of frames of reference, tracing backgrounded versus foregrounded aspects and mapping what Schröter refers to as "meta-discourses" of silence.[62] Importantly, this approach goes beyond merely locating absences and omissions. It seeks to analyse how silence is constituted by and embedded within regimes of (not) listening. The book thus also highlights how silence may function in contexts where speech has occurred but not been attended to. This complicates the assumption that silence always corresponds to a lack of expression. Rather, silence must be analysed relationally – through what is heard, sidelined, ignored, rendered unintelligible. This methodological approach raises deeper epistemological questions: what counts as speech? What is expected to be said? What is presumed to be relevant or legitimate?

One of the core difficulties in researching silence is the methodological issue that silence resists direct citation and conventional forms of documentation and referencing. However, silence can become loud and discursively apparent, for example when silence-as-secrecy is critiqued by parliamentary oversight committees, or when silence-as-acquiescence is debated in legal forums. Investigating such "meta-discourses"[63] on silence – discussions about silence itself – offers a practical methodological entry point for tracing loud silences. This is particularly relevant because loud silence may carry rhetorical weight even in the absence of "actual" silence. Whether silence is perceived in a given context depends fundamentally on the prevailing assumptions and speech expectations within a discourse. As I will show in Chapter 5, silence-as-acquiescence to drone warfare and "targeted killing" practices hinges on speech expectations that centre on formal reactions to US practices in the UN Security Council. Protest articulated in other forums or in response to different actors may go unrecognised, thereby sustaining the perception of silence. Even when protest exists, the invocation of silence in meta-discourses can function to legitimise violence by framing it as uncontested.

Meta-discourses on silence tend to approach silence through a predetermined function, such as acquiescence, secrecy or diplomacy. These loud silences play a crucial political role in legitimising and enabling practices such as drone warfare. I will explore these effects and how they interplay with each other and broader discursive conditions to facilitate and normalise military violence. Yet, it's also important to remember that these silences are not monolithic or self-evident; instead they emerge from complex layers of speech, omissions and interpretations. Their framing – as acquiescence or secrecy – and even their perception as silences are dependent on regimes of (not) listening. These regimes often end up reproducing Western-centric power structures, even within critical discourses that aim to challenge them. For example, when NGOs demand greater transparency and ask states for more information on drone warfare, they may inadvertently reinforce the framing of drone warfare as a secret war and their own positionality – and that of the public – as outsiders. These tensions carry important practical implications which I will elaborate more in Chapter 6, where I will offer alternative ways of dealing with and mobilising silences.

However, this book does not only attend to loud silences which have already been recognised and ascribed meaning in discourses. It also seeks to identify and analyse *deep silences* – those that have not been named, discussed or problematised. Methodologically, I approach these silences through the construction of specific frames of reference, following what Schröter and Taylor have called "comparison as a means to identify absence".[64] This comparative method allows for the identification and mapping of silences by examining discrepancies across sources; for example, noting which aspects are omitted across different accounts of the same topic, which aspects are backgrounded in comparison to foregrounded aspects within the same sources, or observing shifts in emphasis and omission across different time periods.[65] To illustrate, in examining US congressional debates of drone warfare, I show how discussions foreground the hypothetical domestic use of armed drones, while the routine use of armed drones abroad is largely absent from debate.

The book draws on empirical evidence from US congressional and UK parliamentary records, UN Security Council, UN Human Rights Council and General Assembly discussions, NGO reports on armed drones collected through the European Forum on Armed Drones (EFAD), and anglophone media outlets. I analysed 187 legislative debates which were searched through Hansard for the UK

House of Commons and the US Congress website.[66] For UN discourses, I analysed 975 Security Council debates on the use of force generally (such as debates on "threats to international peace and security") or debates referring to the countries and regions within which "targeted killing" claims have been used to justify violence.[67] I also analysed 75 United Nations Yearbook entries between 1950 and 2020 and UN Human Rights Council documents which were accessed through the UN Human Rights Council search engine.[68]

The NGO and think-tank reports were accessed through EFAD, a civil society network of organisations. I analysed all fifty reports published on their website between 2011 and March 2020. Media discourses on current armed drone attacks were analysed by identifying particular drone strikes reported by Airwars and analysing media reporting via LexisNexis for three weeks following the attack.[69] For historical newspaper reporting on police bombing, I searched through the British Newspaper Archive between 1910 and 1935 using the key word "police bombing" and alternative search words.[70] I limited the search to before 1935 because the discursive space became overwhelmed with discussions of the approaching world war.

This methodological approach is not without its challenges and limitations. Analysing textual documents, such as official documents or media reports, offers little insight into individual motivations, intentions or constraints underlying specific silences and omissions. These methods do not reveal the lived experience of institutional and cultural pressure which professionals within different fields may experience in relation to the boundaries of acceptable discourse. Interviews and ethnographic research would be better suited for exploring these dimensions and analysing how actors navigate, internalise or contest the discursive limits they encounter. They would also be valuable for future research aimed at understanding how activists and marginalised actors mobilise voice and silence to resist Western-centric discursive structures.

This book remains focused on tracing the silences that are present within prevalent public and institutional discourses, examining the assumptions and expectations underlying them. My interest lies in the political work these silences do, rather than in reconstructing individual intentions behind them. All the materials analysed for this study are from Western-centric and anglophone platforms. This was not based on a belief that they are the most important institutions or are globally representative but, rather, on the view that they require critical analysis. Much of the existing literature on violence, discursive control, war propaganda and censorship focuses on practices in non-Western states, such as Russia and China, or on political regimes and insurgent groups in the Global South. Comparatively little attention has been paid to the physical and discursive violence enacted by Western states or to the regimes through which such violence is rendered normalised and inaudible. This neglect may reflect an implicit belief in the legitimacy of Western state violence and the presumed robustness of liberal democratic norms that reduce the perceived need for critical inquiry. Based on my empirical findings, I argue that critical interrogation of Western state violence is urgently needed, particularly in light of the everyday regimes of (not) listening that sustain it – regimes that have significant historical continuities with colonial violence.

This book offers critical engagement with discourses surrounding drone warfare and historical practices of police-bombing, focusing on Western-centric platforms. It traces various forms of silences, omissions, secrecies, redactions and unspoken assumptions that are in themselves discursively violent and operate to legitimise and enable physical violence. The aim is not to break the silence nor to give voice to the subaltern. Such gestures, however well intentioned, risk reproducing the power hierarchies they seek to challenge and may end up further essentialising and marginalising the subaltern, a point I will explore further in Chapter 6. Following Spivak, this project instead shifts the analytical focus toward the *listening* practices of the West.

Nonetheless, a critical engagement that centres on Western institutions and discourses is not unproblematic. There is a risk of reproducing a Western-centric epistemology as a form of navel-gazing that once again positions the West "at the centre of all things".[71] This could inadvertently paint a picture of an omnipotent imperial core that unilaterally controls discourses and suppresses dissent. Such an interpretation is neither my intention nor my argument. By building on the concept of regimes of not listening, the book aims to foreground the relational dimensions of power without reducing them to static or unidirectional forces. Power here is understood as embedded in practices, including the everyday and often banal acts of not listening. Focusing on these practices reveals critical potential. While not everyone has equal possibilities to speak, or to speak at dominant platforms, we are all implicated as listeners. Chapter 6 explores how different forms of listening – and of invoking silence – can serve to subvert colonial and hegemonic discourses.

This is not to suggest that I see myself as outside of the silencing processes I critique, or indeed of silencing practices I may not even be aware of. Positionality statements can themselves end up reproducing colonial hierarchies of knowledge production and reaffirming the Western researcher's position of privilege.[72] Yet, I believe it's important to acknowledge the ways in which my background – shaped by imperial, patriarchal and neoliberal ideologies – inevitably limits this research and my abilities for hearing deep silences. These limits are not merely methodological, such as language limitations, but epistemological. My positionality creates what might be described as a deeper epistemic deafness which I am only beginning to understand and unlearn through engagement with works by postcolonial and other critical scholars. Living in Europe and working within a Western anglophone university, I am both spatially distanced from and structurally complicit in the violence of imperial warfare and oppression – whether through taxation, institutional affiliation or indirect benefits from industries such as the arms trade. I do not believe that there is a place of innocence. Thus I write tentatively, conscious of my complicity, aware of my epistemological deafness, but motivated by solidarity and a commitment to *listening otherwise*.

Listening to silence

In this chapter I have developed a conceptualisation of silence as constituted through messy layers that are embedded within regimes of (not) listening. Moving beyond a binary conceptualisation in which silence appears as the opposite to speech, I have proposed understanding it as part of a continuum – interwoven with utterances rather than external to them. Silence does not negate speech;

it works with and through speech. I have argued that it is less productive to attempt rigid typologies of silence, as if it could be classified from the outside. Instead I have suggested that we focus analytically on the listening practices through which silences are perceived, interpreted – or rendered inaudible. Whether silence is perceived at all and becomes "loud" depends on the assumptions and expectations within particular discursive communities.

These listening processes are embedded within material and ideational power relations of what I have referred to as the global economy of silence – a term that encompasses intersecting power structures of coloniality, patriarchy, neoliberal capitalism and other vectors of domination. Attending to such power structures is crucial if we are to challenge dominant listening regimes that sustain the status quo. The following chapters will examine how silences around military violence are produced and gain "currency" within this economy. Secrecy, for instance, functions as a signifier of power, a spectacle that delineates those "in the know" from those outside of knowledge and power.

While loud silences – such as those framed as expressing secrecy or acquiescence – are noted and ascribed meaning, deep silences slip through our expectations and remain unheard. Yet I contend that deep silences, too, can fulfil important communicative functions and indeed cannot be disentangled from other discursive modes. They limit, influence and overlap with utterances and loud silences. Deep silences delineate the boundaries of what cannot be said, in turn reinforcing prevalent expectations of speech. They can convey more effectively than words that certain matters are to be seen as irrelevant, marginal and unimportant. Through unspoken assumptions, presuppositions and implicatures deep silences can, furthermore, signal what is to be taken for granted and thus placed beyond debate. The next chapter will explore how such self-evident assumptions operate within discourses on imperial violence.

Notes

1 Sara Maitland, *A Book of Silence* (Granta, 2009), 118.
2 Maitland, *A Book of Silence*, 118.

3 George Kalamaras, "The Center and Circumference of Silence: Yoga, Poststructuralism, and the Rhetoric of Paradox," *International Journal of Hindu Studies*, 1.1 (1997), 3–18, 3.
4 Oliver Darcy, "Trump Says Right-Wing Voices Are Being Censored. The Data Says Something Else | CNN Business," CNN, May 28, 2020, www.cnn.com/2020/05/28/media/trump-social-media-conservative-censorship/index.html (accessed October 30, 2025).
5 Julian Dodd, "What 4′ 33″ Is," *Australasian Journal of Philosophy*, 2017, 1–13.
6 Andrew Kania, "Silent Music," *The Journal of Aesthetics and Art Criticism* 68, no. 4 (2010): 343–53; David R. Kauffman, "The Theory of Silence," *Musical Offerings* 2, no. 1 (2011): 1.
7 Schröter, *Silence and Concealment in Political Discourse*, 31.
8 Kania, "Silent Music," 346); Julian Dodd, "What 4′ 33″ Is," *Australasian Journal of Philosophy*, 2017, 1–13, 3; David R. Kauffman, "The Theory of Silence," *Musical Offerings*, 2.1 (2011), 1.
9 Dennis Kurzon, "The Right of Silence: A Socio-Pragmatic Model of Interpretation," *Journal of Pragmatics*, 23.1 (1995), 55–69.
10 Andrew Garwood-Gowers, "Israel's Airstrike on Syria's Al-Kibar Facility: A Test Case for the Doctrine of Pre-Emptive Self-Defence?," *Journal of Conflict and Security Law* 16, no. 2 (2011): 265; Schweiger, "'Targeted Killing' and the Lack of Acquiescence," 751; ICCT, "Towards a European Position on the Use of Armed Drones; International Centre for Counter-Terrorism, The Hague," 2016; Krasmann, "Targeted Killing and Its Law"; Theresa Reinold, "State Weakness, Irregular Warfare, and the Right to Self-Defense Post-9/11," *The American Journal of International Law* 105, no. 2 (2011): 244–86, https://doi.org/10.5305/amerjintelaw.105.2.0244; Sean D. Murphy, "The International Legality of US Military Cross-Border Operations from Afghanistan into Pakistan," *International Law Studies* 85 (2009): 109–39.
11 Thomas Huckin, "Textual Silence and the Discourse of Homelessness," *Discourse & Society*, 13.3 (2002), 347–72; Schröter, *Silence and Concealment in Political Discourse.*
12 Schröter, *Silence and Concealment in Political Discourse.*
13 Schröter, *Silence and Concealment in Political Discourse*, 15; Cheryl Glenn, *Unspoken: A Rhetoric of Silence* (Southern Illinois University Press, 2004), 13; Michal Ephratt, "The Functions of Silence," *Journal of Pragmatics*, 40.11 (2008), 1909–38.
14 Huckin, "Textual Silence," 355.
15 International Court of Justice, "Case Concerning Elettronica Sicula S.p.A. (United States of America v. Italy)," 1989, para 54.

16 Brito Vieira et al., "The Nature of Silence," 429.

17 K. Wolfke, "Some Persistent Controversies Regarding Customary International Law," *Netherlands Yearbook of International Law* 24 (December 1993): 8, https://doi.org/10.1017/S0167676800000027; the International Law Commission supports this view: UN Doc A/CN.4/682, *International Law Commission, Report by Special Rapporteur Michael Wood, Third Report on Identification of Customary International Law*, 2015.

18 Raphaël Van Steenberghe, "Self-Defence in Response to Attacks by Non-State Actors in the Light of Recent State Practice: A Step Forward?" *Leiden Journal of International Law*, 23.1 (2010), 183–208 194.

19 International Court of Justice, *Sovereignty over Pedra Branca/Palau Batu Puteh, Middle Rocks and South Ledge (Malaysia/Singapore), Jurisdiction and Admissibility*, Judgment of May 23, 2008 [2008] ICJ Rep. 14, at 51, 2008, para 121.

20 Schweiger, "Listen Closely."

21 Lisa Block De Behar, *A Rhetoric of Silence and Other Selected Writings* (Walter de Gruyter, 1995), 122:7.

22 Michael Freeden, *Concealed Silences and Inaudible Voices in Political Thinking* (Oxford University Press, 2022).

23 Freeden, *Concealed Silences*, 20.

24 Antony Anghie, "Finding the Peripheries: Sovereignty and Colonialism in Nineteenth-Century International Law," *Harvard International Law Journal* 40 (1999): 3; Brigitte Stern, "Custom at the Heart of International Law," *Duke Journal of Comparative & International Law* 11 (2001): 98; Chimni, "Customary International Law."

25 De Behar, *A Rhetoric of Silence*, cxxii.

26 Maggio, "'Can the Subaltern Be Heard?'", 431.

27 Linda Alcoff, "The Problem of Speaking for Others," *Cultural Critique*, no. 20 (1991): 7, https://doi.org/10.2307/1354221

28 Jessica Gantt Shafer, "Donald Trump's 'Political Incorrectness': Neoliberalism as Frontstage Racism on Social Media," *Social Media+ Society* 3, no. 3 (2017): 2056305117733226.

29 Rutazibwa, "Hidden in Plain Sight," 233.

30 Chimni, "Customary International Law"; Dimitri Van Den Meerssche, "Global South Perspectives on Methodology and Critique in International Law," *Leiden Journal of International Law* 37, no. 4 (2024): 763–72, https://doi.org/10.1017/S0922156524000396; Schweiger, "Listen Closely."

31 Lynn Janet Thiesmeyer, *Discourse and Silencing. Representation and the Language of Displacement*, 2003.

32 Banafsheh Ranji, "Traces of Orientalism in Media Studies," *Media, Culture & Society* 43, no. 6 (2021): 1136–46, https://doi.org/10.1177/01634437211022692
33 Freeden, *Concealed Silences*, 22.
34 Alcoff, "The Problem of Speaking for Others," 15.
35 Michel Foucault, *The History of Sexuality: Volume I: An Introduction* (Pantheon Books, 1978), 92.
36 Jean D'Aspremont, "Wording in International Law," *Leiden Journal of International Law*, 25.3 (2012), 575–602, 586; Ian Johnstone, "Security Council Deliberations: The Power of the Better Argument," *European Journal of International Law*, 14.3 (2003), 437–80, 445.
37 Anibal Quijano, "Coloniality of Power and Eurocentrism in Latin America," *International Sociology* 15, no. 2 (2000): 218.
38 Quijano, "Coloniality of Power and Eurocentrism in Latin America," 221.
39 Afonso de Albuquerque, "The Institutional Basis of Anglophone Western Centrality," *Media, Culture & Society*, 43.1 (2021), 180–88, 181.
40 Mignolo, *The Politics of Decolonial Investigations*, 3.
41 John Blenkinsopp and Marissa S. Edwards, "On Not Blowing the Whistle: Quiescent Silence as an Emotion Episode," in *Emotions, Ethics and Decision-Making*, vol. 4, ed. Wilfred J. Zerbe, Charmine E. J. Härtel, and Neal M. Ashkanasy (Emerald Group Publishing Limited, 2008); Brita Bjørkelo et al., *Silence Is Golden? Characteristics and Experiences of Self-Reported Whistleblowers*, Taylor & Francis, 2011; Joyce Rothschild and Terance D. Miethe, "Whistle-Blower Disclosures and Management Retaliation: The Battle to Control Information about Organization Corruption," *Work and Occupations* 26, no. 1 (1999): 107–28; Ester Rocha and Brian H. Kleiner, "To Blow or Not to Blow the Whistle? That Is the Question," *Management Research News* 28, no. 11/12 (2005): 80–87.
42 Oyèrónkẹ́ Oyěwùmí, *The Invention of Women: Making an African Sense of Western Gender Discourses* (University of Minnesota Press, 1997); Paula Gunn Allen, *The Sacred Hoop: Recovering the Feminine in American Indian Traditions* (Beacon Press, 1992).
43 María Lugones, "Heterosexualism and the Colonial/Modern Gender System," *Hypatia* 22, no. 1 (2007): 186–219, https://doi.org/10.1111/j.1527-2001.2007.tb01156.x
44 John M. Hobson, *The Eastern Origins of Western Civilisation* [Electronic Resource] (Cambridge University Press, 2004, 2004).

45 George Klay Kieh, "Neo-Colonialism: American Foreign Policy and the First Liberian Civil War," *The Journal of Pan African Studies* 5, no. 1 (2012): 164–84.
46 G. John Ikenberry, *Liberal Leviathan: The Origins, Crisis, and Transformation of the American World Order* (Princeton University Press, 2011), 67.
47 Lugones, "Heterosexualism and the Colonial/Modern Gender System," 191.
48 Terry Hathaway, "Neoliberalism as Corporate Power," *Competition & Change*, 24.3–4 (2020), 315–37, 317.
49 Hathaway, "Neoliberalism as Corporate Power"; Damien Cahill and Martijn Konings, *Neoliberalism* (John Wiley & Sons, 2017).
50 Manchanda, "The Janus-Faced Nature of Militarization," 4.
51 Manchanda, "The Janus-Faced Nature of Militarization," 4.
52 Thomas Martin, Elisabeth Schweiger and Nick Ritchie, "The Limits of National Security and Foreign Policy Orthodoxy: Labour's Challenge to UK Policy under Jeremy Corbyn," *Critical Studies on Security* (2025): 1–27, https://doi.org/10.1080/21624887.2025.2538361
53 Herman and Chomsky, *Manufacturing Consent*, 284.
54 Herman and Chomsky, *Manufacturing Consent*, 13.
55 Anssi Paasi, "Globalisation, Academic Capitalism, and the Uneven Geographies of International Journal Publishing Spaces," *Environment and Planning A*, 37.5 (2005), 769–89, 769.
56 Paasi, "Globalisation," 771.
57 Bronwyn Davies and Peter Bansel, "The Time of Their Lives? Academic Workers in Neoliberal Time(s)," *Health Sociology Review*, 14.1 (2005), 47–58, https://doi.org/10.5172/hesr.14.1.47
58 Yves Dezalay and Bryant G. Garth, "Marketing and Selling Transnational 'Judges' and Global 'Experts': Building the Credibility of (Quasi)Judicial Regulation," *Socio-Economic Review*, 8.1 (2010), 113–30, 117, https://doi.org/10.1093/ser/mwp022
59 Feyzi Ismail and Sangeeta Kamat, "NGOs, Social Movements and the Neoliberal State: Incorporation, Reinvention, Critique," *Critical Sociology* (SAGE Publications Sage UK, 2018), 569–77, 572.
60 Sangeeta Kamat, "The Privatization of Public Interest: Theorizing NGO Discourse in a Neoliberal Era," *Review of International Political Economy*, 11.1 (2004), 155–76, 163–65, https://doi.org/10.1080/0969229042000179794
61 Muganzi M. Isharaza, "Hierarchies of Editorial Power in International NGOs," *Journalism Studies* 20, no. 12 (2019): 1764–81, https://doi.org/10.1080/1461670X.2019.1638296

62 See for a more extended discussion of methodological approaches to silence Elisabeth Schweiger and Kerstin Tomiak, "Researching Silence: A Methodological Inquiry," *Millennium*, 50.3 (2022), 623–46; Schröter and Taylor, *Exploring Silence and Absence in Discourse*.

63 Schröter, *Silence and Concealment in Political Discourse*, 48.

64 Schröter and Taylor, *Exploring Silence and Absence in Discourse*, 12.

65 Schweiger and Tomiak, "Researching Silence," 639–40.

66 I used the key word "armed drone" between 2005 and 2020 and collected historical records of UK commons debates between 1910 and 1935 through the key word "police bombing". In order to avoid missing crucial debates I also ran searches with similar key words (such as UAV, targeted killing, counterterrorism, insurgency).

67 UN Doc A/HRC/14/24/Add.6, *Report of the Special Rapporteur on Extrajudicial, Summary or Arbitrary Executions, Philip Alston*, 2010. The debates included "the situation in the Middle East", "the situation in Somalia", or "peace and security – terrorist acts: Pakistan". I did not include debates which referred to issue areas or regions less related to "targeted killing" claims, such as "the situation in Timor-Leste" or "election of a member of the International Court of Justice".

68 I used the key word "drone" to search for these documents. This returned 142 results which were further narrowed down by excluding irrelevant documents, duplicates of the above analysis or translations. The remaining 75 documents were searched via key words around drone warfare (UAV, targeted, drone, unmanned).

69 I used the key words "drone" and the country within which the strike took place. I also searched individual newspaper databases, including the *New York Times*, the *Washington Post* and *Fox News* following three weeks after the strike.

70 Including "bombing" AND "rebellion", "bombing" AND "natives", "bombing" AND "tribes".

71 John M. Hobson, "Is Critical Theory Always for the White West and for Western Imperialism? Beyond Westphilian towards a Post-Racist Critical IR," *Review of International Studies* 33, no. S1 (2007): 93, https://doi.org/10.1017/S0260210507007413

72 Jasmine K. Gani and Rabea M. Khan, "Positionality Statements as a Function of Coloniality: Interrogating Reflexive Methodologies," *International Studies Quarterly* 68, no. 2 (2024): sqae038.

2

Unspoken assumptions

Alan Cobham, a pilot and First World War hero, emerged as a public hero and celebrity in the interwar years. In the 1926 film *Flight Commander*, Cobham starred as himself in a dramatised narrative set in a fictional Chinese village. Praised by the British Empire Film Society, the film served as promotional material to show off the purported power and morality of police bombing, portraying bombing campaigns as virtuous means to regain peace in outlying regions of the Empire.[1] As the *Daily Mail* described the plot at the time: "There has been a revolt in the village; the English residents, including the heroine are in imminent danger of being killed by a surging mob of natives. Rescue comes suddenly from the air. Sir Alan in a bombing plane swoops low along the main street, terrifying the rebels and dropping a couple of bombs."[2]

During the 1920s and 1930s, European colonial powers increasingly relied on the new technology of aeroplanes to "control" mandates and colonies. In the British Empire, so-called "police bombing" became a central strategy of imperial governance. Indeed, it was argued at the time that without police bombing, the international "obligations" towards mandates and colonised territories could not have been fulfilled. The argument was made "that bombing from the air is a cheap, rapid, effective, and not in practice a particularly inhumane method of maintaining order in uncivilised and mountainous districts [which] is in itself quite incontrovertible".[3] Even though there was indeed little public discussion of police bombing (see Chapter 3), the argument was not in fact incontrovertible and the practice of police bombing was not entirely free from critique.

This chapter examines the debates – however limited – that did occur around police bombing by drawing on parliamentary records, newspaper coverage and popular-culture representations between the 1910s and the 1930s. My focus is on the unspoken assumptions, implicatures and presuppositions that underpinned these debates. Implicatures refer to meaning that is suggested by an utterance rather than explicitly stated, and presuppositions refer to background information that is taken for granted within an utterance. I argue that these deep silences carry particular discursive power precisely because they frame certain ideas as self-evident and thus place them beyond contestation.[4] Drawing on pragmatics and linguistic scholarship shows how such implicit discursive strategies operate through presupposition accommodation.[5] Because there is a default preference for a smooth linguistic exchange, interlocutors tend to accept and accommodate implicit assumptions.[6] Hidden underneath surface-level messages, presuppositions and implications are thus difficult to challenge. This dynamic continues to resonate in contemporary discussions of drone warfare. As I will demonstrate, unspoken assumptions here still function powerfully in communicating problematic ideas as self-evident, thus placing them beyond debate.

This chapter traces the debates surrounding the practice of police bombing, which focused on whether such bombing was conducted "humanely". I show how underlying these debates lay an unquestioned assumption that guilty individuals and tribes should be targeted. This assumption was deeply entwined with wider orientalist framings of the peoples and areas subjected to imperial control. The debates were infused with implicatures that transmit a sense of moral duty of Britain as a policing power who was assumed to have an obligation to control these spaces. The aeroplane, as a novel military technology, played a central role which embedded the practice into the "rhetoric of modernity" – casting aerial bombing as a symbol of Western technological advancement and civilisational superiority, in contrast to the backwards, colonial "other". These unspoken assumptions have important synergies with contemporary discourses surrounding drone warfare. A similar presupposition persists, namely that the presumed guilty – now framed as "terrorists" – should be killed. This presumption rests on orientalist framings of the places and peoples under surveillance and bombardment, and is supported by implicatures that cast the Western self as inherently virtuous and obligated to act.

This is not to say that there are not also important differences, and, as Loomba has argued, "all 'subordinating' discourses and practices are not the same either over time or across the globe".[7] There are differences in operational rules and ethical standards for bombing practices. Humane bombing in the context of police bombing practices was mainly to be guaranteed by giving advance warning of a bombing raid. In contrast, drone warfare places emphasis on precision targeting and international humanitarian law provisions regarding the distinction between civilians and combatants.[8] Yet, these differences rest on a shared bedrock of unquestioned assumptions, deep silences which shape the limits of the discourse.

Across both contexts, ethical concern that focuses on the "innocent" presupposes that those presumed guilty can and even should be killed. The debates about *how* bombing should be conducted obscure the deeper, unquestioned logic that military violence should be waged at all. These assumptions can only remain self-evident, deep silences, due to a host of orientalist and racialised understandings of the "other" and a self-image of Western moral superiority which themselves remain largely implied as self-evident assumptions. While they are more noticeable in the context of colonial police bombing, I argue that they continue to underpin contemporary warfare. Indeed, comparing the discourses across historical periods helps to make audible the often taken-for-granted deep silences within our own, more familiar regimes of not listening.

Humanely bombing the outlying regions of the Empire

The rules for bombing humanely were referenced both by critics of police bombing who argued that they had been broken and by supporters who invoked adherence to them in order to justify bombing practices. I use the term "rule" here as opposed to law because, even though there were some links to legal frameworks in international law, I am also interested in the less tangible, ethical considerations that are audible in debates of what constitutes "humane" and ethically acceptable bombing. These rules were concerned with the (purported) goal of sparing "innocent" lives. The legal category of "civilian" was starting to emerge in international law discourses at the time, most notably through the drafting of the Hague Rules of Aerial Warfare in 1922,[9] though the category did not become formalised until 1949.[10] Importantly, the emerging concept was restricted to white Europeans in international law discourses at the time through a "silent exclusion of non-European non-combatants from the civilian category".[11]

While not framed in legal terms, the protection of those deemed "innocent" played a central role in debates about the morality of police bombing in British parliamentary and media discussions. This was linked to two ethical provisions purportedly made to show mercy to colonised subjects. The first provision centred on giving advance warning to inhabitants before bombing an area. This rule was often invoked in justifications of police bombing practices: "In independent air operations, bombing is never resorted to unless at least 24 hours' notice is given to enable tribesmen and their families to evacuate the area."[12] The length of time between warning and attack seemed to be positively associated with the humaneness of the practice: "in all cases except one not less than two days' warning was given to enable the inhabitants to withdraw".[13]

The stated goal of this rule was to spare the lives of innocent colonial subjects who could evacuate the area. There were some doubts as to the effectiveness of the method. An article in the *Daily Herald*, for example, argued that despite giving prior warning, "the women, the children, and the peasantry, all of them innocent, will suffer from the destruction of the village".[14] Public opposition was not insignificant; for example at a demonstration in Birmingham in June, the bishop of Birmingham called attention to the indiscriminate nature of air bombing, calling it "morally indefensible".[15] Mostly, though, the discussion centred on whether advance warning was indeed given, with supporters insisting that this was routinely done: "The policy is to give warning before employing this weapon on the Frontier."[16]

Critics of the practice invoked gender and age as markers of innocence, with women and children presupposed as a particular social category[17] that differentiated them from those supposed guilty: "was it right that our officers should be engaged in killing women and children because the real culprits could not be discovered?"[18] However, the attention to "women and children" as a social category was subsumed within wider narratives that framed police bombing as a collective punitive action directed against entire tribes: "Those conditions do not exist in the Middle and Far East. There are no railways and very few and very bad roads. Therefore, if a peaceful population is to be protected from raids by marauding tribes, it can only be done from the air."[19] It was entire tribes who were framed as guilty, and thus legitimate targets, in juxtaposition to peaceful, obedient tribes: "Throughout bombing operations no villages were touched other than those of certain tribes which had probably above all others been consistently and actively hostile to Government."[20] This reflected international law discourses, which at times similarly argued that the emerging category of "civilian" was inapplicable to non-Europeans, as "among savages, war includes everyone".[21]

This understanding of entire tribes as punishable explains the second provision behind so-called "humane" bombing, which stressed the importance of offering tribes an opportunity to mend their ways and surrender: "Very seldom, indeed not at all during the last year, has bombing taken place for punitive purposes. Pamphlets are dropped in every case, and very often a loud speaker is used to give warning to the tribesmen that if they do not behave themselves aircraft will take action against them."[22] The provision of offering tribes an opportunity for reform and submission thus silently presupposed that tribes needed "to behave themselves".

The effectiveness of police bombing in upholding the opportunity for surrender was questioned by some commentators, who argued that aerial warfare inherently undermined the possibility for surrender, as there were no direct means for those on the ground to communicate submission: "People may have repented, but there is no one to whom they can express their repentance when it is a case of attack from the air."[23] Generally, though, the ability to follow this rule was positively compared to traditional ground war: "The people on the ground, if bombed, can always hold out a white sheet to show that they are endeavouring to surrender, whereas in the case of artillery fire, they cannot do so."[24]

There was, therefore, some debate over the extent to which police bombing conformed to the stated principles of "humane" warfare and fulfilled the purported goal of sparing innocent lives. However, these debates presupposed that people under imperial rule had to "behave themselves", and also presupposed the legitimacy of targeting those deemed to be guilty. Killing them was neither discussed nor problematised. The guilty were labelled "raiders",[25] "brigands",[26] or "rebels",[27] yet the nature of their alleged guilt was little discussed. Offences were vaguely defined with references to actions such as "raids" or "unrest". There was some discussion as to whether offences, such as a tribe's refusal to surrender a wanted individual,[28] or the non-payment of taxes, could justify "bombing of Arabs in Mesopotamia 'or elsewhere'".[29] Overall, however, the guilt of individuals or tribes was little discussed and instead was linked to orientalist framings of tribes as inherently violent and dangerous: "To present-day Europeans, at all events, modern war has become something utterly horrible, wasteful, and destructive. Not so to a Pathan of the North-West Frontier ... War is still to the Pathan the be-all and end-all of his existence. It is his hobby. He makes it an extremely profitable hobby when he gets the chance. The Pathans are a very large body of fighting men."[30]

Terms commonly used in discourses on police bombing – such as "tribes", "natives" or "barbarians" – carried inherently othering connotations that served to dehumanise people subjected to bombing. Notably, such language appeared even in critical accounts of bombing operations. For example, members of the British Red Cross and Near and Middle East Association stated in an open letter published in the *Daily Mail* that "we hope that never again will the Royal Air Force be employed in similar operations against *natives*, either in Iraq or elsewhere".[31] A critical article in the *Manchester Guardian* stated that "the 'collective' bombing of *tribes* and the destruction of their villages cannot be contemplated without revulsion".[32] The use of othering terms such as "tribes" and "natives" was embedded within broader discursive framings that portrayed entire regions as inherently wild and lawless, filled with dangerous men where "there are now probably 500,000 hardy, armed men in the tribal hills on both sides of the frontier".[33]

As Edward Said has argued, such perceptions are rooted in centuries of orientalist constructions of the colonial "other" in which Islam, in particular, has been framed through a lens of hostility and fear.[34] To Europeans, Islam and the Middle East have long been constructed "to symbolize terror, devastation, the demonic hordes of hated barbarians".[35] In the context of police bombing discourses, these orientalist tropes were further reinforced by depictions of the geography itself and – typically perhaps, for a British discourse – the weather. Both geography and climate were framed through notions of wilderness and hostility, further reinforcing the idea that such environments necessitated the control with bombing planes:

> The tribal territory [...] is one of the most tangled masses of ragged mountain country in the world. Limestone ranges and deep gorges running up in the case of the Safed Koh to 14,000 feet, incredibly rough, incredibly jagged, yet carrying, relative to its apparent resources, a very thick population. The country is further fortified by a very severe climate terrifically hot in the summer and exceedingly cold in the winter.[36]

While there was some debate over the use of police bombing – particularly whether the rules for humane warfare were always observed and the innocent spared – what remained largely unquestioned was the assumption that those deemed guilty of not submitting to the authority of the British and "behaving themselves" should be killed. The criteria for guilt were vague and linked to orientalist assumptions that portrayed entire regions as unruly and violent. These areas were imagined as rugged, dangerous places, populated by violent tribes, effectively naturalising the use of force without explicitly doing so. The racialised depictions of "certain outlying regions", *presumed* violence as necessary to check "refractory tribes"[37] and presented this assumption as self-evident and beyond debate. Military violence was understood as necessary not merely for security but also for advancing the supposed civilising mission and even safeguarding the "particular advantage to 'colonial' nations"[38] themselves.

An obligation to police

Underlying debates around police bombing was an unquestioned assumption, not only of the colonial "other" as wild and dangerous but of Britain as an inherently moral actor with a civilisational duty to use violence to maintain control over its colonies and mandates. This duty was framed as an obligation towards the colonies and mandates themselves, an obligation legally expressed in the mandate system of the League of Nations to protect those peoples stipulated as "not yet able to stand by themselves under the strenuous conditions of the modern world".[39] As will be evident in British parliamentary debates, this sense of duty was broadly grasped as a responsibility towards the world, civilisation and Christianity, three concepts often used interchangeably.

Within this framework, police bombing was understood as a crucial tool in fulfilling the duty of governing the colonies and mandates, most notably because it was regarded as more cost-effective and "safer" than traditional ground warfare. It was thus, for example, argued that "the financial saving in Iraq has made the fulfilment of our commitments under the mandate possible, and I do feel that if we had not developed this new technique, and brought the Budget of the last military year down from about £10,000,000 to a comparatively infinitesimal sum for the protection of that country, we should have been unable to fulfil that obligation".[40] Some people questioned the necessity of police bombing on the basis that it had been possible to control these territories even in "the times when there were no aeroplanes, when we still had to police those areas, when there were wilder tribes in existence which were more numerous and armed more on an equality with our land forces than they are to-day".[41]

Most, however, maintained that "police bombing" was the best or even the only means of fulfilling international obligations: "The continued free use of aircraft is in existing circumstances the *sole* economical means available of discharging our treaty obligations in certain territories."[42] This might have been at least partly down to the strategic way in which the Royal Air Force (RAF) had justified its existence and budget against the opposition of traditional military arms:[43] "Nobody in this Committee will dispute the intrinsic strength of the case for police bombing [...]. It is beyond question that the Government has been saved a considerable expense, in money and in the lives of her soldiers, by this method of dealing with outlying districts."[44] Presupposing that "outlying districts have to be dealt with", the whole rationale for police bombing rested on orientalist assumptions framing Britain's use of military violence as self-evidently necessary.

While the necessity and ethics of the method of bombing were thus somewhat debated, even critics of the practice of police bombing tended to assume or reassert the obligation to violently oppress and control outlying regions: "I am not so simple as to imagine that the policing of outlying parts is not going to be necessary for a very long time. Of course it will. [But] if we really believe in the security of Christendom we have to sacrifice our own convenience in this particular."[45] It is notable here how the speaker invoked the phrases "of course it will" and "I am not so simple as to imagine" as a way of demarcating the proposition – that policing is necessary – as self-evident and beyond debate. This unquestioned assumption of the necessity of policing was linked to portrayals of Britain as fulfilling a heroic role within civilisation and the world, since "we have to police the wild places of the earth on behalf of civilisation generally".[46]

Most of the opposition to police bombing was tied less to objections about the practice itself and more to concerns over how its use might affect the prospects of the European Disarmament Conference which took place in the 1930s – a point explored in more detail in Chapter 3. While a few isolated voices did question the morality of the practice in its own right, even these critics tended to rest on the assumption that Britain had an obligation to control the colonies and a sense of ethical superiority and civilisationism:[47]

> If you abolished that particular arm it might be more expensive in our men's lives and in our cash, to keep the frontiers of India and of Iraq and elsewhere [...]. But the question of its cheapness as a method of warfare is not the final test to which we should submit the use of force. There are certain things that we do not do [...]. In this category is bombing; such as the bombing of the Bondelzworts natives in

> South Africa. That is inhuman and you do not use inhuman weapons if you are a civilised State and if you consider the feelings of your own people and the traditions of your own race.[48]

These notions of ethical superiority were often invoked through unspoken assumptions, such as the existential presupposition that "there are civilised states", with the implication that Britain was one of them. Maintaining the values of Britain as an inherently "civilised State" was argued to be important in its own right, but also in terms of the "reputation which we have for being a little ahead of the rest of the world in the humane treatment of these problems".[49] While presumed to be effective, the practice of bombing was here seen as impacting negatively on the image of Britain and its role in promoting civilisation: "This is a moral problem and not merely a question of efficiency. It is not a question of the safety and convenience of the State but a question of justice and of our standards of civilisation and Christianity."[50] The existential proposition that "we have standards of civilisation and Christianity" was at times juxtaposed to the possibility of other states using the same techniques: "My primary objection to police bombing or bombing of any kind being in the hands of any sovereign Power, is that the sovereign Power would be liable at any moment and in any situation to be imitated by some other sovereign Power."[51]

Supporters of police bombing maintained that the method was ethical and indeed exemplified a more advanced and modern approach to imperial governance – what Satia has described as the imaginary of a "liberal empire in the sky".[52] Police bombing in the colonies and mandates was cast as saving lives, an argument almost always made in comparison to ground warfare, showing that "this kind of raid [with ground forces], with its consequent loss of life, has been almost entirely abolished by the measures taken by the Air Force".[53] Particularly when the European Disarmament Conference made the abolition of all bombing capacity a real possibility, there were concerns about the potential "reversion to older forms of ground warfare involving heavier casualties".[54] Crucially, the emphasis on reduced casualties in these arguments largely referred to the lives of British soldiers: "If we do away with that reservation, we shall have to go back to expeditions like those which have been necessary in the past for the maintenance of order on the North West Frontier of India, at Aden, and at other places, where cholera was rife, and where casualties of killed and wounded among the infantry were quite out of proportion to the work to be carried out."[55]

If casualties other than British soldiers were mentioned, they generally appeared as a side note: "In this period there have been no casualties to the Royal Air Force in Iraq during bombing operations. As regards casualties inflicted by the operations, none have been reported to Air Headquarters."[56] Only rarely was police bombing also more explicitly argued to be a method that saved the lives of so-called "natives":

> I do submit that the first concern of this House should be the lives of our own soldiers and not the lives of those at war against us. Even in their case, I think it can be shown clearly from the figures of campaigns, particularly on the North West Frontier of India in the last few years when the Air Force has been employed, as compared with the years when we used the old cumbersome methods of small but very expensive expeditions, that the new system of bombing from the air is far more merciful, in the matter of life to the people against whom these expeditions are made, than the old system of embarking on a regular war.[57]

The notion that police bombing was a more "merciful" form of warfare was rarely elaborated in detail but it seemed to rest on its supposedly preventive function: "I believe the aeroplane as a fighting machine is the most humane instrument that you can employ. I will give one reason only, and that is the speed with which you can act and the ability, therefore, to nip trouble in the bud, and prevent it spreading."[58] Police bombing was thus framed as a deterrent and "silent warning"[59] to tribes, tied to the rules for humane bombing: "Aircraft are, first, extremely swift in their operations. Within a few hours a squadron of aeroplanes can penetrate to the most remote villages, to the actual point of disturbance or disaffection and, not only that, but they are able from their very nature to give precise warning by dropping messages to the people who, if they do not mend their ways, will receive swift punishment."[60]

Debates tended to compare police bombing to other forms of warfare, rather than to unarmed policing, or indeed the possibility of ending occupation and violent oppression – alternatives that were notably absent from discussion. The positive comparison of police bombing to ground war serves a dual purpose. On the one hand it normalised the practice by aligning it with conventional forms of war, thereby legitimising the killing of "those at war against us".[61] At the same time, police bombing was directly contrasted to the brutality of traditional ground war as a new, more humane way of policing:

> The hon. Gentleman wants us, I suppose, to go back to the older methods. I have here a passage from Haldane's Insurrection of Mesopotamia, published in 1920, which will indicate to those who want to go back to the old methods the kind of methods to which they would be going back. It quotes from a published military order: "Villages will be razed to the ground, and all woodwork removed. Pressure will be brought on all inhabitants by cutting off water power and destroying water lifts [...]." How our pacifists must glory in the knowledge that they are going back to that charming, humane method of warfare when they abandon the reservation with regard to bombing in outlying areas.[62]

Altogether, the practice was positively compared to methods of ground war as a benign and restrained measure which needed to happen very rarely, followed the rules for humane killing and at times did not even use bombs but acted "only by means of a machine gun, or two machine guns, mounted on aeroplanes to scatter the rebels who are creating the disturbance".[63] As the name itself suggests, the practice was framed as a form of policing, described as the "policing of outlying parts",[64] "action"[65] or "measures taken by the Air Force"[66] which are "necessary for the preservation of order in outlying parts of our Empire".[67] This portrayal of police bombing rests on the presupposed moral authority of Britain, cast as fulfilling its civilisational duty to administer and control the colonies and mandates. The morality of the Western self is rarely explicitly addressed but is instead assumed and thus reinforced as a self-evident fact that does not need to be said out loud.

While some critics contended that police bombing was an inappropriate method and others defended it as the most humane and merciful way of "controlling" colonial territories with minimal casualties, both shared an unquestioned belief in the moral superiority of the civilised self. This belief was often not overtly stated but functioned through implicatures and presuppositions, deep silences that reinforced orientalist constructions of Western virtue as self-evident and beyond debate. Violence was not only justified but reconfigured as a moral obligation towards civilisation and the world. No figure embodied this heroic self-conception of virtuous, military masculinity more distinctly than the pilot. In the interwar years "airmen were not simply the heroes of modern warfare, the ultimate technological warriors, they had become the elite, the guardians of empire and international order".[68] First World War veterans, like pilot Alan Cobham, featured in documentaries sponsored by Imperial Airways and in films which documented the power of air policing, such as *Flight Commander*, where Alan Cobham "flies to the rescue, scaring the wits out of the rebels with his aerial prowess and bombing power, and peace is restored amid the waving of the Union Jack".[69] The following section will examine the wider context surrounding the emergence of aeroplane technology and its implications for conceptions of bombing as a humane practice.

The pinnacle of modernity

During the 1920s and 1930s, there was widespread fascination with "the novelty and modernity of the aeroplane, distant or near, and the sheer excitement it conveys as synecdochic of modernity as a whole".[70] This cultural excitement had a significant economic dimension, as major companies, such as Shell Oil, played a central role in developing aviation infrastructure and actively promoted positive representations of aircraft through air shows, specialist aircraft magazines, advertisements and films.[71] The positive representation of aircraft was not always a given, since the military capacities of the new technology also provoked widespread anxiety about aerial warfare and the threat to civilians stemming from enemy air attacks.[72] This fear was reflected in popular culture, such as the 1927 RAF Hendon Air Display, which featured a frightening mock air raid on London,[73] and in films like *Things to Come* (1936), which opened with an air attack on a British city and depicted a devastating global war culminating in the collapse of civilisation.[74] Nonetheless, the advancement of the air industry was widely perceived as an inevitable expression of progress. Even the film ended with an optimistic vision of future air power featuring "an international organization of 'airmen' called 'Wings Over the World' that ends the global war and leads to a peaceful future of technological advances".[75]

Across Western states, governments subsidised the new industry and competitively developed civilian airlines and military air forces. As Van Vleck has argued, the development of civilian and military aviation functioned as "a conduit of power – military, economic, and ideological".[76] In Britain, one of the first states to establish an independent military air force wing (the RAF),[77] aviation carried not only a military but also an imperial significance as a new instrument for global domination: "Naval strength had underpinned Britain's rise as an imperial power and aviation promised to reconfigure Britain's place in the globalised world of the future."[78] While most accounts of aerial development and culture in the interwar years relegate colonial aspects to the margins, they were in fact central to that development. As an instrument for imperialism, aeroplanes connected far-flung territories and facilitated the movement of civil servants, traders, goods and letters through the Imperial Mail System.[79] Imperial Airways (later to become British Airways) was a fusion of several private airlines which received considerable subsidies from the state to develop routes to India, South Africa and Australia.[80] Aerial surveillance and bombing gave rise to a new mode of imperial rule, which Satia has called "covert empire",[81] a form of control that departed from overt occupation and ground war, relying instead on air power to enforce imperial power from a distance.

The cultural representation of aviation was deeply entwined with imperial relations. As scholars have noted "modernity is represented by the aeroplane and/or its pilot; the gaze is that of the ground-based observer looking skywards".[82] This dynamic became even more compelling when imagined through the eyes of colonised subjects. In a newspaper report on Italian bombings in Abyssinia, for example, the technology was described through the real or imagined words of "natives" who described the aircraft as "monstrous metal birds that rain death out of the sky".[83] Here, the technological force of "modernity" was juxtaposed with the figure of the backwards, traditional "other", reinforcing a civilisational hierarchy. The aeroplane thus functioned not only as a symbol of progress and harbinger of modernity but as a means of constructing colonial difference. This included military and civilian aviation, which was framed within a discourse of Western "development". For example, the documentary *African Skyways*, which was selected for the British pavilion at the New York World's Fair in 1939, showed British civilian aviation as connecting and improving prosperity to African peoples:[84]

> An Imperial Airways plane landing "on a lake the size of Ireland" brings mail and facilitates the arrival of Western doctors and engineers to a nation where women are shown carrying large ceramic pots of water on their heads and where naked families live in straw huts. "Under British Colonial policy", intones the commentary, "the African combines the cultures of the west with his own traditions so that this country may one day rule itself."[85]

In addition to documentaries and films, air shows – or "air displays" – emerged as a popular medium through which the public encountered the new technology and its possibilities. Among these, the RAF show at Hendon attracted particularly large audiences, with hundreds of thousands of visitors – far surpassing sports events like the Football Association Cup final at Wembley.[86] These shows featured aerobatic displays, flight formations and mock battles in the air, but they also regularly included re-enactments of colonial police bombing operations.[87] A striking example is the 1927 Hendon display, which staged a dramatised scenario in an "Eastern village" where "natives" were depicted to attack European settlers. Following the evacuation of (white) women and children, a squadron of Fairey Fox bombers launched an aerial attack on the natives.[88] This imperial context helps to explain why British audiences were not only impressed by the military potential of air power but also knew to fear it: "The alleged prematurity with which Britons began to fear aerial bombardment in the early 1930s, before any apparent material international development, seems less remarkable when we look, as they did, beyond the European horizon of history to the distant happenings in the deserts of Arabia."[89]

Understanding the significance of the aeroplane within its economic and cultural context is essential to grasp the underpinnings of political debates surrounding "police bombing". The new practice was on the one hand depicted as a terrifying spectacle that subjugated colonised populations through fear, while it was on the other hand framed as a rational, restrained, even humane form of policing. This contradictory logic became even more evident in the context of the fears and moral outrage associated with aerial bombing in Europe – where air bombing was negatively compared to ground warfare. The 1927 air display at Hendon thus featured both a dystopian air raid of London and a triumphant representation of a mock attack of an "Eastern village". In so doing, it captured the ambivalence of the period's aerial imaginary in which air power was simultaneously feared as a terrifying, apocalyptic threat and celebrated as an instrument of civilisational control.

Mass killings of colonised populations and the use of violence to intimidate and control people have long been central to colonial rule, and it is important not to exaggerate the novelty of aerial police bombing as a radical departure from earlier forms of imperial violence.[90] What distinguished police bombing was not the nature, scale or purpose of violence, nor the identity of those subjected to it, but the technological means of conducting imperial violence. Nevertheless, the new technology and its symbolic representations gave rise to a powerful narrative of modernity that reframed the continuity of violence as innovation. The legitimacy of police bombing was therefore deeply embedded in what has been called the "rhetoric of modernity"[91] – a discursive framework which bound Western self-conceptions of rationality, moral superiority and scientific advancement and the depravity and backwardness of the colonised "other" to a story of progress. As postcolonial scholars have shown, colonialism universalised specific Western constructs – such as "scientific" knowledge, capitalist economic structures and centralised state authority – as self-evident characteristics of modernity.[92] Through this framework, violence enacted from the air could be presented not only as technological mastery but also as a symbol of and instrument for ethical advancement and superiority.

The film *Flight Commander* offers a telling example. It was praised by the British Empire Film Society for exposing both the ideals and the material resources of the Empire.[93] As previously discussed, this presumption of ethical superiority was implied not only through the acts enabled by the technology but, rather, through what the technology demonstrated *the self* to be: rational, modern and advanced. This fetishisation of aviation technology was intertwined with constructions of white military masculinity, often represented in stereotypical fantasies in which "aeroplanes can penetrate to the most remote villages, to the actual point of disturbance or disaffection".[94] Despite, or indeed through, these hyper-masculine tropes, the technology was framed as a symbol of civilisation and moral restraint. The scientific and rational dimensions of the "rhetoric of modernity" played a crucial role in these discourses. They served what Pugliese has called the "prosthetics of war"[95] – where killing conducted via advanced technologies appears as rational and detached from the harm it causes. Within this framework, police bombing could be represented as simply "the most efficient weapon for the suppression of barbarians".[96]

By focusing on technology, this discourse privileges an operational military perspective – what might be termed the bird's-eye view of the bomber pilot. From this vantage point the main concerns are logistics, tactics and effectiveness, rather than political or moral implications of violence. Even when debates approach questions of legitimacy or ethics, they become redirected towards technical discussions of method and implementation. Thus, the core question is not *whether* military violence should be inflicted but, rather, *how* it should be administered: "For such operations as we may take in a wide country where land troops can move only very slowly and with a great train of supplies – it may be in the Sudan or it may be in Iraq – I say that not only am I unable to distinguish morally between the use of the bomb and other means, but that

I believe the aeroplane as a fighting machine is the most humane instrument that you can employ."[97]

Police bombing as a practice was thus linked to conceptions of the material technology of the bombing aeroplane, a technology which was seen as a symbolic expression of Western modernity. Significant state and corporate funding reinforced the positive promotion of the image of aeroplanes, investing in air shows, magazines and films to advertise the power and significance of aviation technologies to the public. Embedded within the "rhetoric of modernity", police bombing was framed not only as an expression of technological superiority but as an enactment of ethical authority. The emphasis on technological capability shaped public discourses and privileged an operational military perspective, in which the main concerns were those of logistics, tactics and effectiveness. Crucially, these narratives were underpinned by a civilisational narrative of the innate technological and moral superiority of the Western "self" and the presumed backwardness and irrationality of the colonial "other". The following section turns to contemporary discourses around drone warfare. While there are clear differences in context and technology, I argue that important synergies in the unspoken assumptions underpinning the debates can be identified.

A new war

The emphasis on technology outlined in the previous section is important when examining contemporary discourses around "drone warfare" and, more broadly, the military deployment of AI and robotic systems. These discourses frequently focus on the technological capabilities of these weapon systems and reflect a broader cultural fascination with technological innovation. Public and strategic discourses on drone warfare often revolve around the enhanced operational capacities drones provide, positioning them as a natural progression in the evolution of warfare where "the role of those [remotely piloted aircraft] systems in armed conflicts will only increase over time, whether to gain a more complex level of situational awareness for tactical crews and military commanders or to attack positively identified targets when required".[98]

Such descriptions frame drone warfare in terms of the military superiority the new weapons systems provide, invoking echoes of colonial hierarchies: "It is our remotely piloted aircraft that the terrorists fear most. They know just as well as we do that these systems contribute massively to our identifying them and their weapons."[99]

This intense focus on technology amounts to a form of fetishisation where drone technologies – and increasingly AI-assisted technologies – become a centrepiece of discussions, attaining symbolic currency independent of the political or historical context of their actual deployment. As Parks and Kaplan have argued, they are constructed as "the most highly remediated 'new' things of the present moment – removing most traces or connections to the past".[100] This rhetoric of novelty not only masks the enduring colonial logics underpinning contemporary military violence but also implicitly embeds the practice within a broader narrative of technological and moral progress. Much like earlier discourses surrounding colonial police bombing, the technological framing of drone warfare invokes a scientific, rationalist rhetoric of modernity. Armed drone attacks are described in ultra-technical ways which abstract from the actual violence taking place, such as when the bombing of human beings is described as an attack on "positively identified targets".[101]

The focus on technology privileges an operational military perspective – what might be called the view from the drone – from which everything centres on logistics, target selection and the efficiency of methods of violence. Within this framework, drone technology is frequently justified as a tool for enhancing the precision of strikes, thereby purportedly ensuring compliance with contemporary rules for humane bombing: "Uniquely, UAVs [unmanned aerial vehicles] provide an unblinking and persistent ISR [intelligence, surveillance and reconnaissance] presence that can be exploited with crews being relieved while the aircraft remain airborne […]. Persistent surveillance provides a significantly more complete intelligence picture, which decreases the risk of misidentifying targets of interest."[102]

Of course, the norms governing what constitutes "humane bombing" have changed substantively since the era of colonial police bombing. Earlier doctrines focused on advance warning and the opportunity for entire tribal communities to "mend their ways".[103] In contrast, drone warfare is framed within a contemporary discourse of "precision" and individualisation. Linked to a shifting context of international law frameworks,[104] the emphasis is now on differentiating between combatants and civilians. The purported goal of sparing innocent lives is argued to be enabled through precise targeting of those deemed "terrorists", encapsulated in claims of "pinpoint-accurate strike capability".[105] The goal is presented less as putting pressure on entire groups to change their behaviour (though I will discuss later that this is not absent) and more as eliminating guilty individuals.

Another notable development is the prominent role played by claims of compliance with international law frameworks and the preoccupation with procedures and protocols in discourses around drone warfare. Unlike police bombing discourses, drone warfare is frequently framed through the lens of legality. In particular, justifications of drone warfare often invoke the central role of lawyers and legal frameworks in targeting decisions – though it is often unclear which legal frameworks: "There is a legal framework for each operation and that is supported by the legal service. It surprises some people that each strike has a legal sign-off, with lawyers who agree what can and cannot be done, including, as I know from my time in office, a chain that sometimes includes Ministers who have to agree to those sign-offs."[106] Discussions around drone warfare revolve around targeting procedures, such as how often the list of imminent threats is updated.[107] In British debates, there is an emphasis on "protocols about the way in which the UK Government target sites",[108] as well as the American rules of engagement which might differ from British laws.[109]

One the one hand, this legalistic framing appears to be heavily linked to the worry "that our serving personnel were not subject to legal threats",[110] a point I will explore more in the next chapter. On the other hand, it is tied to broader claims of legitimacy and moral restraint. Procedural adherence is often conflated with ethical responsibility, with the implication that observance of legal protocols and the involvement of lawyers is itself presented as evidence of the moral integrity of military violence:

> It is difficult for anyone in the chain of command to take a decision, from the person executing the mission on the ground right up to a Minister signing something off. That is not an easy process. Can things go wrong all the way through? Yes. However, I would argue that as long as a decision is underpinned by our legal processes right the way through to authorisation by a Minister to ensure that it is legally watertight, we should be okay. Mistakes will happen. What a lot of the public find strange is that in cells that deal with targeting, there are MOD [Ministry of Defence] or RAF lawyers sat there, saying, I am sorry, you cannot do that.[111]

This legalistic framing is closely linked to the construction of drone strikes as police-like actions rather than conventional warfare. Similar to the framing of police bombing previously discussed, this serves to distance drone warfare from the connotations of traditional military interventions, presenting it as not quite amounting to military violence at all: "Politically, drones have allowed the US in particular to pursue strategic objectives without needing to put boots on the ground in an era when, as we all know, there is very little appetite among western electorates for their countries to engage in further overseas military adventures."[112] Drone warfare is thus contrasted to ground war, not merely in method but in its ontological constitution, presenting it as something less than – or outside of – conventional warfare which does not count as an "overseas military adventure". Similar to colonial police bombing, drone warfare is cast as a rational form of preventive force which keeps local populations in check by its mere presence: "The fact of the matter is that they are put in some places as a deterrent, without firing at anything, because the sight of them apparently discourages insurgents."[113]

Supporters of drone warfare frequently justify its use through claims that the tactic saves lives, echoing the ambiguous and racialised notions of lives underlying police bombing justifications. Drone technology is described as an "exceptionally useful tool [that] contributes greatly toward protecting and defending UK forces and civilians".[114] However, the concept of protection is understood in markedly asymmetrical terms, with a strong focus on the safety of British personnel. As one account puts it: "They are apparently largely riskless, with very little chance of loss of human lives on our side."[115] Indeed, the notion of lives is at times expanded to include British national interests, economic stability and industrial employment: "And the RAF will receive a new fighter system, harnessing artificial intelligence and drone technology to defeat any adversary in air-to-air combat. Our plans will safeguard hundreds of thousands of jobs in the defence industry, protecting livelihoods across the UK and keeping the British people safe."[116]

Bad men in bad places

The ambivalent framing of drone warfare as simultaneously a form of war and not quite a war is apparent in depictions of drone pilots within contemporary popular culture. The martial identity of drone operators has been called into question and they have derisively been called "desk-jockey warriors".[117] The unease surrounding the quasi-civilian life of remote warfare is a central theme in films such as *Eye in the Sky* (2015) or *Drones* (2010). While these films highlight the psychological tensions faced by drone operators, they also reinforce the "precision myth" of armed drones and present them as a punitive technology against "bad guys". In doing so, such representations of drone warfare "perpetuate remnants of traditional gendered and racialized narratives that reconfigure the white male drone operator as morally courageous and a potential savior".[118]

Unlike the obvious civilising assumptions underlying earlier police bombing discourses – where Western violence was justified as a duty towards the colonies and the civilised world – contemporary discussions of drone warfare rarely invoke such tropes explicitly. Nevertheless, echoes of these civilisational narratives persist. Drone warfare is often cast as part of a broader moral struggle of good versus evil, with evil unequivocally located on the side of those labelled "terrorists". While critics may challenge the legality or accuracy of armed drone strikes, the overarching objectives of Western counterterrorism are rarely questioned. As one parliamentary comment illustrates: "Does he agree that, while we regret the loss of civilian lives, the drones' military objective of taking on terrorism is vastly important?"[119] The use of armed drones is framed not only as necessary but as serving a global good, implicitly reinforcing the moral superiority of the Western self.

As with historical discussions of police bombing, contemporary debates on drone warfare focus on whether the rules for humane bombing – purported to spare the innocent – are being observed. Critics of drone warfare argue that mistakes are made and "it may not be the bad guys who end up on the receiving end of drone strikes",[120] and worry about "the number of civilians caught up in some of those strikes".[121] However, underlying these debates a foundational assumption persists: that the so-called "bad guys" are legitimate targets and should be killed. In the discourse around drone warfare these "bad guys" are often labelled "terrorists" – a term that is not only heavily contested but also has racialised connotations. As Rabea Khan has shown, the concept of terrorism has a long, colonial history of being employed to delegitimise violence of the racialised or colonial "other" while simultaneously legitimising state violence by the West. She concludes "that 'terrorism' is a pejorative rather than analytical term because of its racial underpinnings and connotations".[122]

In contrast to police bombing discourses, contemporary discourses on drone warfare emphasise the targeting of individuals rather than entire tribes or villages. The prevailing norms for humane bombing today centre on the precise identification and killing of specific individuals, with much of the critical discourse focused on questioning this precision claim. Terms like "tribes" and "natives" are largely absent from contemporary public debates. However, there is a recurrent slippage from the language of individual "terrorists" and "targets" to broader and more ambiguous categories, such as "combatants" or the "enemy".[123] These are war-based classifications that implicitly designate entire regions as war zones or "theatres of conflict",[124] regardless of whether locations meet the threshold for armed conflict under international law.[125] This framing rests on a stark spatial and moral dichotomy between the violence "over there", presumed to be a war zone, and the stability and legality presumed "at home" – a point explored further in Chapter 3: "You can argue that, well that is war over there, and that is a lower standard, and I can accept it."[126]

This discursive slippage is enabled through implicit orientalist constructions – not only of the individuals targeted but of entire regions where armed drones are used: "It is now possible, through satellite technology and drones, to collect video footage of battle zones and run the information collected through facial recognition software, which allows us to track much more forensically and accurately the movement, habits, working lives and leisure of bad people in bad places."[127] The presupposition that there are "bad people" as well as "bad places" is not overtly stated as a point for discussion but is implied as self-evident and beyond debate, a side note added to the technological capacity of armed drones. These so-called "bad places" are portrayed along orientalist lines as wild and lawless areas, "the ungoverned parts of the world where Five Eyes co-operation is often strongest: Iraq, Pakistan, Afghanistan and, more recently, parts of Syria".[128]

Such representations evoke colonial imaginaries of disorder and violence inherent in the peoples and places subjected to bombing: "Reports from the federally administered tribal areas in Pakistan suggest that it is a matter of honour under the tribal code for the families of drone attack victims to seek revenge."[129] Even NGO and human rights discourses at times reproduce such orientalist tropes, framing areas subjected to bombing as ungoverned and dangerous, for example when Amnesty International describes the "remote and lawless nature of the region".[130] Such "imagined geographies"[131] – to borrow Said's term – have long underpinned imperial logics and continue to implicitly shape contemporary understandings of military violence. Even critical accounts, such as those noting the difficulty of investigating drone strikes due to "the danger and remoteness of the places where targets are located",[132] implicitly reinforce the idea that these places are ungovernable, wild and thus appropriate sites for technologically mediated violence: "This is, of course, one reason why remotely piloted systems like armed UAVs may have been chosen for use in the first place."[133]

Despite the shifts in legal and normative frameworks for humane bombing, significant continuities remain in terms of the unspoken assumptions underpinning debates on aerial bombing of the Global South. Both drone warfare and police bombing practices rely on the unquestioned assumption that "terrorists" or "rebels" should be killed by technologically advanced, Western states, and that using bombs for this purpose is justified because "over there" is presumed to be a war zone. These assumptions fundamentally rely on racialised castings of the areas and peoples in which bombing takes place. The depiction of rugged mountains and violent, tribal chaos is linked to a presumed necessity for the civilisational corrections of the virtuous West in its rational use of advanced military technologies. While these bombing practices may appear to be ethically contested in public debates, they are staged in a discourse which fundamentally accepts these orientalist assumptions as self-evident and beyond debate. The focus remains on the methods used for *how* to control the outlying regions of the Empire, reproducing a deep silence on the question of *whether* violence and oppression are morally or politically legitimate in the first place.

Communicating self-evidence

This chapter has analysed discourses on police bombing and drone warfare in UK parliamentary, media and popular culture representations and has argued that both discourses are underpinned by a set of shared, unspoken assumptions, presuppositions and implications. While many of these assumptions – particularly those rooted in stark orientalist binaries between the civilised self and the barbaric other – are louder in the case of police bombing, they remain subtly embedded in contemporary drone narratives. Comparing the two cases enables us to make assumptions audible which might otherwise be taken for granted. This, of course, is one of the reasons why presuppositions, inferences and implicatures are so powerful in the first place. By not being said out loud, they are signalled to be self-evident truths which are not up for debate. It is more difficult to challenge presuppositions and unspoken assumptions precisely because they remain unarticulated.

While this chapter has focused on convergences between the two practices in terms of their underlying assumptions, I have also shown significant divergences, particularly in terms of the rules and normative frameworks for "humane" bombing. In the context of police bombing, bombing procedures centred on whether advance warning had been given and whether tribes had been offered a chance to "mend their ways" and surrender. In the context of drone warfare, the rules are focused on precision bombing, and "humane" conduct is defined by the accurate targeting and elimination of those deemed guilty, supported by detailed legal processes and the technological capacity of drones.

Despite these differences, both practices rely on a shared bedrock of unspoken assumptions. Discussions on whether the innocent have been spared presuppose that those deemed guilty – the so-called "bad guys" – should be killed. This act of killing is consistently framed not as warfare but as a form of policing which is cast as preventive, restrained and ultimately life preserving. In both cases, the lives presumed as worth saving are primarily Western lives. The construction of bombing as a benign form of violence is inherently linked to racialised depictions of the people and places subjected to bombing. While colonial-era police bombing discourses more explicitly drew on orientalist notions of "violent tribes" which necessitate "control", echoes of these logics persist implicitly in contemporary debates on drone warfare, particularly through the portrayal of entire regions as hostile, wild and inherently threatening. These spatial imaginaries sustain the construction and normalisation of war zones "over there" and legitimate ongoing military intervention. These ideas and imaginaries are not overtly stated but are implied as self-evident and thus reinforced as truths that are beyond debate.

As a result, bombing is not merely rendered permissible but can become framed as a positive duty towards the colonies, civilisation, Christianity or the world at large. Even critiques of the practice often presuppose the ethical superiority of the West, often tethered to its material and technological advancement. The focus on the new technology functions to embed these discourses within a broader rhetoric of modernity which demarcates military violence as novel, rational and progressive – thereby masking continuities with past systems of violence and oppression. The technological focus further shifts the discursive lens towards an operational, militarised viewpoint – the view from above – from which the focus is on effectiveness, targeting methods and protocols. On the bedrock of these unspoken assumptions, military violence is not only justified but normalised. As deep silences, these unspoken assumptions and presuppositions function to communicate such matters as self-evident and beyond debate. The following chapter will explore how this process of normalisation is sustained through a broader architecture of silence and neglect in Western discourses of imperial warfare.

Notes

All URLs were last accessed on October 30, 2025.

1 Gordon H. Pirie, "Cinema and British Imperial Civil Aviation, 1919–1939," *Historical Journal of Film, Radio and Television* 23, no. 2 (2003): 120, https://doi.org/10.1080/0143968032000091068

2 *Daily Mail*, "Sir A. Cobham's Film 'Swoop,'" July 18, 1927.

3 *The Times*, "Police Bombing," May 30, 1933.

4 Robyn Carston and Alison Hall, "3. Implicature and Explicature," in *Cognitive Pragmatics*, ed. Hans-Jörg Schmid (De Gruyter, 2012); Sbisà, "Presupposition and Implicature."

5 Sbisà, "Presupposition and Implicature," 178.

6 Sbisà, "Presupposition and Implicature," 178.

7 Loomba, *Colonialism/Postcolonialism*, 17.

8 K. J. Heller, "'One Hell of a Killing Machine': Signature Strikes and International Law," *Journal of International Criminal Justice* 11, no. 1 (2013): 89–119, https://doi.org/10.1093/jicj/mqs093; Nehaluddin Ahmad et al., "Can International Humanitarian Law Regulate Recent Drone Strikes?: A Case Study," *Journal of East Asia and International Law* 17 (2024): 159; Christof Heyns et al., "The International Law Framework Regulating the Use of Armed Drones," *International & Comparative Law Quarterly* 65, no. 4 (2016): 791–827, https://doi.org/10.1017/S0020589316000385

9 Amanda Alexander, "The Genesis of the Civilian," *Leiden Journal of International Law* 20, no. 2 (2007): 359–76, https://doi.org/10.1017/S0922156506003347; Christiane Wilke and Helyeh Doutaghi, "Legal Technologies: Conceptualizing the Legacy of the 1923 Hague Rules of Aerial Warfare," *Leiden Journal of International Law* 37, no. 1 (2024): 88–110, https://doi.org/10.1017/S0922156523000493

10 Helen Kinsella, *The Image before the Weapon: A Critical History of the Distinction between Combatant and Civilian*, 1st ed. (Cornell University Press, 2011), 10.

11 Christiane Wilke and Helyeh Doutaghi, "Legal Technologies: Conceptualizing the Legacy of the 1923 Hague Rules of Aerial Warfare." *Leiden Journal of International Law* 37, no. 1 (2024): 88–110, 104; see also page 100, https://doi.org/10.1017/S0922156523000493
12 UK House of Commons, *HC Debates*, June 16, 1938, Vol. 337, Aerial Warfare, Cc395–7.
13 UK House of Commons, *HC Debates*, July 3, 1924, Vol. 175, Bombing Operations, Iraq, Cc1490–2.
14 *Daily Herald*, "Bombs for Natives," n.d.
15 *Manchester Guardian*, "Right to Police Bombing: Effect in Wartime: Dr Barnes's Example: Birmingham Protest," June 19, 1933.
16 UK House of Commons, *HC Debates*, April 29, 1932, Vol. 265, India Office, Cc703–84, 1932.
17 Sbisà, "Presupposition and Implicature."
18 *Daily Mail*, "Mespot Waste," March 2, 1923.
19 UK House of Commons, *HC Debates*, June 13, 1933, Vol. 279, Foreign Office, Cc29–146.
20 *Daily Mail*, "Secret of a Gorge," June 12, 1924.
21 Elbridge Colby, "How to Fight Savage Tribes," *American Journal of International Law* 21, no. 2 (1927): 281.
22 UK House of Commons, *HC Debates*, March 14, 1933, Vol. 275, Supply, Cc1795–896.
23 UK House of Commons, *HC Debates*, June 13, 1933, Vol. 279, Foreign Office, Cc29–146.
24 UK House of Commons, *HC Debates*, June 13, 1933, Vol. 279, Foreign Office, Cc29–146.
25 UK House of Commons, *HC Debates*, June 13, 1933, Vol. 279, Foreign Office, Cc29–146.
26 *Daily Mail*, "British in Frontier Skirmish," July 28, 1933.
27 UK House of Commons, *HC Debates*, March 14, 1933, Vol. 275, Supply, Cc1795–896.
28 *Manchester Guardian*, "Letters to the Editor: Police Bombing: Does Use in India Mean Use in Europe?" August 16, 1933.
29 *Daily Mail*, "Bombing for Taxes," February 24, 1923.
30 UK House of Commons, *HC Debates*, April 29, 1932, Vol. 265, India Office, Cc703–84, 29.
31 *Daily Mail*, "Bombing for Taxes," February 12, 1924, emphasis added; see for a notable exception the open letter by the Humane Education Society, who demand a stop of the use of air bombing and liquid and poison gas "upon human beings and animals" in the *Manchester Guardian*, "Police bombing," August 28, 1933.

32 *Manchester Guardian*, "Police Bombing," May 29, 1933, see also reporting on a film project by John Amery, where the *Daily Mail* states that "some of the proposed scenes have aroused protests. They include the bombing of natives, the rescue of a European from natives by means of an aeroplane, and the blowing up of a native village", in *Daily Mail*, "Mr. Amery's Son and a Film," March 17, 1932.
33 *Daily Mail*, "British in Frontier Skirmish," July 28, 1933.
34 Said, *Orientalism*, 74.
35 Said, *Orientalism*, 59.
36 UK House of Commons, *HC Debates*, April 29, 1932, Vol. 265, India Office, Cc703–84, 29.
37 *Manchester Guardian*, "Police Bombing," May 29, 1933.
38 *Manchester Guardian*, "Police Bombing," May 29, 1933.
39 Covenant of the League of Nations, Art. 22; see also Leonard V. Smith, "Sovereignty under the League of Nations Mandates: The Jurists' Debates," *Journal of the History of International Law / Revue d'histoire Du Droit International* 21, no. 4 (2019): 563–87, https://doi.org/10.1163/15718050-12340133; Anghie, "Colonialism and the Birth of International Institutions."
40 UK House of Commons, *HC Debates*, June 13, 1933, Vol. 279, Foreign Office, Cc29–146, 13.
41 UK House of Commons, *HC Debates*, June 13, 1933, Vol. 279, Foreign Office, Cc29–146, 13.
42 UK House of Commons, *HC Debates*, June 26, 1933, Vol. 279, Disarmament (Draft Convention), Cc1161–62, 1933, emphasis added.
43 Michael Paris, *Warrior Nation: Images of War in British Popular Culture, 1850–2000* (Reaktion, 2000), 158.
44 UK House of Commons, *HC Debates*, June 13, 1933, Vol. 279, Foreign Office, Cc29–146, 13.
45 UK House of Commons, *HC Debates*, June 13, 1933, Vol. 279, Foreign Office, Cc29–146, 13.
46 UK House of Commons, *HC Debates*, June 13, 1933, Vol. 279, Foreign Office, Cc29–146, 13.
47 See, for a notable exception, *HC Debates*, June 13, 1922, Vol. 279, Foreign Office, Cc29–146: "We send out missionaries to convert the people to our religion, and we send our bombers to send them to that Heaven which we are trying to convert them to believe in, more speedily than they would go in the natural course."
48 UK House of Commons, *HC Debates*, July 5, 1933, Vol. 280, Foreign Office, Cc339–457, 1933.

49 UK House of Commons, *HC Debates*, July 5, 1933, Vol. 280, Foreign Office, Cc339–457.
50 UK House of Commons, *HC Debates*, July 5, 1933, Vol. 280, Foreign Office, Cc339–457.
51 UK House of Commons, *HC Debates*, December 13, 1933, Vol. 284, International Police Force, Cc445–502, 1933.
52 Satia, *Spies in Arabia*, 245.
53 UK House of Commons, *HC Debates*, July 3, 1924, Vol. 175, Bombing Operations, Iraq, Cc1490–2.
54 UK House of Commons, *HC Debates*, June 26, 1933, Vol. 279, Disarmament (Draft Convention), Cc1161–62.
55 UK House of Commons, *HC Debates*, June 13, 1933, Vol. 279, Foreign Office, Cc29–146.
56 UK House of Commons, *HC Debates*, July 3, 1924, Vol. 175, Bombing Operations, Iraq, Cc1490–92.
57 UK House of Commons, *HC Debates*, June 13, 1933, Vol. 279, Foreign Office, Cc29–146.
58 UK House of Commons, *HC Debates*, July 5, 1933, Vol. 280, Foreign Office, Cc339–457.
59 Wilson quoted in Satia, *Spies in Arabia*, 245.
60 UK House of Commons, *HC Debates*, April 29, 1932, Vol. 265, India Office, Cc703–84.
61 UK House of Commons, *HC Debates*, June 13, 1933, Vol. 279, Foreign Office, Cc29–146.
62 UK House of Commons, *HC Debates*, June 13, 1933, Vol. 279, Foreign Office, Cc29–146.
63 UK House of Commons, *HC Debates*, March 14, 1933, Vol. 275, Supply, Cc1795–896.
64 UK House of Commons, *HC Debates*, June 13, 1933, Vol. 279, Foreign Office, Cc29–146.
65 UK House of Commons, *HC Debates*, March 14, 1933, Vol. 275, Supply, Cc1795–896.
66 UK House of Commons, *HC Debates*, July 3, 1924, Vol. 175, Bombing Operations, Iraq, Cc1490–92.
67 UK House of Commons, *HC Debates*, June 13, 1933, Vol. 279, Foreign Office, Cc29–146.
68 Paris, *Warrior Nation*, 158.
69 The Flight Commander script, British Film Institute Library, London; in Tony Shaw, "Early Warnings of the Red Peril: A Pre-History of Cold War British Cinema, 1917–1939," *Film History* 14, no. 3/4 (2002): 365.

70 Luke Seaber, "'From This New Culture of the Air We Finally See': 'Groundmindedness' in the 1930s," in *Aviation in the Literature and Culture of Interwar Britain*, ed. Michael McCluskey and Luke Seaber (Springer International Publishing, 2020), 43.
71 McCluskey and Seaber, *Aviation in the Literature and Culture of Interwar Britain*, 12.
72 Alexander, "The Genesis of the Civilian," 372.
73 Brett Holman, "Spectre and Spectacle: Mock Air Raids as Aerial Theatre in Interwar Britain," in *Aviation in the Literature and Culture of Interwar Britain*, ed. Michael McCluskey and Luke Seaber (Springer International Publishing, 2020), 489.
74 McCluskey and Seaber, *Aviation in the Literature and Culture of Interwar Britain*, 13.
75 McCluskey and Seaber, *Aviation in the Literature and Culture of Interwar Britain*, 13.
76 Jenifer Van Vleck, *Empire of the Air: Aviation and the American Ascendancy* (Harvard University Press, 2013), 3, https://doi.org/10.4159/harvard.9780674726246
77 Holman, "Spectre and Spectacle," 487.
78 Scott Anthony, "The Future's in the Air: Imperial Airways and the British Documentary Film Movement," *Journal of British Cinema and Television* 8, no. 3 (2011): 301–21, https://doi.org/10.3366/jbctv.2011.0041; see also Richard Overy, *The Morbid Age: Britain between the Wars* (London, 2009), 313.
79 McCluskey and Seaber, *Aviation in the Literature and Culture of Interwar Britain*, 7–8.
80 Anthony, "The Future's in the Air," 302.
81 Satia, *Spies in Arabia*, 7.
82 Seaber, "'From This New Culture of the Air We Finally See'", 44.
83 *Daily Mail*, "Warplanes Disperse Massed Warriors," October 9, 1935.
84 Anthony, "The Future's in the Air," 308.
85 Anthony, "The Future's in the Air," 308.
86 Holman, "Spectre and Spectacle," 490.
87 Paris, *Warrior Nation*, 158.
88 Holman, "Spectre and Spectacle," 489.
89 Satia, *Spies in Arabia*, 254.
90 Satia, *Spies in Arabia*, 11.
91 Mignolo, *The Politics of Decolonial Investigations*, 7.
92 Mignolo, *The Politics of Decolonial Investigations*, 37; Quijano, "Coloniality of Power and Eurocentrism in Latin America."

93 Pirie, "Cinema and British Imperial Civil Aviation, 1919–1939," 120.
94 UK House of Commons, *HC Debates*, April 29, 1932, Vol. 265, India Office, Cc703–84.
95 Joseph Pugliese, "Prosthetics of Law and the Anomic Violence of Drones," *Griffith Law Review* 20 (2011): 931.
96 UK House of Commons, *HC Debates*, July 5, 1933, Vol. 280, Foreign Office, Cc339–457.
97 UK House of Commons, *HC Debates*, July 5, 1933, Vol. 280, Foreign Office, Cc339–457.
98 UK House of Commons, *HC Debates*, October 13, 2015, Vol. 600, Drones in Conflict, Cc288–94, 2015.
99 UK House of Commons, *HC Debates*, December 1, 2015, Vol. 603, Westminster Hall, Armed Drones, Cc50WH–72WH, 2015.
100 Lisa Parks and Caren Kaplan, *Life in the Age of Drone Warfare* (Duke University Press, 2020), 161.
101 UK House of Commons, *HC Debates*, October 13, 2015, Vol. 600, Drones in Conflict, Cc288–94.
102 UK House of Commons, *HC Debates*, November 6, 2012, Vol. 552, Westminster Hall, Unmanned Aerial Vehicles, Cc197WH–204WH, 2012.
103 UK House of Commons, *HC Debates*, April 29, 1932, Vol. 265, India Office, Cc703–84.
104 Amanda Alexander, "A Short History of International Humanitarian Law," *European Journal of International Law* 26, no. 1 (2015): 109–38, https://doi.org/10.1093/ejil/chv002; Kinsella, *The Image before the Weapon.*
105 UK House of Commons, *HC Debates*, December 1, 2015, Vol. 603, Westminster Hall, Armed Drones, Cc50WH–72WH.
106 UK House of Commons, *HC Debates*, October 14, 2020, Public Bill Committees, Overseas Operations (Service Personnel and Veterans) Bill (Fifth Sitting), Cc131–62, 2020.
107 "If article 51, which states that there has to be an imminent threat, is to mean anything, the security services and, indeed, Ministers who are considering the issue need to be in a position to update such a list constantly", in UK House of Commons, *HC Debates*, December 1, 2015, Vol. 603, Westminster Hall, Armed Drones, Cc50WH–72WH.
108 UK House of Commons, *HC Debates*, November 7, 2012, Vol. 552, Westminster Hall, Combat Troop Withdrawal (Afghanistan), Cc224WH–245WH.
109 UK House of Commons, *HC Debates*, March 20, 2018, Public Bill Committees, Data Protection Bill [Lords] (Fifth Sitting), Cc161–94.

110 UK House of Commons, *HC Debates*, March 20, 2018, Public Bill Committees, Data Protection Bill [Lords] (Fifth Sitting), Cc161–94.
111 UK House of Commons, *HC Debates*, October 14, 2020, Public Bill Committees, Overseas Operations (Service Personnel and Veterans) Bill (Fifth Sitting), Cc131–62.
112 UK House of Commons, *HC Debates*, December 1, 2015, Vol. 603, Westminster Hall, Armed Drones, Cc50wh–72WH.
113 UK House of Commons, *HC Debates*, November 7, 2012, Vol. 552, Westminster Hall, Combat Troop Withdrawal (Afghanistan), Cc224WH–245WH.
114 UK House of Commons, *HC Debates*, December 1, 2015, Vol. 603, Westminster Hall, Armed Drones, Cc50wh–72WH.
115 UK House of Commons, *HC Debates*, December 1, 2015, Vol. 603, Westminster Hall, Armed Drones, Cc50WH–72WH.
116 UK House of Commons, *HC Debates*, November 19, 2020, Vol. 684, Integrated Review, Cc487–505.
117 Robert Sparrow, "War without Virtue?" in *Killing by Remote Control*, by Jeff McMahan, ed. Bradley Jay Strawser (Oxford University Press, 2013).
118 Thomas Ærvold Bjerre, "Unmanned? Military Masculinities in Filmic Representations of US Drone Operators," *Men and Masculinities* 26, no. 1 (2023): 25, https://doi.org/10.1177/1097184X221139820
119 Mahmood Ahmad, "The Legality of Unmanned Aerial Vehicles Outside the Combat Zone: A Case Study of the Federally Administered Tribal Areas of Pakistan†," *Defense & Security Analysis*, www.tandfonline.com/doi/abs/10.1080/14751798.2014.921448
120 UK House of Commons, *HC Debates*, December 1, 2015, Vol. 603, Westminster Hall, Armed Drones, Cc50WH–72WH.
121 UK House of Commons, *HC Debates*, March 20, 2018, Public Bill Committees, Data Protection Bill [Lords] (Fifth Sitting), Cc161–94.
122 Rabea M. Khan, "A Case for the Abolition of 'Terrorism' and Its Industry," *Critical Studies on Terrorism* 0, no. 0 (n.d.): 2, https://doi.org/10.1080/17539153.2024.2327727
123 UK House of Commons, *HC Debates*, March 20, 2018, Public Bill Committees, Data Protection Bill [Lords] (Fifth Sitting), Cc161–94.
124 See for example UK House of Commons, *HC Debates*, November 6, 2012, Vol. 552, Westminster Hall, Unmanned Aerial Vehicles, Cc197WH–204WH.
125 Gloria Gaggioli and Pavle Kilibarda, "Counterterrorism and the Risk of Over-Classification of Situations of Violence," *International Review of the Red Cross* 103, nos. 916–17 (2021): 203–36,

https://doi.org/10.1017/S1816383121000424; Mary Ellen O'Connell, "Combatants and the Combat Zone," *University of Richmond Law Review* 43 (2008): 845.

126 US Congress, *Congressional Record*, Vol. 159 (32), Senate, March 6, 2013, S1181–226, 2013, 06.

127 UK House of Commons, *HC Debates*, March 20, 2018, Public Bill Committees, Data Protection Bill [Lords] (Fifth Sitting), Cc161–94.

128 UK House of Commons, *HC Debates*, December 1, 2015, Vol. 603, Westminster Hall, Armed Drones, Cc50WH–72WH.

129 UK House of Commons, *HC Debates*, December 1, 2015, Vol. 603, Westminster Hall, Armed Drones, Cc50wh–72WH.

130 Amnesty International, "*Will I Be Next?" US Drone Strikes in Pakistan*, 2013, www.amnestyusa.org/reports/will-i-be-next-us-drone-strikes-in-pakistan/

131 Said, *Orientalism*.

132 UNIDIR, *Increasing Transparency, Oversight and Accountability of Armed Unmanned Aerial Vehicles, United Nations Institute for Disarmament Research*, 2017, https://unidir.org/publication/increasing-transparency-oversight-and-accountability-of-armed-unmanned-aerial-vehicles/

133 UNIDIR, *Increasing Transparency, Oversight and Accountability*.

3

Neglect

This chapter maps out a broader architecture of deep silences that underpins discourses on imperial violence. I use the term "deep silences" because these silences have remained unrecognised and hidden – unlike the loud silences I will explore in the following chapters – and because they are deeply engrained within our regimes of not listening. These silences are not monolithic absences but manifest through the neglect and backgrounding of certain aspects, while others are foregrounded and emphasised. For example, in UK parliamentary debates, there is a notable focus on the welfare of drone operators, contrasting sharply with the lack of attention to the wellbeing of people living under drones.

The deep silences investigated in this chapter carry with them muffled undertones of racialised registers that render some individuals and populations killable and their death "ungrievable". As Judith Butler has argued in a similar context, such silences should prompt us to question and oppose "the conditions under which certain human lives are more vulnerable than others, and thus certain human lives are more grievable than others."[1] For example, in US Congress the absence of discussions of drone warfare "abroad" starkly contrasts with the extensive debates on the hypothetical use of armed drones "at home" within the United States. Deep silences thus reflect assumptions about worth and disposability, determining, in Achille Mbembe's words, "who matters and who does not, who is *disposable* and who is not".[2]

The neglect of the death of the colonial "other" is haunted by a historical silence on coloniality itself and is embedded within a history of absence. Mapping deep silences in the colonial context of police bombing thus reveals notable similarities with contemporary discourses. Parliamentary and media discourses at the time thus primarily discussed police bombing in terms of how it might affect the "Empire at its heart", for example in terms of the cost of bombing operations or the success of the European Disarmament Conference. Deep silences thus persist and overlap in discourses about bombing campaigns in imperial wars "abroad". These silences are not merely historically significant but have real-world implications. As Rutazibwa reminds us, "a people's systematically denied and erased suffering allows for the re-enactment of their premature death in the material world".[3]

The act of mapping silences inevitably raises questions of intentionality and accountability. Are individuals or institutions silent because they are unable to speak, is silence a deliberate choice, or even a non-choice stemming from a lack of knowledge about the issue? Rather than pursuing questions of motive, this chapter investigates how, regardless of intentionality, such silences illuminate what is rendered ir/relevant and un/important. Deep silences can have an illocutionary – or performative – effect that *does* something. Not speaking about an issue can more powerfully denote its insignificance than explicit statements ever could. Silence here communicatively produces the notion that an issue is – and is to be considered – irrelevant. In this way, deep silence demarcates zones of irrelevance around violence and its consequences, thereby facilitating its continuation. As Block De Behar observes, "silence is often an efficient instrument of obliteration, and one that leaves no traces."[4]

Building on and contributing to scholarship on state censorship, this chapter examines the crucial role of deep silence in war propaganda. I adopt the term *banal silencings* to indicate that these silences are not neutral but embedded within power relations of who is listened to. However, these are not necessarily centralised or monolithic acts of silencing but are multiple and fragmented. Departing from an agential model of propaganda which focuses on state mechanisms for top-down censorship and control, my analysis emphasises the subtler regimes of not listening that sustain these networks of silences. These dynamics are embedded within material and institutional structures, but they also exceed them. I draw on postcolonial scholarship, and particularly on Stoler's concept of colonial aphasia, which denotes a cultural inability to articulate or meaningfully engage with colonial violence.[5] While embedded in power relations, these absences are also part of banal, everyday acts of not speaking and not listening.

A history of absence

Colonial violence has a long history of being silenced, not just at the moment of its enactment but through consistent sidelining, forgetting and dis-remembering over subsequent decades.[6] Scholarship on the Mau Mau uprising in Kenya, for instance, has demonstrated how reporting at the time foregrounded narratives of Mau Mau terrorism while largely omitting information on the hundreds of thousands of black Kenyans who were killed.[7] Government records documenting such violence were deliberately concealed for decades, reinforcing this erasure.[8] However, it is important to resist framing these dynamics through simplistic binaries of absence and presence, as if colonial violence were entirely silenced and forgotten until suddenly revealed. As Bijl has shown in the case of Dutch colonial discourses, detailed information and photographic evidence of colonial violence often existed at the time. However, when such evidence was presented, it was ignored, unintegrated or assimilated into more recognisable frames in dominant discourses.[9] Stoler has used the term "colonial aphasia" to refer to an underlying blockage as "a dismembering, a difficulty speaking, a difficulty generating a vocabulary that associates appropriate words and concepts with appropriate things" when it comes to colonial violence.[10] Following Stoler, this difficulty of speaking and hearing is part of a wider condition that consists of active as well as subconscious processes of ignoring and forgetting colonial violence within our regimes of not listening.[11]

The concept of colonial aphasia helps to see how colonial police bombing practices are actively dis-remembered and erased from contemporary discourses. The concept also sheds light on the ways in which the topic of police bombing practices was backgrounded and omitted in public discourses at the time. When "police bombing" was brought up in Parliament, it was often as a side note, for example when referring to the repression of "political opinion in India by a great show of force, and, under modern conditions, a great show of force means the use of aeroplanes for bombing purposes".[12] There was awareness of aeroplanes being used for bombing purposes as part of the government's imperial policies. The British government's imperial policies – particularly its involvement in the Middle East – were often met with scepticism, largely due to concerns about financial cost and suspicions regarding who stood to benefit, including powerful corporate interests in the Middle East, such as those tied to oil. This distrust was further increased by the covertness of imperialism in the Middle East.[13] As Satia has argued, in the economic struggle of the interwar years, fiscal concern "was the starting point of the halting critique of government secrecy about the Middle East".[14] While questions were raised about the policies and practices in the Middle East – particularly in regard to the use of public funds – this did not culminate in a sustained interrogation of police bombing itself.

During the European Disarmament Conference, which took place between 1932 and 1934, the practice of police bombing was subject to some debate. The issue arose in connection with the British Draft Convention, which proposed "'the complete abolition of bombing' from the air (except for police purposes 'in certain outlying regions')".[15] Controversy emerged regarding the significance of the British exception to the abolition of bombing: some viewed it as marginal, while others argued that it held up an agreement on disarmament more generally. Critics argued that "our proposals [to the Conference] were handicapped by our reservation in favour of bombing in outlying districts for police purposes".[16] Justifications of the bombing campaigns, on the other hand, doubted "that it was this entirely insignificant little reservation that was holding up the work".[17]

Some fundamental debates regarding the legitimacy of police bombing emerged within this context, with objections raised on both practical and moral grounds: "I doubt very much whether bombing in outlying regions is justifiable. I do not see a nice point of ethics between bombing an Indian village or an Arab encampment and dropping bombs on a great Western city. I do not believe that bombing is really effective or that it is economic."[18] As I showed in Chapter 2, there were concerns about the impact of police bombing on those understood as innocent. However, these points of critique were shaped by orientalist assumptions, remained relatively isolated and tended to become reabsorbed into the primary question – how police bombing affected the Disarmament Conference and with it the possibility of aerial bombing in Europe – which remained the dominant frame of reference. The main question thus centred on how bombing might affect the self – even by those opposing the practice: "The hon. and gallant Gentleman may be entirely right in all the practical considerations that he has put before us, but surely it is insanity to weigh the police considerations on the extremities of the Empire beside the safety of the Empire itself at its heart."[19]

In the summer of 1933, shortly after the policy of retaining the exception for aerial bombing in the context of imperial policing was made public, a group of dissenting Members of Parliament issued an open letter with *The Times*, expressing their disagreement with the decision: "we believe that it would be a political mistake of the first magnitude for Great Britain in isolation to seek to perpetuate the principle of air bombing. We should inevitably be imitated by other Imperial Powers."[20] Public demonstrations were organised and a number of organisations, such as the Humane Education Society[21] or the Quarterly Meeting of the Society of Friends[22] voiced opposition to the practice of police bombing. Certain newspapers, such as the *Manchester Guardian*, engaged critically with these concerns. However, as with debates in Parliament, this coverage redirected the discussion back to the Disarmament Conference and the question "is it worth running the risk of defeating the objects of a general convention [against aerial bombing] for the sake of this particular advantage to 'colonial' nations?"[23]

Within dominant public and political discourses, critiques of bombing "the extremities of the Empire" largely failed to gain traction on ethical or political implications; instead such concerns were refracted through the lens of imperial security, focusing on the implications for "the safety of the Empire at its heart".[24] Newspaper responses to the issue varied depending on the political position of the newspaper. *The Times* and the *Manchester Guardian* questioned the value of maintaining the exception, while the *Daily Mail* was more inclined to echo the Prime Minister's position, who "defended Britain's right to retain aerial bombing for its own special needs, and scoffed at Socialists who would abolish all air bombing".[25] Despite these differences, what unified the coverage was a shared emphasis on the ramifications of the police bombing exception for the Disarmament Conference, rather than sustained engagement with the practice of police bombing per se.

In the few instances where specific aerial bombing attacks in the colonial context were discussed in the media, such references were typically treated as peripheral, appearing as a side note rather than a subject of engagement, for example in 1927 when "The Waliabi Sheik Feisal ed Dowish, is reported to be gathering a force of more than 5,000 tribesmen at a village 100 miles south-east of here [Basra] for an attack on Iraq territory" and "British bombing aeroplanes are keeping a constant watch".[26] Coverage of such instances was also frequently reframed through dominant frames, particularly those emphasising financial cost and the implications for the Disarmament Conference. For example, the *Daily Mail* reported in 1933 that a British force "has been sent to support the friendly Halimzei tribe on the Mohmand border against repetition of recent raids by Upper Mohmands".[27] This instance was significant because of "a reversion to the use of ground troops for controlling the border country instead of using bombing aeroplanes of the RAF as police, a method which in the past three years has saved the Indian taxpayer masses of money, and avoided military casualties".[28]

Following Stoler, it is important not to interpret this phenomenon as one of absolute silence, or a complete lack of knowledge or concern regarding colonial violence. Critical voices did exist, and during the height of debates on the Disarmament Conference such perspectives were represented in parliamentary discourse and the media. Yet, fundamental critiques of police bombing were rarely articulated and received as such. Instead, they were subsumed within the parameters of the dominant discourse which remained focused on the "Empire at its heart" – such as the economic burden on Britain, threats to Britain's democratic accountability due to state secrecy, or the potential consequences of the bombing exception for the success of the Disarmament Conference. As discussed in Chapter 2, the deep silences that emerged from this dynamic were rooted in racialised registers, which were, at times, overtly expressed: "There is no such thing as a special machine to bomb yellow races or black races which could not be used against the white races, and, if an exception had been made in favour of the British Empire for bombers at all, the result would have been that we should have had bombers and no other country would have had any. They were not so foolish as to agree to that."[29]

The failure to engage with colonial police bombing as a practice worthy of scrutiny in its own right produced a deep silence around the devastating impact of the practice on people subjected to bombing. This deep silence recreates a racialised hierarchy of relevance, wherein the deaths of people classified as belonging to the "black or yellow races" in the outlying parts of the Empire are rendered politically inconsequential. This deep silence has important effects. As Rutazibwa has argued, "a people's systematically denied and erased suffering allows for the re-enactment of their premature death in the material world and in the present".[30] While the explicitly racialised language invoked in the 1920s and 1930s might no longer be acceptable in contemporary Western discourses, the following section will demonstrate how similar structures of deep silences sustain modern practices of drone warfare.

Irrelevant and unimportant

The United States, often in collaboration with allies such as the United Kingdom, has carried out armed drone attacks and other forms of so-called "targeted" counterterrorism operations in places including Afghanistan, Pakistan, Yemen, Syria and Somalia. Given the number of attacks and the controversy surrounding the use of the new technology – critiqued by scholars, NGOs and human rights activists – one might reasonably expect sustained discussion of the ethical, legal and political implications of the practice in the US Congress and UK Parliament. This, however, is not the case. Armed drone attacks have been discussed little in Parliament, and when such debates have occurred, the experiences and suffering of those living in targeted regions have been utterly backgrounded and neglected. This section examines the deep silences that pervade

US congressional and UK House of Commons debates on drone warfare, exploring how these deep silences function to signal irrelevance and reproduce racialised registers of who and what is to be considered un/important.

A search of US congressional records from 2005 to 2020 using the keyword "armed drone" yields just twenty-four sessions. These mainly engage with drone warfare in a side note, for example looking at "rules and regulations relating to small UAS [Unmanned Aircraft Systems] flown for recreational or educational use",[31] or armed drones used by other actors, such as when "Houthis, supported by Iran, have used missiles, armed drones, and explosive boats to attack civilian and military targets".[32] The proliferation of drones to actors like the United Arab Emirates (UAE) has attracted some attention where "selling F-35s and MQ-9 Reaper drones into the heart of the Middle East" raises questions around "whether the UAE is ready for this technology or whether their behavior over the past several years makes them an unworthy partner for this set of highly complicated U.S. defense technology".[33] However, the deployment and use of this "highly complicated … defense technology"[34] by the US itself has received comparatively little scrutiny or discussion.

This relative silence does not imply a complete absence of debate or awareness regarding US drone warfare within legislative settings. It can reasonably be assumed that legislators have been aware of the US drone programme, given the extensive reporting and analysis provided by NGOs, journalists and scholars. Some degree of debate has occurred within legislative arenas in the US. The Senate Committee on the Judiciary, for example, held a hearing on drone warfare in 2013, and again in 2022, including witnesses from the American Civil Liberties Union and the Yemen-based human rights organisation Mwatama.[35] Yet, there is a paucity of discussion of drone strikes in Congress, with little initiative to bring the topic to attention, and it seems like party and committee leaders have blocked procedural votes to open floor debates on bills addressing armed drone attacks.[36]

In 2013, congressional discussion of drone warfare became more substantive following the leak of a Department of Justice White Paper which outlined the legal rationale for drone strikes, including the contentious assertion that American citizens suspected of terrorism may be targeted by armed drones overseas.[37] This revelation sparked debate on drone warfare in the Senate, including an almost thirteen-hour-long filibuster.[38] However, the primary focus of the debate centred on the targeting of American citizens, with particular concern given to the potential domestic use of armed drones, raising the primary question: "Can you kill an American in America with a drone strike?"[39] While the debate encompassed broader critique of the drone programme, such as the opacity surrounding targeting processes,[40] these issues were predominantly framed within the context of hypothetical drone employment "at home" in the US. This framing echoes the dynamics of earlier debates on police bombing in the 1930s, where moral questions were absorbed into the primary concern of how this might affect the imperial self: "I am not saying we should not use drones. I am not saying they are not a valuable weapon that has helped us to decimate our enemies. I am just saying it is different in a warzone than it is in our country."[41]

Building on the concept of colonial aphasia, the deep silences in Congress are rooted in racialised and orientalist constructions. As Said has argued, centuries of orientalist thought have produced a dichotomy in which the "Oriental other" is constructed as irrational, deviant and uncivilised – juxtaposed to the West, which is imagined as rational, civilised and morally superior. This binary serves to naturalise and legitimise Western violence and oppression, particularly in contexts involving the Middle East.[42] Said notes that such dynamics are particularly evident in representations of "Islam and the Arab",[43] where orientalist narratives sustain the dehumanisation of targeted populations. This orientalist logic leads to a normalisation of violence against the Oriental "other", thus rendering it unremarkable – unless such violence affects the interests of the "self". This asymmetry is apparent in the US debates on drone warfare, where concern is primarily directed to the hypothetical possibility of the use of armed drones within US borders or against US citizens. The issue becomes politically salient only when the violence is imagined as directed at American citizens "at home" in America, while the use of armed drones "abroad" – predominantly in Muslim-majority regions – is cast as irrelevant and unworthy of attention:

> The problem I have is that in foreign countries – I do not know the exact number because it is classified, but in foreign countries many of the people being killed are not actively engaged in combat. I am not saying that is right or wrong or making an opinion on that matter. But I am saying that is not a standard I can live with in the United States. So let's say one-third of the drone strikes are going against people who are eating dinner with their family or walking down the road or sleeping in their house. If that is our standard and we are going to do drone strikes in America, I could not tolerate or live with myself if I would accept a standard in the United States that would allow that to happen.[44]

Violence inflicted on non-American bodies abroad is thus dismissed, even as it is invoked. It is not articulated as morally problematic in itself, but only becomes an object of concern if it highlights problems about the possibility of the practice being adopted against Americans within the US. These deep silences render the suffering of racialised others inconsequential, their deaths invoked as not mattering in their own right. Even when critical issues are raised – such as the expansive interpretation of pre-emptive self-defence – they are discussed primarily in terms of how intolerable such standards would be if applied domestically: "So we say that unless you can prove that you are not attacking us, because we know the history of al-Qaida is to continue to attack us, we can preemptively attack you. But now we are talking about bringing that kind of gobbledygook, jumbled logic to the United States. Are these going to be the standards by which we kill Americans?"[45] Particularly casual methods of authorising lethal force, such as the reported practice of determining targets through PowerPoint presentations in the Oval Office on Tuesdays, are invoked as an almost comedic ploy to stress the absurdity of such a practice at home: "The President should say unequivocally we are not going to kill noncombatants, we are not going to do PowerPoint presentations in the Oval Office on Tuesdays. We are not going to have Terrorist Tuesdays *for Americans*."[46]

As with colonial-era discourses surrounding police bombing, contemporary legislative debates on aerial bombing campaigns are marked by deep silences concerning the lived experience and suffering of those targeted by such violence. These debates are largely framed around the implications for the Western self rather than engaging substantively with the moral or political implications of the practice for affected populations. This self-referential framing is also evident in the predominance of concerns around democratic accountability – a theme explored more in Chapter 4. In the US Congress, the majority of policy proposals do not seek to challenge morally and legally questionable acts, such as the use of armed drones outside of armed conflict, but merely to gain more information about them. The Oversight of Sensitive Military Operations Act, successfully implemented in 2013, thus stipulates that the military would notify the House and Senate Armed Services Committee of drone strikes outside recognised war zones within sixty days.[47] In British parliamentary debates, the lack of democratic oversight is also a sticking point, especially in cases involving the potential targeting of British citizens. Yet here, too, the dominant concern is not with the broader ethical consequences of extraterritorial violence but with the legal risks and implications for British citizens: "The prospect of UK Government officials deciding behind closed doors on whether or not to kill a British citizen extrajudicially at all, let alone on the basis of a secretive and vague process, should alarm the public."[48]

Returning to Stoler's concept of aphasia, it is crucial to avoid portraying these discursive patterns in simplistic ways as exhibiting total silence or an absolute lack of debate. Drone warfare is indeed subject to critique and there is evidence of understanding – both within and beyond legislative spaces – of the practice and its morally troubling aspects. Yet, these aspects rarely form the subject of legislative debate. On the rare occasions when the harm and suffering caused by drone strikes are acknowledged, such references are swiftly subsumed within the dominant frame centred on the Western "self", its democratic functioning, the legality of targeting American or British citizens, or the hypothetical use of armed drones within domestic borders. This selective discourse produces a corresponding silencing of the morality of such violence and the experiences of those who are subjected to drone surveillance and bombing abroad. Their suffering is systematically backgrounded and thus rendered irrelevant, their deaths reaffirmed as politically insignificant. In this way, deep silences do not simply reflect racialised hierarchies but actively reproduce what is to be considered irrelevant.

A similar asymmetry between what is foregrounded and what is backgrounded is evident in British parliamentary discourses. Legislative debates on drone warfare here frequently focus on the psychological impact of drone warfare on drone pilots – in stark contrast to the deep silence on the wellbeing of those subjected to surveillance and bombing. Concerns are raised about the dissonance drone operators face when they "head home in their cars, thousands of miles from the results of their day's work and crucially remote from the opportunity to assimilate their experiences with those of colleagues".[49] The intimacy provided by drone footage as well as the distance created between soldiers and their "targets" is thus a focus point of debates – in terms of the psychological toll this has on drone pilots. Concern for the wellbeing of drone operators is arguably instrumentalist and embedded within military effectiveness before the background of drone operators who are "keen to transfer to conventional crews, and consideration now being given to financial incentives to persuade pilots to remain on drone crews, where numbers are becoming critical".[50]

Independent of the intention or instrumental value of this focus on the psychological wellbeing of drone operators, it contrasts with a striking silence on the wellbeing of those subjected to surveillance and bombing. This erasure reinforces a racialised hierarchy in which the Western subject is foregrounded, while the lives of those subjected to drone violence are backgrounded, neglected and silenced:

> They [the pilots] witness the violence, whereas most people who are involved in a war are distanced, at least to some extent, from the people who suffer from their weapon system. The sheer fidelity of the drone systems makes the witnessing very close and personal, in some senses. The sheer number of kills that some armed drone squadrons achieve increases the stress. One squadron was attributed with 1,626 kills, which is far more than any normal aircraft squadron would carry out. There is a long-distance version of post-traumatic stress disorder.[51]

Within such discourses, Western drone pilots are cast as the central subjects – protagonists affected by the weapon systems they operate. The "people who suffer from their weapon system" are referenced only insofar as their suffering generates psychological strain on pilots because the technology enables a form of witnessing that is "very close and personal". This framing centres the emotional and psychological burden borne by the perpetrators of violence, while systematically ignoring or backgrounding the wellbeing of those subjected to continuous surveillance and bombardment, thus creating deep silences of what is deemed irrelevant. Importantly, the suffering and death of the colonial "other" are not entirely absent from these discourses. They are invoked as marginal references, side notes that signal limited awareness of their existence. Yet, these acknowledgements tend to surface only insofar as they intersect with the interests of the Western self, such as the emotional toll that witnessing the suffering of drone victims may impose on British drone operators. This process of backgrounding does more than reflect a lack of speech expectations within Western regimes of not listening; it actively reinforces them.

Deep silences thus reproduce a profound asymmetry in whose experiences are to be deemed politically and morally salient. Even when concerns are raised – such as the recognition that "when strikes begin to be made from above there will be mistakes"[52] – the consequences of bombing are often framed as a problem only insofar as they could cause legal challenges to service personnel. A driving motivator of discussions is thus "to protect the pilots and the armed forces from prosecution".[53] This is often linked to the different standards used by the US, which is seen to potentially cause legal issues for UK military staff and "potentially places the UK military, and our own workers, in a legal quagmire".[54]

The deep silences that characterise legislative debates on drone warfare are not mere absences but serve to recreate racialised hierarchies of whose lives are deemed (not) to matter. References to deaths "abroad" are not entirely absent from discourses but are often deployed merely as a rhetorical device – for example, to generate shock over the possible use of drones domestically or to emphasise the psychological burden on Western drone pilots. In doing so, these discourses create deep silences on the death and suffering of those subjected to continuous drone surveillance and bombardment as an issue in its own right. These deep silences reflect racialised registers of who matters and who does not. As Judith Butler has asked: "What defense against the apprehension of loss is at work in the blithe way in which we accept deaths caused by military means with a shrug or with self-righteousness or with clear vindictiveness? To what extent have Arab peoples, predominantly practitioners of Islam, fallen outside the 'human' as it has been naturalized in its 'Western' mold by the contemporary workings of humanism?"[55]

Echoing earlier patterns of imperial discourse and the ways in which police bombing was properly discussed only insofar as it affected the "Empire at its heart", contemporary discourses on drone warfare are similarly subsumed under concerns related to the Western "self". Legislative debates on drone warfare predominantly focus on questions of democratic oversight, the implications of targeting American or British citizens (especially within domestic borders), the psychological wellbeing of drone operators, or the potential legal repercussions for military personnel. In these discussions, the suffering and death of the "other" caused by drone warfare – primarily racialised others in the Global South – are consistently ignored, instrumentalised or backgrounded. These deep silences carry significant illocutionary and performative consequences. To omit or background an issue in public discourse is to denote it as irrelevant, as unworthy of political or ethical attention, as outside the bounds of this discursive space. In doing so, the death and suffering of those targeted by drone strikes is actively constituted as insignificant. This recreates racialised hierarchies and enables and legitimises ongoing violence. As the following section will discuss, it also sanitises aerial bombing by portraying it as a clean and ethically unproblematic measure that is dissociated from the realities of the death and suffering it produces.

Sanitising violence

On February 23, 2019, a teacher and his twenty-month-old baby were killed in a US drone attack in Somalia. USAFRICOM first reported that the strike had killed "two terrorists", yet local newspapers reported the death of civilians, including in their coverage photos of the dead body of the baby. After pressure from NGOs and investigative journalists, USAFRICOM later admitted that "it is likely that two civilians were regrettably and unintentionally killed".[56] Western newspapers largely failed to cover the attack. A review of British newspapers and major American outlets in the three weeks following the attack[57] revealed no coverage whatsoever. This absence is not an isolated incident but reflects a broader pattern in media responses to armed drone attacks. A similar lack of reporting is evident in relation to three other drone strikes with confirmed civilian casualties between 2019 and 2020.[58] Despite verified loss of civilian life, these attacks receive little to no attention in the mainstream Western press. On the rare occasion when a strike is reported on, coverage tends to rely heavily on official state narratives, omitting or minimising allegations of civilian death made by independent sources, such as NGOs, international organisations or investigative journalism.

For example, in a drone strike in Idlib in October 2020, two humanitarian aid workers were injured – one of whom later died – and reports also indicated the death of a small child, alongside those of the two suspected militants who were targeted. These accounts emerged from local sources, such as the Syrian Observatory for Human Rights,[59] and were acknowledged by the UN Regional Humanitarian Coordinator.[60] The accounts of at least one civilian death were, nearly two years later, assessed as "credible" even by the Combined Joint Task Force conducting the strikes.[61] Despite this, major Western newspapers, such as the *Washington Post* and the *New York Times* did not report on the attack. *Fox News* did cover the attack with the headline "US Drone Strike Kills Two Senior Al-Qaeda Operatives in Syria", but does not mention any allegations of civilian death.[62] Instead, the article quotes US Central Command and discusses the continuing threat of al-Qaeda, Assad and Russia, accusing Russia of "covering up their attacks on civilians" in Syria.[63]

This is not to suggest that armed drone attacks are entirely absent from Western media coverage. Notably, independent investigative outlets, such as the Bureau of Investigative Journalism – a non-profit organisation based in London – tracked US drone strikes from 2010 to 2020, providing detailed documentation of individual

…s, civilian casualty numbers and, where possible, the names of victims.[64] In addition, some mainstream Western media outlets have offered space to journalists from regions subjected to drone warfare. For example, the *Guardian* and the *New Yorker* have published stories on the work of photojournalist Noor Behram, whose efforts to document the aftermath of drone strikes are discussed in greater detail in Chapter 6. Moreover, large-scale investigate projects have examined the civilian toll of Western bombing practices. For example, in 2023 the NGO Airwars, in collaboration with the *Guardian*, released a comprehensive investigation into civilian deaths resulting from US-led bombing campaigns against ISIS in Iraq and Syria.[65] The investigation is based on previously classified material as well as on-the-ground research and interviews with survivors, thus supplementing what Airwars has called a "semi-passive approach to casualty monitoring"[66] by Western states.

In part due to the pervasive secrecy surrounding military operations, journalists face significant obstacles in uncovering reliable evidence about drone strikes, which helps to explain the limited news coverage of strikes at the time they take place.[67] Investigative work that challenges official state narratives – for example, by disproving claims that no civilian casualties occurred – does take place, but it is often slow and "by the time [the claims] are refuted, the news cycle has moved on".[68] The absence of timely reporting on strikes and their human cost is politically significant. Early coverage in the immediate aftermath of an attack has the potential to translate the abstract deployment of military weapons into a recognisable, tangible form of violence – one that is morally and emotionally legible, particularly if civilians have died, and carries political momentum for public inquiry. Such immediacy in reporting has mediated Western understanding of the violence used by other actors, but is conspicuously rare when military violence originates from Western states, who deploy violence in the Middle East and Africa.[69]

When drone strikes are covered in Western media discourses, they are often presented in a general or sanitised way. Visual imagery tends to focus on the drone technology or depict the abstract remnants of violence, such as residue or debris, rather than the human suffering inflicted.[70] The language employed in mainstream newspaper reporting typically adheres to a military-operational framework, with headlines such as "Al-Qaeda leader killed in US drone strike in Afghanistan",[71] or "American Drone Strike in Libya Kills Top Qaeda Recruiter".[72] This mode of reporting ends up abstracting the violence and backgrounding its human toll, thus constructing a sanitised and delusional understanding of imperial warfare in which the suffering of those targeted is rendered irrelevant and inaudible and the reader assumes the perspective of the perpetrator. As Judith Butler has argued, "In the silence of the newspaper, there was no event, no loss, and this failure of recognition is mandated through an identification with those who identify with the perpetrators of that violence."[73]

Legislative debates reflect a similar discursive logic. Discussions of drone warfare are largely situated within a strategic or operational framework that foregrounds military effectiveness while obscuring the real-life consequences of military violence. Proponents of armed drones often highlight their military effectiveness and strategic advantages, focusing on technological features such as their ability to "provide an unblinking and persistent ISR [intelligence, surveillance and reconnaissance] presence".[74] Even critical perspectives tend to remain within this operational frame, questioning armed drone attacks on the grounds that they may prove strategically ineffective because "drone strikes arouse anger, which coalesces populations around extremists"[75] and "radicalises and militarises civilians, and unites militants".[76] In both lines of argumentation, the discussion is centred on the achievement of Western military objectives: "If we want to win the hearts and minds of the public, we must carry them with us, but when they see hundreds of lives lost in drone strikes, they turn against the west and pose a danger to our national security."[77] Even when civilian deaths are raised, such references often become reabsorbed into discussions of military effectiveness as the main concern – framed not as a moral question in its own right but as potential obstacles to strategic success:

> The first question I would like the Minister to address is, what is the Government's policy on the use of drones, particularly in Afghanistan and Pakistan? My second question is, how many civilians have been killed by UK drone strikes in Afghanistan? My third question,

e agree that the death of civilians in
of winning hearts and minds, and

aw often functions as a further
ctual violence inflicted on bodies
or the lives lost.[79] Justifications
hasise legal compliance – for
each strike has a legal sign-off"[80] – thereby
presenting drone violence as lawful but implying that strikes are morally legitimate. As scholars of international law have argued, international humanitarian law operates through a fundamental paradox of both restraining military violence and its effects on populations and simultaneously morally legitimising it by delineating the – purposely broad – conditions under which committing mass murder is permitted.[81] Even when invoked to critique drone warfare, legal framings retain this paradoxical effect. Discussing military violence in terms of its legal compliance leaves no room for emotive or moral questions;[82] it closes off inquiry into broader moral and political questions about bombing itself. The discussion becomes one of strategic effectiveness or procedural legality – focused on *how* killing should be conducted, rather than a critical inquiry into *whether* such violence should take place at all. In this way, the legal discourse brackets the moral stakes of military violence. An elaborate discussion on how bombing should take place implicitly assumes that the practice is acceptable in principle – and denotes that broader questions are not up for debate.

The deep silences in media and legislative discourses on drone warfare are thus not mere absences but have performative effects. The failure to report on armed drone attacks as they occur, or the tendency to focus on their technical, legal and abstract dimensions, systematically backgrounds the death and suffering these strikes inflict. As deep silences, these omissions shape the epistemic and moral contours of public discourse of imperial violence, reinforcing the boundaries of what is considered relevant or irrelevant. The consistent exclusion, backgrounding or marginalisation of the death and grief caused by drone warfare contributes to a sanitised portrayal of military violence. Drone warfare is within a military-operational framework, assessed in strategic effectiveness or legal compliance rather tha ethical or political interrogation of the harm it causes. This fosters a delusional understanding of contemporary warfare that obscures its brutality and dislocates it from the lives it impa As such, these deep silences do quite significant ideological work to legitimise, normalise and enable ongoing imperial violence by rendering it intelligible only within the narrow confines of state interest and procedural legality.

Censorship and silencings

If war propaganda loudly proclaims the barbarity of the enemy, the censorship of evidence of one's own brutality and its human consequences is equally central to enabling military campaigns. Those who raise concerns about impending or ongoing wars are frequently dismissed, threatened or criminalised.[83] The stark binarism that war reproduces – casting the self as virtuous and the enemy as irredeemably evil – leaves little room for dissenting voices.[84] The treatment of whistleblowers, who often face intimidation, surveillance and incarceration, underscores both the imperative and the institutional capacity of states to suppress and silence inconvenient narratives.[85] For war propaganda to function effectively, alternative narratives and critical accounts need to be excluded. This imperative is often pursued through targeting journalists and the media infrastructure. It is no coincidence that military forces often attack communication facilities in occupied or invaded territories. During the 2003 Iraq war, for example, the United States bombed Iraqi radio and television transmitters, telephone lines and government media offices, while also seizing Iraqi radio frequencies to broadcast pro-American messages.[86] In the onslaught of genocidal violence in Gaza in 2023–25, Israel seems to have similarly targeted journalists and communication centres.[87] On the domestic front, military efforts have long relied on the control and censorship of media narratives. Traditionally, martial law was invoked for direct censorship, for example during the Second World War in the UK, where the Defence Regulations forbade newspapers to foment opposition to the war and introduced heavy censorship of broadcasting, with switch censors standing by to cut off unauthorised content.[88] It has been argued that contemporary Western states rely less heavily on direct control, instead influencing media content more indirectly through control of personnel and finances, in what has been termed the "military-media-complex".[89]

Much of existing scholarship on silencing focuses on direct censorship, particularly within non-Western authoritarian contexts. Considerable attention has been paid to the silencing strategies employed by states, such as China and Russia, including the use of firewalls, the criminalisation of dissent and state control of media content.[90] Yet, even within these contexts, scholars have noted a shift away from overt censorship and towards more indirect forms of media influence, through financial, institutional and algorithmic means.[91] In the age of social media, it is arguably no longer possible for states to directly censor information effectively. Conflicts – including the most recent horrors in Gaza – are now documented in real time via smartphones, with images, video clips and testimonies disseminated by actors who have been described as "citizen-journalists".[92]

However, these new information flows do not signify that silencing does not take place. Especially when a conflict is characterised by both military asymmetry and "information asymmetry",[93] certain narratives are systematically marginalised. This is particularly relevant in the case of imperial warfare, where states not only physically target alternative communication channels (e.g., by targeting information infrastructure and journalists) but also exert institutional control over information flows. As will be discussed more fully in Chapter 4, legislators in the UK and the US have, for example, been obstructed from accessing information on the war, and journalistic reporting on drone warfare has been shaped and constrained by state secrecy.

The focus solely on top-down censorship and state suppression of information, however, risks overlooking how propaganda in imperial contexts also – and perhaps predominantly – relies on decentralised silencing and registers of colonial aphasia deeply engrained into our regimes of not listening. These are not always coercive or intentional but manifest through mundane and routinised forms of neglect or backgrounding. I refer to such processes as *banal silencings*, drawing on Hannah Arendt's concept of the banality of evil,[94] which invites us to shift analytical attention from evil protagonists towards seemingly banal, everyday decisions and omissions that enable systemic harm.

What is left out of media reporting and other discourses is therefore a matter not simply of top-down suppression but also of differential audibility – of who is listened to and who is not. As Alcoff has put it, "how what is said gets heard depends on who says it, and who says it will affect the style and language in which it is stated, which will in turn affect its perceived significance (for specific hearers)".[95] This is not merely an abstract concern but has tangible implications, for example in terms of who gets contacted and cited in newspaper reports. As discussed above, even when reporters on the ground, Human Rights activists, NGOs and international organisations provide evidence of the effects of bombing campaigns, their accounts are often ignored. Instead, mainstream reporting continues to prioritise state and military sources, treating them as the primary if not exclusive producers of authoritative knowledge. This reliance on state sources persists even though the little (and often delayed) information provided by state authorities has systematically been disproven in later, more thorough investigations by NGOs, journalists or the military itself.[96]

The focus on state sources is not incidental but is structurally embedded within the material and ideational structures of the global economy of silence. Government bodies have invested significant resources into public information operations and relations with the media, organising press conferences and photo opportunities in a way that gives the media easy access to news bites which sell.[97] Apart from the ideational advantage of invoking "trustworthy sources", relying on state sources saves investigative expense and avoids libel claims for journalists.[98] This is particularly relevant in the context of asymmetric warfare. As Tasseron and Lawson have shown in the context of media coverage of Israel–Palestine, Israel Defense Force spokespersons provide constant opportunities for media briefings – in contrast to Hamas representatives, who are often in hiding.[99] What is not said in media reporting on asymmetric warfare is thus entrenched in material and institutional power structures.

My aim here is not to evidence a line of censorship, a conspiracy of top-down suppression of information by the state. Indeed, such a line of inquiry would risk reinforcing regimes of not listening that are focused on the words and actions by political and military elites. It is overly reductive to conceptualise such silences as forming a linear hierarchy, starting with government secrecy at the top, which then results in a lack of parliamentary debate, subsequently limiting media reporting, which ultimately leads to an absence of public debate. We might also consider public disengagement as the starting point, offering an explanation for why parliamentarians have not prioritised drone warfare as a politically salient issue in terms of electoral appeal. In the US in particular, where public opinion polls have suggested unwavering support of drone warfare, it is reasonable to suggest "that the opposition party in Congress had few direct electoral incentives to contest the executive's policies".[100] Indeed, lack of pressure from the public might not only been seen as responsible for parliamentary silences but even to cause state secrecy, because "the public does not exert pressure on the US government to be accountable for potential civilian harm".[101]

Rather than framing these silences as the outcome of a unidirectional causal chain at all, I suggest understanding them as interconnected webs within a wider economy of silence. This approach draws our attention towards the discursive and institutional registers through which certain issues are systematically deemed unnewsworthy, irrelevant or unsayable across various fields. Not necessarily caused only – or predominantly – by direct censorship or state secrecy does not mean that these silences are arbitrary or disconnected. Instead they are shaped by the assumptions of dominant regimes of not listening that determine which voices and positions are acknowledged – or marginalised – across discursive spaces. These regimes are underpinned by material power structures, such as the structural ties between the military and the media, or institutional constraints on parliamentary inquiry. But they are also shaped by ideational power structures, and most notably the racialised logics embedded in dominant epistemologies of attention and recognition.

To underestimate the significance of these silences in the absence of direct censorship or overt state control is, I argue, a serious oversight. In the context of war propaganda in support of imperial warfare – and arguably military violence more broadly – such banal silencings play a crucial role. Regardless of the intention or intentionality behind these silences, their effects are to consistently efface the suffering of those subjected to violence and to signal that their deaths and injuries are irrelevant. The systematic erasure of the real consequences of bombing creates a delusional understanding of military "operations" – one that, I argue, plays a significant role in legitimising such violence. Through silence, omission and the systematic relegation of suffering and death to the background, military violence is thus downplayed, naturalised and sanitised.

Silence and neglect

This chapter has traced the contours of silences within UK House of Commons and US congressional debates, as well as in media representations of drone warfare. I have demonstrated that while armed drone attacks – and the effects of armed drone attacks – are not entirely absent from public discourse, they are systematically backgrounded and absorbed within dominant discursive frames. This is not a silence of total omission but one of structured layers of neglect, where particular aspects and voices are ignored. In US congressional debates, for example, intense concern over the hypothetical use of armed drones against American citizens on US soil starkly contrasts with the near total disregard of the actual practice of drone strikes, killing non-Americans abroad. While critical points about drone warfare abroad occasionally emerge, they become subsumed within the narrow parameters of the main debate on whether it could become possible to "kill an American in America with a drone strike".[102]

Following Stoler's concept of colonial aphasia, I contend that the issue is not a complete lack of critique or awareness of ethical problems regarding drone warfare but, rather, a discursive condition in which these problems cannot be fully articulated, heard or made sense of in their own right. These deep silences recreate a racialised hierarchy of political relevance – differentiating between what is to be considered un/important, whose lives matter and whose suffering is rendered inconsequential. This hierarchy is embedded within a long history of absence. Discourses on police bombing in the 1920s and 1930s thus similarly prioritised concerns central to the "Empire at its heart" – such as the success of the European Disarmament Conference or the lack of democratic oversight of imperial affairs. Concerns about the effects of bombing on colonised people were systematically ignored, instrumentalised or backgrounded.

These deep silences are not merely discursive gaps; they have important illocutionary and performative force which enables military violence. By not speaking about it, the death and suffering of people categorised as "black races" is systematically reaffirmed as irrelevant. By ignoring the chaos, terror, death and suffering inflicted by Western military violence, such violence is discursively reconstituted as rational, riskless, lawful and clean. As such, public and political discussions of drone warfare often remain confined within a military-operational logic. They are preoccupied with legal targeting procedures, strategic effectiveness and technological innovation, rather than the human and political consequences of military violence.

Deep silences thus have important effects in enabling military violence and, I argue, function as a form of war propaganda. Indeed, the sanitised framing of imperial warfare as a "high-tech intervention" fundamentally depends on what is left out and silenced, what is omitted and hidden. These deep silences are embedded within registers of racialised and orientalist assumptions, as outlined in Chapter 2. They are also sustained by a wider economy of material and institutional power structures – including restrictions on congressional oversight, limitations on media access to sources and the institutionalisation of state secrecy. The following chapter will discuss the central role of such silences in enabling and defining imperial warfare as "secret, unaccountable, borderless wars".[103]

Notes

All URLs were last accessed on October 30, 2025.

1 Butler, *Precarious Life*, 22.
2 Mbembe, "Necropolitics," 27.
3 Rutazibwa, "Hidden in Plain Sight," 224.
4 De Behar, *A Rhetoric of Silence*, 122:9.
5 Stoler, "Colonial Archives and the Arts of Governance."
6 Anne Donadey, "Between Amnesia and Anamnesis: Re-Membering the Fractures of Colonial History," *Studies in 20th & 21st Century Literature* 23, no. 1 (1999), https://doi.org/10.4148/2334-4415.1457; Robert Fletcher, "The Art of Forgetting: Imperialist Amnesia and Public Secrecy," *Third World Quarterly* 33, no. 3 (2012): 423–39, https://doi.org/10.1080/01436597.2012.657476
7 Muadi Mukenge, "Sensationalism at Work: Creating the Myth of the Mau Mau," *Ufahamu: A Journal of African Studies* 21, nos. 1–2 (1993), https://doi.org/10.5070/F7211-2016741; Caroline Elkins, *Britain's Gulag: The Brutal End of Empire in Kenya* (Random House, 2005).
8 Tim Livsey, "Open Secrets: The British 'Migrated Archives,'" Colonial History, and Postcolonial History," *History Workshop Journal* 93, no. 1 (2022): 95–116, https://doi.org/10.1093/hwj/dbac002
9 Paul Bijl, "Colonial Memory and Forgetting in the Netherlands and Indonesia," in *Colonial Counterinsurgency and Mass Violence*, ed. Bart Luttikhuis and A. Dirk Moses (Routledge, 2018), www.taylorfrancis.com/chapters/edit/10.4324/9781315767345-13/colonial-memory-forgetting-netherlands-indonesia-paul-bijl
10 Stoler, "Colonial Archives and the Arts of Governance," 125.
11 Stoler, "Colonial Archives and the Arts of Governance," 141.
12 UK House of Commons, *HC Debates*, May 26, 1930, Vol. 239, India Office, Cc825–949, 1930.
13 Satia, *Spies in Arabia*, 291.
14 Satia, *Spies in Arabia*, 293.
15 *The Times*, "Police Bombing," May 30, 1933.
16 UK House of Commons, *HC Debates*, March 19, 1935, Vol. 299, Air Estimates, Cc1015–117, 1935.
17 UK House of Commons, *HC Debates*, July 11, 1935, Vol. 304, Foreign Office, Cc509–631, 1935.
18 UK House of Commons, *HC Debates*, June 13, 1933, Vol. 279, Foreign Office, Cc29–146.

19 UK House of Commons, *HC Debates*, July 5, 1933, Vol. 280, Foreign Office, Cc339–457.
20 *The Times*, "Police Bombing," June 21, 1933.
21 *Manchester Guardian*, "Police Bombing," August 28, 1933.
22 *Manchester Guardian*, "Britain and Police Bombing," June 26, 1933.
23 *Manchester Guardian*, "Police Bombing," May 29, 1933.
24 UK House of Commons, *HC Debates*, July 5, 1933, Vol. 280, Foreign Office, Cc339–457.
25 *Daily Mail*, "Premier and Air Rights," November 14, 1933.
26 *Daily Mail*, "5,000 Men," November 22, 1927.
27 *Daily Mail*, "British in Frontier Skirmish," July 28, 1933.
28 *Daily Mail*, "British in Frontier Skirmish," July 28, 1933.
29 UK House of Commons, *HC Debates*, July 11, 1935, Vol. 304, Foreign Office, Cc509–631.
30 Rutazibwa, "Hidden in Plain Sight," 224.
31 US Congress, *Congressional Record*, Vol. 164 (68), House of Representatives, April 26, 2018, H3643–88, 2018.
32 US Congress, *Congressional Record*, Vol. 165 (69), Senate, April 29, 2019, S2469–84, 2019.
33 US Congress, *Congressional Record*, Vol. 166 (208), Senate, December 9, 2020, S7296–317, 2020.
34 US Congress, *Congressional Record*, Vol. 166 (208), Senate, December 9, 2020, S7296–317.
35 US Senate Committee on the Judiciary, Hearing on "Targeted Killing and the Rule of Law," at www.judiciary.senate.gov/committee-activity/hearings/targeted-killing-and-the-rule-of-law_the-legal-and-human-costs-of-20-years-of-us-drone-strikes
36 Marcus Müller and Florian Böller, "The Tug-of-War over Drone Strike Oversight: Congress and the Politics of Drone Warfare during the Obama Presidency," *Congress & the Presidency* 0, no. 0 (2022): 10, https://doi.org/10.1080/07343469.2022.2070298
37 "Drones and the War on Terror: When Can the US Target Alleged American Terrorists Overseas; Hearing before the Committee on the Judiciary House of Representatives, 113th Congress, Serial No. 113–2," 2013, www.congress.gov/event/113th-congress/house-event/LC646/text
38 Müller and Böller, "The Tug-of-War over Drone Strike Oversight," 12.
39 US Congress, *Congressional Record*, Vol. 159 (32), Senate, March 6, 2013, S1181–226, S1181.
40 US Congress, *Congressional Record*, Vol. 159 (32), Senate, March 6, 2013, S1181–226.

41 US Congress, *Congressional Record*, Vol. 159 (32), Senate, March 6, 2013, S1181–226, S1189.
42 Said, *Orientalism*, 40.
43 Said, *Orientalism*, 287.
44 US Congress, *Congressional Record*, Vol. 159 (32), Senate, March 6, 2013, S1181–226, S1181.
45 US Congress, *Congressional Record*, Vol. 159 (32), Senate, March 6, 2013, S1181–226, S1187.
46 US Congress, *Congressional Record*, Vol. 159 (32), Senate, March 6, 2013, S1181–226, S1188. Emphasis added.
47 Müller and Böller, "The Tug-of-War over Drone Strike Oversight," 14.
48 Barnaby Pace and Menwith Hill Accountability Campaign and Yorkshire CND, "Menwith Hill in 3D: Domes, Data and Drone Strikes," 2021, 22, www.themhac.uk/sites/default/files/2021-10/MHAC%20Domes%20Data%20and%20Drones%2003.08.21.pdf
49 UK House of Commons, *HC Debates*, December 1, 2015, Vol. 603, Westminster Hall, Armed Drones, Cc50WH–72WH, 01.
50 UK House of Commons, *HC Debates*, December 1, 2015, Vol. 603, Westminster Hall, Armed Drones, Cc50WH–72WH, 01.
51 UK House of Commons, *HC Debates*, December 1, 2015, Vol. 603, Westminster Hall, Armed Drones, Cc50WH–72WH, 01.
52 UK House of Commons, *HC Debates*, June 18, 2019, Vol. 662, Westminster Hall, International Humanitarian Law: Protecting Civilians in Conflict, Cc28WH–47WH, 2019.
53 UK House of Commons, *HC Debates*, December 1, 2015, Vol. 603, Westminster Hall, Armed Drones, Cc50WH–72WH, 01.
54 UK House of Commons, *HC Debates*, December 1, 2015, Vol. 603, Westminster Hall, Armed Drones, Cc50WH–72WH, 01.
55 Butler, *Precarious Life*.
56 AFRICOM, Initial U.S. Africa Command Civilian Casualty Assessment Quarterly Report, Apr 27, 2020, www.africom.mil/pressrelease/32740/initial-us-africa-command-civilian-casualty-assessment-quarterly-report
57 Including LexisNexis for British newspaper coverage, the *New York Times*, *Washington Post* and *Fox News* for American newspaper coverage, as well as *Frankfurter Allgemeine*, *Süddeutsche Zeitung* for German news coverage.
58 A strike in Idlib in 2020, in Jilib in February 2020 and in Al Bayda in Yemen in January 2019, searching NexisLexis for British newspaper reporting as well as the *New York Times*, *Washington Post* and *Fox News* for American newspaper coverage.

59 Airwars, "Civilian Casualties, Airwars Assessment, CS 1950, Idlib Syria," n.d., https://airwars.org/civilian-casualties/cs1950-october-15-2020/
60 UN, Office of the Regional Humanitarian Coordinator for the Syria Crisis, *Statement by Kevin Kennedy, Regional Humanitarian Coordinator for the Syria Crisis, on Violence Impacting Aid Workers in North-West Syria Amman*, October 18, 2020.
61 Combined Joint Task Force – Operation Inherent Resolve, "Civilian Casualty Assessment," March 10, 2022; Release No. 20210310, CJTF-OIR CIVCAS Press release Mar 22.pdf.
62 Lucas Tomlinson, "US Drone Strike Kills 2 Senior Al Qaeda Operatives in Syria," *Fox News*, October 15, 2020, www.foxnews.com/world/us-drone-strike-kills-2-senior-al-qaeda-operatives-in-syria
63 Tomlinson, "US Drone Strike Kills 2 Senior Al Qaeda Operatives in Syria."
64 The Bureau of Investigative Journalism, Projects, Drone Warfare, at www.thebureauinvestigates.com/projects/drone-war/
65 Emma Graham-Harrison and Joe Dyke, "Lives Torn Apart by British Airstrikes in Mosul Give Lie to UK's 'Perfect' Precision War," *The Guardian*, March 21, 2023, www.theguardian.com/world/2023/mar/21/british-airstrikes-mosul-civilian-victims-iraq
66 Airwars, *Limited Accountability: A Transparency Audit of the Coalition Air War against So-Called Islamic State*. Remote Control, Oxford Research Group, 2016, https://airwars.org/wp-content/uploads/2016/12/Airwars-report_Web-FINAL1.compressed.pdf
67 Muhammad Idrees Ahmad, "The Magical Realism of Body Counts: How Media Credulity and Flawed Statistics Sustain a Controversial Policy." *Journalism* 17, no. 1 (2016): 18–34. https://doi.org/10.1177/1464884915593237
68 Ahmad, "The Magical Realism of Body Counts," 22.
69 Opeoluwa Dayo Dada, "A Look at Media Subtle Act of Bias and Framing in Russia–Ukraine Crisis," SSRN Scholarly Paper 4277332, Rochester, NY, November 15, 2022. https://doi.org/10.2139/ssrn.4277332
70 Oliver Kearns, "Secrecy and Absence in the Residue of Covert Drone Strikes," *Political Geography* 57 (2017): 14.
71 BBC News, "Al-Qaeda Leader Killed in US Drone Strike in Afghanistan," *BBC News*, November 5, 2016, www.bbc.com/news/world-asia-37882010
72 Eric Schmitt, "American Drone Strike in Libya Kills Top Qaeda Recruiter," *New York Times*, March 28, 2018, www.nytimes.com/2018/03/28/world/africa/us-drone-strike-libya-qaeda.html

73 Butler, *Precarious Life*, 24.
74 UK House of Commons, *HC Debates*, November 6, 2012, Vol. 552, Westminster Hall, Unmanned Aerial Vehicles, Cc197WH–204WH.
75 UK House of Commons, *HC Debates*, December 1, 2015, Vol. 603, Westminster Hall, Armed Drones, Cc50WH–72WH.
76 UK House of Commons, *HC Debates*, December 1, 2015, Vol. 603, Westminster Hall, Armed Drones, Cc50WH–72WH.
77 UK House of Commons, *HC Debates*, December 11, 2012, Vol. 555, Westminster Hall, Unmanned Aerial Vehicles, Cc27WH–48WH, 2012.
78 UK House of Commons, *HC Debates*, November 6, 2012, Vol. 552, Westminster Hall, Unmanned Aerial Vehicles, Cc197WH–204WH.
79 Thomas Gregory, "Drones, Targeted Killings, and the Limitations of International Law," *International Political Sociology* 9, no. 3 (2015): 197–212, https://doi.org/10.1111/ips.12093
80 UK House of Commons, *HC Debates*, October 14, 2020, Public Bill Committees, Overseas Operations (Service Personnel and Veterans) Bill (Fifth Sitting), Cc131–62.
81 Helen M. Kinsella, "Discourses of Difference: Civilians, Combatants, and Compliance with the Laws of War," *Review of International Studies* 31, no. S1 (2005): 163–85, https://doi.org/10.1017/S0260210505006844; Amanda Alexander, "The 'Good War': Preparations for a War against Civilians," *Law, Culture and the Humanities* 15, no. 1 (2019): 227–52, https://doi.org/10.1177/1743872116651224
82 Gregory, "Drones, Targeted Killings, and the Limitations of International Law"; Pugliese, "Prosthetics of Law and the Anomic Violence of Drones."
83 David Altheide and Jennifer Grimes, "War Programming: The Propaganda Project and the Iraq War," *The Sociological Quarterly* 46 (September 2005): 622, https://doi.org/10.1111/j.1533-8525.2005.00029.x
84 Butler, *Precarious Life*.
85 Kevin Howley, "Violence, Intimidation and Incarceration: America's War on Whistleblowers," *Communication & Theatre Faculty Publications*, August 1, 2020, https://scholarship.depauw.edu/commtheatre_facpubs/3
86 Ray Eldon Hiebert, "Public Relations and Propaganda in Framing the Iraq War: A Preliminary Review," *Public Relations Review* 29, no. 3 (2003): 247–48.
87 UN Human Rights Office, *Media Statement: UN Human Rights Office Condemns Targeting Journalists and Attacks on Hospitals*,

June 6, 2025, www.un.org/unispal/document/un-human-rights-office-condemns-targeting-journalists-and-attacks-on-hospitals/

88 P. M. H. Bell, "Censorship, Propaganda and Public Opinion: The Case of the Katyn Graves, 1943," *Transactions of the Royal Historical Society* 39 (December 1989): 68, https://doi.org/10.2307/3678978

89 See, for example, Altheide and Grimes, "War Programming," 621; Dwayne Winseck, "Information Operations 'Blowback': Communication, Propaganda and Surveillance in the Global War on Terrorism," *International Communication Gazette* 70, no. 6 (2008): 419–41, https://doi.org/10.1177/1748048508096141

90 David Kaye, *Online Propaganda, Censorship and Human Rights in Russia's War against Reality*, Cambridge University Press, 2022; Veronica Ma, "Propaganda and Censorship: Adapting to the Modern Age," *Harvard International Review* 37, no. 2 (2016): 46–50.

91 Sergei M. Guriev and Daniel Treisman, "How Modern Dictators Survive: Cooptation, Censorship, Propaganda, and Repression," *SSRN Electronic Journal*, ahead of print, 2015, https://doi.org/10.2139/ssrn.2571905

92 Bader Alakklouk and Birol Gülnar, "The Impact of Citizen Journalism and Social Media in News Coverage of the Israeli Attacks on Gaza," *South Asian Journal of Social Sciences and Humanities* 4, no. 4 (2023): 76–100.

93 Michael Tasseron and Brendan T. Lawson, "Legitimizing Military Action through Statistics and Discourse in the 2014 IDF Assault on Gaza," *Media, War & Conflict* 15, no. 2 (2022): 238–56, https://doi.org/10.1177/1750635220917692

94 Hannah Arendt and Jens Kroh, *Eichmann in Jerusalem* (Viking Press, 1964).

95 Linda Alcoff, "The Problem of Speaking for Others." *Cultural Critique*, no. 20 (1991): 5–32, 13, https://doi.org/10.2307/1354221

96 Ahmad, "The Magical Realism of Body Counts."

97 Herman and Chomsky, *Manufacturing Consent*, 21.

98 Herman and Chomsky, *Manufacturing Consent*, 18.

99 Tasseron and Lawson, "Legitimizing Military Action through Statistics and Discourse in the 2014 IDF Assault on Gaza," 250.

100 Müller and Böller, "The Tug-of-War over Drone Strike Oversight," 9.

101 Human Rights Clinic and Center for Civilians in Conflict, "The Civilian Impact of Drones: Unexamined Costs, Unanswered Questions," 2012, https://civiliansinconflict.org/publications/research/civilian-impact-drones-unexamined-costs-unanswered-questions/; see also Drone

Wars UK, at https://dronewars.net/2023/10/12/new-protector-armed-drones-to-begin-flying-in-uk-join-the-protest-on-13-november/

102 US Congress, *Congressional Record*, Vol. 159 (32), Senate, March 6, 2013, S1181–226, S1181.

103 ECCHR, *Litigating Drone Strikes*.

4

Secrecy

Secrecy has been central in shaping discussions of drone warfare and similar military practices and has been a core point of critique. The secrecy of contemporary warfare is often associated with new developments in warfare and its increasing reliance on secret services, new, obscure weapon technologies and transnational cooperation among intelligence agencies.[1] While such characteristics undoubtedly contribute to the layers of omission I will discuss in this chapter, interpreting them as an entirely new phenomenon risks overlooking the long trajectory of secrecy as a defining feature of imperial violence and oppression. British policies in the Middle East during the era of police bombing were similarly grasped as shrouded in governmental opacity which deliberately obstructed public oversight and debate. As Satia has argued, "The palpable press silence – on details if not on demands for them – was not wilful but officially contrived."[2]

State secrecy is typically theorised in one of two dominant ways. First, as "arcanum" – a state instrument to hide information and shield state actors from public inquiry. While it is justified by some in the name of national security – allowing state agents to operate without the glare of publicity – critiques understand it as endangering democratic oversight and accountability. Secrecy can have both material consequences – such as the denial of compensation – and broader legitimating effects by concealing key aspects of warfare. In response, international lawyers and human rights actors have often championed transparency and called on state actors to reveal more information. However, positioning transparency as a liberal panacea for curbing state violence is, I argue, overly simplistic.

Secrecy is not a discrete entity that can be opposed in binary terms to transparency. Rather, it is constituted of layers that operate with and through revelations. These layers are deeply entrenched in liberal modes of warfare and are institutionalised through legal frameworks, bureaucratic mechanisms and court proceedings. Secrecy and transparency are not the clear oppositional binary they are often presumed to be, and instead are closely entangled with each other. Transparency creates its own systems of exclusions, while secrecy becomes legible and performative only through partial disclosures.

The second conceptualisation of secrecy – as "secretum" – emphasises its performative and symbolic dimensions. Here, secrecy functions as a spectacle that generates relations of inclusion and exclusion.[3] Open secrets are constituted through hierarchies of access that are embedded within global power relations. These hierarchies not only determine how much information someone receives but also become a performative element of their status and authority. In the context of warfare, secrecy creates a bifurcated epistemological field of an inner circle of elite knowledge holders, such as intelligence agents, and a periphery of actors cast as ignorant and uninformed. This is reflected in popular culture depictions of covert state agents, where secrecy gains a spectacular quality that is imbued with power and mystique.

Building on these theorisations of secrecy, I argue that a critical analysis of secrecy must be situated within a broader economy of silence that shapes whether secrecy is perceived as a loud, expressive silence and how it is interpreted in the first place. Analysing NGO reports, UN Human Rights Council documents and parliamentary debates, this chapter shows that secrecy is not a monolithic unit but is encountered through layers of silences and utterances which are ordered and interpreted in specific ways – ways that often serve the interests of dominant actors. This is particularly important, given how central secrecy has been to the framing of imperial warfare *as* covert warfare. In the case of colonial police bombing, secrecy became the defining feature and focus of critique in public debate of the government's policies in Mesopotamia. Likewise, the framing of drone warfare as "a secretive program of surveillance and killings"[4] has been crucial in its public perception and in politically enabling it by creating a subject position of exclusion from which it becomes difficult to know and speak about the war. These processes of omission do not merely obscure warfare – they constitute it.

Secrecy as a loud, expressive silence is perceived not as the mere absence of speech but through messy layers of utterances and silences. It is not the binary opposite of disclosure, but takes shape through the organisation and interpretation of complex layers of denials, redactions, classifications, delays. These interpretive processes both reflect and further perpetuate existing power relations. For example, even though extensive information on drone strikes has been gathered by local witnesses, NGOs, human rights activists, journalists and academics, the US government and its transnational intelligence network continue to be positioned as the authoritative sources of knowledge. Prevalent expectations of speech – who we expect to speak and to demand information from – therefore actively contribute to creating the political functions of secrecy. The production and interpretation of silences (who can speak, who is heard and how their words are perceived) is embedded in imperial relations of knowledge production that define this war and make it possible. When these fractured layers of silences are interpreted as secrecy, the interpretive act itself can serve to legitimise and further enable military violence.

Shielding from oversight

Secrecy is often theorised as a protective mechanism that shields state actors from negative repercussions of their actions. By concealing compromising information, it creates a space within which officials can operate without facing immediate accountability. This concealment is frequently justified in the name of national security, with secrecy framed as a necessary condition for finding effective solutions in sensitive contexts. In the context of covert warfare, secrecy is further justified as helping to avoid escalation because it "reduces mobilization of external audiences, the reputational and domestic stakes involved in an incident, and hard-to control escalation pressure".[5] From this perspective, the "glare of publicity"[6] is a liability, an exposure that might hinder pragmatic or "necessary" solutions. Secrecy functions to protect actions that might transgress accepted legal and moral boundaries, by shielding state actors from public inquiry and protecting them from the negative repercussions that exposure entails. If complete obscurity is not possible, secrecy at least allows states – or particular state agents – to claim plausible deniability of their involvement in such activities.[7] This logic of secrecy is not just upheld in academic and policy discourses but exists in popular culture as well, in the portrayal of the covert agent as a heroic figure who is going beyond the law in order to protect the state.[8]

This same logic of secrecy – as a state instrument for concealing information and thus shielding officials from public scrutiny – has also been the centre of critique. From this perspective, transparency is not a liability but a democratic and legal imperative. It is a means to shed light on potentially corrupt, illegal or immoral acts, keeping government transgressions in check. Transparency is often upheld as essential to the functioning of liberal democracies and the rule of law, where public oversight is understood as a safeguard against state overreach.[9] The global rules-based order underpinning international law has likewise been understood as grounded in commitments to transparency, clarity and publicity.[10] While secrecy is still conceptualised as a shield between state actors and the public, its normative evaluation shifts. Coming from the other side, secrecy is seen as an obstacle that prevents publics from fully understanding, evaluating and sanctioning state conduct. Without access to information, responsibility for past wrongs cannot be properly attributed, and the lack of public pressure allows immoral or corrupt acts to be perpetuated in the future.[11]

This logic of secrecy as a shield – underlying both its justification and its critique – has been pervasive in debates surrounding drone warfare. Nowhere is this more evident than in the controversy over civilian casualties resulting from drone strikes. For human rights advocates, NGOs and international lawyers, secrecy presents a significant barrier to evaluating whether attacks comply with international law, particularly the principles of distinction and proportionality under international humanitarian law. This fuels suspicion that states are deliberately withholding information about civilian harm, a suspicion amplified by the consistently low civilian casualty figures reported by state actors. As a British MP put it in Parliament: "The right hon. Lady referred to the figure for RAF casualties, and the claim that there was only one civilian casualty after 4,000 munitions were dropped in the war against Isis ... The RAF is effective and efficient and has tight safeguards over the use of munitions, but to suggest that there was only one civilian casualty after 4,000 attacks is challenging in terms of credibility."[12]

NGOs have noted absences in strike reports when contrasting "the fact that some air strikes are described in detail, particularly those that seem the most palatable", which then shows "the absence of detail in others".[13] When allegations of civilian harm are submitted to government agencies to initiate further inquiry, this is often met with rebuttals, the details of which are kept secret, such as when "AFRICOM stated they [the allegations of civilian death] 'do not appear likely based on contradictory intelligence that cannot be disclosed because of operational security limitations'".[14] This dynamic has been particularly pronounced in the context of drone warfare. In 2016, a study conducted for the British All Party Parliamentary Group on Drones examined the Ministry of Defence's public reporting of air strikes carried out by both manned and unmanned aircraft during 2014 and 2015. The study found that while 76 per cent of the reports of manned aircraft strikes included location details with a high level of precision (the name of a specific town or village), only 13 per cent of drone strikes included such details.[15]

Civil society organisations, including Reprieve and the American Civil Liberties Union, have sought to challenge this lack of transparency through Freedom of Information Act litigation, aiming to obtain access to legal justifications, policy memoranda and intelligence records related to air strikes.[16] However, such legal efforts have frequently been unsuccessful, further highlighting the structural obstacles to transparency. The concealment of information about drone strikes and resulting civilian harm is widely regarded as a problem. Secrecy causes difficulties in evaluating compliance with international law and is seen to obstruct "the requirement to hold persons criminally accountable for crimes under international law".[17] Secrecy around civilian death also has concrete material consequences when it blocks "the right to a remedy and reparation".[18]

The failure to acknowledge harm caused by drone strikes directly affects processes of attribution and recompense.[19] When civilian casualties are not officially recognised, the basis for providing reparations – such as financial compensation, medical care or formal apologies – is effectively undermined. In this context, lack of acknowledgement serves to justify the denial of responsibility and the avoidance of legal and moral obligations towards those harmed by military violence: "In response to a specific query on this from Amnesty International, a DoD spokesperson confirmed in March 2019 that the USA had made no solatia or ex-gratia payments in Somalia *because* 'as previously stated, there are no assessed civilian casualties resulting from U.S. military operations.'"[20]

Secrecy can be understood as a mechanism that shields state actors not only from material and legal repercussions for potentially unlawful acts but also from the political consequences associated with negative public opinion. The lack of specific information – such as accurate data on civilian death – has been identified as a key factor in rendering drone warfare more palatable to the electorate. Public support for, or indifference towards, drone warfare has therefore been understood as partially produced by this lack of transparency. In turn, limited public awareness reduces the pressure on state actors to disclose information, thereby reinforcing the conditions under which secrecy persists: "secrecy, framed as preservation of national security, further diminishes the public's interest in exerting pressure on the government to justify lethal operations".[21]

The shielding of acts of war from public scrutiny is further reinforced by the transnational character of contemporary warfare, which diffuses responsibility and accountability between states. For instance, an appeal by Reprieve to the UK High Court to examine Britain's role in US armed drone attacks was rejected in 2016. The High Court did not engage with the substance of the issue at all and refused to grant permission for the case on the basis of the Act of State doctrine: "The court argued that any attempt to examine Britain's role would necessarily require it to sit in judgment of the legality of US actions and in doing so, potentially 'imperil relations between the states.'"[22] Questions in Parliament are similarly rebuffed on the basis of transnational cooperation:

"My hon. Friend raised some questions regarding the use of armed UAVs by the United States. I am not going to comment on the operations of our allies and this is long-standing Government policy for reasons of operational security, the Ministry of Defence does not comment on its intelligence-sharing arrangements with coalition partners."[23]

Secrecy is also tied to the increasing reliance on intelligence services and special forces, whose actions evade standard mechanisms of legal and political oversight.[24] In the UK, for example, special forces benefit from an official "no comment" policy that effectively shields their actions from parliamentary scrutiny.[25] This institutionalised opacity reflects the extent to which secrecy is integrated in the operational logic of this type of warfare where "not one parliamentary committee has the mandate to conduct comprehensive investigations into all aspects of a drone strike".[26] As a result, parliamentary engagement with this type of warfare is characterised less by substantive debate and more by a ritualised interaction, a dance of questions asked but systematically left unanswered: "Many of us have asked questions, including on the all-party group on drones, and have not received full information."[27] The lack of reply by government actors or non-cooperation with inquiries is frequently noted, with MPs humbly asking, "will the Minister, in her response, confirm that the Committee will get the Ministry's full co-operation, obviously within the parameters of what it can say on this matter?"[28]

In the US, the military's reliance on the Central Intelligence Agency (CIA) and special forces has similarly drawn significant critique. When drone strikes are designated as "covert actions", statutory briefing requirements are limited to a small group within Congress – namely the leadership of House and Senate and the chairs and ranking members of the Intelligence Committees.[29] As a result, oversight is restricted to a narrow and controlled circle. Due to the compartmentalised character of congressional oversight, which operates through distinct committees, information related to covert wars is effectively "siloed". Members of other committees often are not only excluded from key briefings but are not even aware of the information they are missing.[30] Some representatives have voiced concern "about the complete lack of oversight by this

Congress in the armed drone program".[31] Congress, in this context, comes to be understood as largely excluded from information flows between military and governmental elites: "We have not been told anything. We have been told to go and sit in a corner – including the Senate and Congress – and be quiet."[32]

It is not surprising that there have been efforts to reform this dynamic – though, as discussed in Chapter 3, such initiatives have been fewer and more limited than one might expect. Congressional pressure, including threats to withhold funding, did lead to some improvements in oversight for the drone programme, with the introduction of the so-called Oversight of Sensitive Military Operations Act under the Obama administration.[33] Yet, important aspects, including a proposed amendment which would shift "sole responsibility for conducting lethal military action using weaponized drones in the hands of the Department of Defense",[34] were defeated. Rather than a simple stand-off between government and Congress, opposition also came from within Congress by senior leaders of both parties, spearheaded by the chairwoman of the Senate Select Committee on Intelligence.[35] In 2023, US representatives Lee and Burgess unsuccessfully introduced the "Drone Reform Act" in an effort to shift the structural conditions of secrecy around drone warfare, transfer authority from intelligence agencies to the Department of Defence and increase transparency "so that Americans can stay fully aware of when, why, and how our military takes action through the use of drones".[36]

There have also been persistent demands from civil society actors, NGOs and international organisations for greater transparency around drone strikes. These calls have urged state actors to "be transparent about the legal criteria that were applied including when, where, and against whom lethal force could be used, as well as the number of casualties".[37] State actors have consistently resisted such requests, often in the name of national security. For example, the CIA denied a request by the American Civil Liberties Union, stating "that it could not confirm or deny even an 'intelligence interest' in the drone program without compromising national security".[38] Secrecy in the context of warfare thus appears as a shield between the state and the public, with each side pushing in different directions. State actors invoke national security to justify the withholding of information, framing secrecy as necessary to protect operational effectiveness. In contrast, civil society actors – including international organisations, human rights advocates and NGOs – critique secrecy as a structural barrier to democratic oversight.

Entire UN reports – or substantial sections within them – have been dedicated to emphasising the need for greater transparency.[39] A central demand articulated in the UN Human Rights Council resolution on armed drones is for states "to ensure transparency in their records on the use of remotely piloted aircraft or armed drones".[40] Transparency is often positioned in direct opposition to secrecy, upheld as a normative good and a cornerstone of accountable governance. This framing draws on a longer historical tradition in which transparency has been central to the political self-understanding of Western liberal democracies, institutionalised through measures such as Freedom of Information requests in the twentieth century.[41] Within this ideological framework, elites often profess commitment to transparency – as exemplified by the Obama administration's Open Government Directive, which sought to establish "accountability by providing the public with information about what the Government is doing".[42] However, the conventional dichotomy between secrecy and transparency overlooks how closely entangled they are and how long they have operated in tandem.

Fighting for transparency

Pushing against the shield of secrecy was an experience all too familiar to critics of British colonial warfare during the interwar years. As Satia notes, the covert nature of police bombing operations became so pronounced "that the RAF was stopped from decorating John Glubb for fear of parliamentary questions about the undisclosed actions for which he was being recognized".[43] Public discourse at the time absorbed and reflected this culture of secrecy, often linked to conspiracy-laden critique of imperial policy. These narratives were embedded in orientalist imagery and a vision of Arabia as a land "full of veils" where "hidden hands [could] operate freely".[44] In this context, state secrecy was seen as a mechanism to conceal private interests – in particular those related to oil – which were widely believed to influence British imperial strategies in the Middle East.[45]

Calls for greater transparency intensified, including around the policy of police bombing, with demands such as "the appointment of a British or International Commission to examine the conditions under which police bombing takes place".[46] Arguably, this resistance to secrecy stemmed less from opposition to the practice itself and more from a broader suspicion of the government and the perceived institutional threat that secrecy posed to democratic governance.[47] Secrecy was thus portrayed as an obstacle to democratic accountability, and opposition to it emerged in media and parliamentary discussions in a familiar dance of questions: "Will his Department print a White Paper giving the full particulars of why and where bombing has taken place, together with the fact that no one but the airman concerned is ever present to know whether any of the inhabitants have been killed?"[48] In response, the Colonial Office and other state bodies attempted to assuage public concern through the publication of reports and White Papers. Yet, these gestures often failed to resolve the underlying suspicion. This is perhaps unsurprising, given that secrecy and transparency are not simple opposites, nor monolithic categories. Rather, they are mutually constituted through layers of revelation, omission and selective disclosure.

It is perhaps no coincidence that the institutionalisation of Freedom of Information requests in the twentieth century occurred alongside the formal entrenchment of intelligence services.[49] Nor is it incidental that the emergence of Britain's "covert empire" in Mesopotamia – where police bombing became a central method – coincided with the rise of mass democracy and increasing public engagement with foreign policy.[50] Satia has argued that "the more the British public strove to hold the government to account by ambushing it in the press, the less information was made available".[51] The growing reliance on police bombing was itself partly a response to public pressure: its relatively low cost and perceived effectiveness were seen as means to placate public concerns over how taxpayer money was spent.[52]

Framing secrecy as an exceptional moment in liberal democracies – an anomaly that can be remedied through transparency – fails to account for these entanglements within liberal governance. The Obama administration, often praised for its commitment to transparency, prosecuted more whistleblowers under the Espionage Act than all previous administrations combined.[53] Understanding secrecy as an exceptional, undemocratic state measure underestimates how deeply engrained it is in Western institutional structures. The contest between secrecy and transparency in liberal democracies is thus not a balanced struggle between freedom and security. While even the *potential* risks of exposure for state security are legally codified and addressed through institutional processes, the dangers posed by secrecy itself are rarely granted any formal recognition when it might affect "national security".[54] This is mirrored in international law: while international human rights law recognises the public's right to know, international humanitarian law does not extend such recognition.[55] As one US court remarked in response to a request for information on CIA drone strikes, this causes "frustration about the laws that, in its view, precluded it from requiring the government to release more information".[56]

Moreover, the common framing of secrecy as a shield separating the government from its domestic public overlooks the wider imperial power structures within which knowledge production and information flows are embedded. For example, during the 1960s and 1970s, various states from the Global South invested billions in cypher machines from the renowned Swiss company Crypto-AG in order to codify sensitive information, unaware that the company was secretly owned by the CIA and the German foreign intelligence agency. The devices were deliberately designed to leave communications vulnerable to interception by the US and its allies.[57] This episode illustrates that secrecy is not confined to internal state dynamics but is deeply embedded within global power relations and material possibilities. These wider structures shape who can know what, under what conditions.

Secrecy and transparency do not simply function as opposing forces but are coexisting modalities embedded within institutional architectures. This helps to explain the frequent dissonance in political discourse, for example when former UK Secretary of State for Defence Gavin Williamson declared: "As the hon. Gentleman knows, the Government do not comment on the activity of special forces, but we are absolutely committed to keeping this House regularly updated on our operations in Iraq and Syria."[58] Here, a ritualistic commitment to transparency is invoked in the very same breath as the denial to access of crucial information. Revelations and disclosures are embedded within hierarchies of knowledge production that will hide and obscure. Indeed, the proliferation of publicly available information can itself obscure perspectives which get buried within an overwhelming volume of data.[59] Transparency – far from being a universally beneficial principle – produces systems of exclusion within institutional structures of power. In the US context, for example, the institutionalisation of transparency in Congress through classified briefings to oversight committees might paradoxically have resulted in less public oversight and diminished debate. As civil rights actors have pointed out, "the CIA's disclosures to the congressional oversight committees have the perverse effect of insulating the agency from public scrutiny".[60] In this context, transparency often becomes a managed performance, curated to project legitimacy.

The moral elevation of transparency as a liberal good – something that is "universally perceived as a positive value"[61] – thus requires closer scrutiny. Closely aligned with Western hegemonic norms, transparency functions as a regulatory ideal of good governance reinforcing power asymmetries. The regulatory ideal of transparency has become an important aspect in discourses around drone warfare, where whole typologies of transparency have been developed, ranking states based on how much they reveal about bombing campaigns. Such typologies have the unintended effect of casting some of the most prolific perpetrators of air strikes – such as the US and Israel – as exemplary models because of their selective openness about them.[62] In this way, transparency becomes a performative practice by elites to carefully select information in the name of increasing democratic legitimacy. As Penny Mordaunt, then UK Minister of State for the Armed Forces, candidly remarked in response to a parliamentary inquiry about increased cooperation with the Joint Committee on Human Rights: "We certainly wish to co-operate, because putting more information into the public domain about the seriousness with which we take such issues will reassure hon. Members."[63]

Calls for increased transparency – premised on the belief that more information revealed by the executive will enhance public control of military violence – is problematic. While efforts to challenge secrecy can be strategically valuable in raising awareness and challenging the presumed legitimacy of violent military acts, they risk distracting from the actual violence itself. As Oliver Kearns's study of newspaper reporting on drone strikes illustrates, the framing of these events as enigmatic and unknowable often leads audiences to fixate on the mysterious quality of the attacks rather than engage with the underlying moral and political questions concerning the use of violence.[64] In this way, demands for transparency about violence risk distracting from – or even legitimising – the violence itself. If the problem is consistently framed as the lack of transparency, the use of violence can become implicitly framed as acceptable – as long as it is conducted in the open. In fact, the strategic openness surrounding "targeted killing" processes and their purported grounding in international law may have contributed to the practice being framed and perceived in legal terms in the first place, thus further legitimising it.[65]

It is thus overly simplistic to frame secrecy as the main problem impeding public control of wrongful state acts, while transparency is presumed to function as its antidote. Such a binary framing of secrecy and transparency obscures the complex interplay between the two and the layered discursive structures through which they both operate. Transparency is not an inherently emancipatory force; it generates its own hierarchies of exclusion and can serve a performative function, lending legitimacy to acts of violence and oppression. The demand for more information in order to understand what is going on misses how secrecy itself contributes to *shaping* what is going on. Secrecy is not merely an obstacle to knowledge about military violence but a productive force that shapes how violence is perceived, narrated and legitimised. Rather than theorising secrecy solely as a shield that facilitates state transgressions and could be pierced by greater openness, the following section turns to a second conceptualisation: secrecy as a spectacle. Here secrecy is understood not simply as a lack of transparency but as an active generator of political subjectivities and relations of inclusion and exclusion.

A spectacle of power

For silences to be interpreted as secrecy, some information must have been revealed to someone, otherwise there would be no recognition that something is being concealed. In existing literature this has sometimes been theorised through the distinction between "closed" and "open" secrets.[66] A closed secret refers to a situation in which there is no awareness of concealment, so that people "are in the dark about the fact that they are being kept in the dark".[67] An open secret, on the other hand, is a secret that is known about in some way, even if obliquely. Once knowledge of a secret exists, even partially, secrecy gains performative effects through a "public demonstration that one will not reveal".[68] In this sense, secrecy does more than obscure – it acquires political and affective force. I argue, therefore, that secrecy should be understood not merely as a barrier to comprehending the war but as playing a constitutive role in shaping how the war is defined, imagined and related to.

Two key considerations – which follow from the conceptual groundwork laid in Chapter 1 – are important here. First, silences interpreted as secrecy are not pre-existing, static entities; they emerge through complex processes of (not) listening, and of organising and interpreting that which has (not) been heard. I return to these processes in the final section of this chapter. Second, the classification of silence-as-secrecy is not universal but always relational and contextual. The political effects of secrecy – and whether secrecy is perceived at all – vary depending on the audience. While the terms "closed" or "open" secret may appear to describe intrinsic characteristics of a secret, secrecy is always mediated by specific configurations of actors, positionalities and historical discursive context.

Secrecy works through hierarchies of access that are contingent upon specific cultural and political circumstances. A striking example is the British government's implementation of Operation Legacy during the period of decolonisation. British authorities reviewed, destroyed or concealed documents of former colonial countries prior to handing over administrative control to newly independent states. As part of this process, thousands of documents were destroyed in what has since been described as an "enormous covert operation of selecting, burning and concealing the remains of the empire".[69] The secrecy of Operation Legacy did not only lie in the concealment or destruction of documentation but in a calibration of who would have access to which versions of the past. Not all officers of the British Empire were privy to Operation Legacy even taking place. In Kenya and Uganda, for example, the operation was supposed to be known about and carried out only by civil service officers who were British subjects of European descent, that is, white British officers.[70]

The hierarchies of access through which secrecy works do more than determine the quantity of information to which individuals are exposed: they also confer symbolic status. The extent of one's access to information becomes performative, shaping perceptions of status and authority. Secrecy thus produces relations of exclusion and inclusion that are sustained through everyday social rituals. As Walters shows in his study of the top-secret site Orford Ness during the Cold War, even seemingly small practices such as wearing badges denoting a high level of access "contributes to feelings of 'distinction and privilege'".[71] Interviews with staff members showed how the act of clearance before being employed conferred a notion of being special and in-the-know.[72] When silences are interpreted as secrecy, they acquire social and political force – secrecy does things. It draws attention, provokes speculation and shapes how events are interpreted. This is why secrecy is often strategically mobilised to generate anticipation, as exemplified by Apple's use of secrecy in product development to create hype around a new product.[73]

This performative dimension is often missed in conceptualisations of secrecy as a shield for states to conceal information from the public. In such a framing of secrecy, leaks or partial disclosures are interpreted as ruptures in the shield of secrecy. Yet this understanding overlooks the more complex and fragmented ways in which secrecy operates. Contemporary forms of covert war – such as drone warfare – are rarely entirely hidden. Acts of covert warfare have always encompassed an element of what might be called "implausible deniability",[74] and the proliferation of modern communication technologies has further rendered total concealment untenable.[75] Implausible deniability refers to a situation in which both the actions and the actors are widely suspected or are known by domestic and international audiences but are not *officially acknowledged.*

Far from being a liability, this ambiguity can serve the interests of powerful state actors. Open secrets and implausible deniability offer strategic advantages. In the context of drone warfare, the blurry status of the acts – known but framed as covert – not only functions as a mechanism to avoid accountability and deflect calls for redress. The openness of the secret also contributes to wider performative effects by generating epistemic uncertainty about what is understood – or can be claimed to be understood. Open secrets and practices of implausible deniability, even when limited to specific aspects of an act, produce uncertainty and a kind of cognitive and political paralysis. Creating conditions in which knowledge is affirmed and discredited, they leave observers suspended. As one interlocutor noted in the US Congress: "When we talk to people around here, they say there are no signature strikes. What are we supposed to believe? A lot of people are saying they have evidence and have heard there are signature strikes. Those in power who have the secret say we are not. It is hard to know what to believe."[76] Open secrets thus sustain a zone of doubt which renders the grounds for objection unstable, leaving publics unsure of how, or even whether, to respond.

This zone of uncertainty is embedded within the epistemic hierarchies of open secrets. Secrecy produces relations of inclusion and exclusion, generating a powerful core of insiders who are perceived to possess privileged knowledge about covert operations. This core is typically associated with the US government, its intelligence agencies and a network of allied secret services that together constitute what might be termed a transnational targeting regime.[77] It is a tightly circumscribed group of individuals operating across a fragmented security architecture in which accountability is often obscured. Drone operations which are conducted by different military branches, secret agencies and special operations forces are understood as so inscrutable that "even higher-level policymakers do not know whether drone operations are conducted by CIA or JSOC [Joint Special Operations Command] personnel".[78]

The authority of the insider status is amplified and reflected in popular culture. Being "in the know" about secret state practices carries a symbolic power which is cultivated and reproduced in the film industry. Films such as *Zero Dark Thirty* (2012) have received considerable government support, including access to CIA headquarters and classified documents. These films function not only as entertainment but as instruments of state projection of power. By associating themselves with these cinematic representations of the intelligence world, state actors seek to cultivate a favourable image of heroism.[79] Popular culture constructs secret agencies as elite sites of state authority, and through this lens the emphasis on such institutions and methods allows state actors to project narratives of military strength and political resolve.[80] In this context, secrecy is transformed into a performative spectacle, serving as a symbolic marker of the power held by dominant state actors.

Constructing a powerful core of actors who are "in-the-know", secrecy simultaneously creates a subject position of exclusion, relegating ordinary citizens, journalists, NGOs, courts, parliaments and even senior policy makers to subordinated epistemic status. Through a gradated hierarchical order, all those who do not frequent the top-secret corridors of the transnational targeting regime are rendered epistemically marginal. This epistemic exclusion has significant political implications for how publics – and the conditions for public political life – are conceptualised. It fosters a sense of unaccountability and limited comprehension because "when the public is only privy to partial, biased, and at times incorrect information, it is unable to serve as a check on its representatives – a critical element of representative democracy".[81]

The public's perceived inability to access adequate information regarding military violence is understood to lead to a situation where "a lack of disclosure gives States a virtual and impermissible license to kill".[82] Secrecy itself is seen as entangled with diminished possibilities for accountability and public control, thus effectively creating a "license to kill". When international law practitioners warn about a lack of transparency, this is not just as a hurdle to understanding and judging the acts. Instead, there is a sense that secrecy undermines the authority and clarity of the law itself:

"OHCHR [Office of the United Nations High Commissioner for Human Rights] notes with concern the lack of transparency surrounding the use of armed drones for targeted killings in Yemen. This contributes to a lack of clarity on the legal bases for the use of lethal force through drone strikes."[83]

Yet, much of this political work of secrecy depends precisely on the openness of the secret, on awareness of what is not known. The performative power of secrecy – as a spectacle of power that shapes what is seen as knowable and creates epistemic hierarchies of inclusion and exclusion – depends on revelations, text, disclosures, rumours. As an American congressional member put it: "The whole world knows these are CIA strikes operating on behalf of the American people, without transparency, accountability or oversight."[84] Secrecy, therefore, is not merely an obstacle to understanding the war; it is constitutive of the war. Secrecy shapes how the war is defined as "opaque, ambiguous and effectively unaccountable",[85] how the conditions of deciding on acts of war are envisioned and how the power of those in-the-know is reproduced. These effects depend on the openness of the secret, and are sustained through a spectrum of omissions, revelations, rumours, declassifications, delayed information etc. through which secrecy becomes known and performative.

How to know

The preceding sections have outlined two distinct conceptualisations of state secrecy, as a shield that inhibits public inquiry and as a spectacle that performs and enacts relations of power. While differing in their understandings of secrecy, both approaches tend to treat secrecy as an instrument – a coherent, monolithic unit that is defined and wielded by the state. This section shifts the focus towards a more fluid and processual understanding of secrecy, one that foregrounds its constitution from silences. I argue that secrecy emerges through messy layers of silences and revelations that are embedded within regimes of (not) listening in the broader economy of silence. This economy shapes not only what is (and what is not) heard in the first place, but also how silences come to be perceived and interpreted as secrecy and the value – or political currency – accorded to such interpretations.

Secrecy is not simply the antithesis of speech but operates through and within discourse – through layers of textual practice that include denials, explicit withholding of information, retractions, delays and the absence of details.[86] For example, critiques regarding the difficulties of evaluating the lawfulness of military operations rarely stem from a complete lack of data; instead, they arise from layers of silences and partial omissions, such as the withholding of details, for instance on the location and timing of attacks. NGOs, such as Airwars, which monitor state violence have expressed frustration with this lack of detail: "Three months later, Defence Command scaled back the level of geographic detail by omitting city names. And from March 2015 a caveat was added noting that strikes took place 'primarily' in for example Anbar province, thus leaving open the possibility of strikes elsewhere."[87] Secrecy is encountered as reluctance to respond to calls for transparency, for example when failing to provide information requested by the UN Human Rights Council.[88] It materialises through interpretations of partial omissions, ambiguities or delays in providing information, for example when NGOs note how "in Iraq, it would take 15 months for the Coalition to admit its first non-combatant casualties".[89]

Secrecy should therefore not merely be understood as a monolithic absence of speech but as a layered discursive formation, produced through omissions entangled with text. In the context of civilian death from drone strikes, secrecy is noted through a combination of claims, vague statements, absence of details or non-responses to requests. This includes overall denial of civilian death, for example when "UK officials have very publicly boasted of Britain having caused no civilian casualties in Iraq and Syria – despite more than 1,000 RAF airstrikes since 2014".[90] There is a general "lack of transparency concerning the circumstances in which armed drones were used",[91] as well as more particular absences of reporting on civilians in government reports, for example when "96% of reports make no mention of civilians".[92] It also includes non-responses to requests by NGOs for more information, for example when "AFRICOM refused to provide further information about the strike or those named by Amnesty International as the civilians found to have been killed in the attack".[93]

Secrecy, in this context, should be understood as a particular interpretative framework applied to the messy, layered interplay of both omissions and revelations. It is embedded within broader regimes of not listening that shape which voices are heard and whose knowledge is considered authoritative. Crucially, secrecy is not only about what is hidden but also about who is – and is not – expected to speak. Human rights actors have conducted intricate research to evidence civilian harm, including the analysis of leaked documents, interviews with eyewitnesses, forensic investigations and satellite image analysis.[94] These investigations frequently yield findings that diverge significantly from official state accounts. As UN Special Rapporteur Emmerson notes, "the figures provided by the Government [of the US] are very significantly lower than those tallied by civil society monitoring organizations".[95] Indeed, as argued above, state representatives have often completely denied any civilian deaths at all, for example when representatives "assert that the USA killed no civilians in Somalia in 2018, despite the fact that there have been no credible or onsite investigations into allegations of civilians killed in air strikes, and no mechanism enabling those affected by air strikes to report civilian deaths or injuries".[96]

Opposition to secrecy, preoccupied with what remains hidden and what must be revealed, fails to register the extensive documentation that is already available. Despite apparent shortcomings, official state narratives continue to be positioned as the most authoritative sources of knowledge. Secrecy both relies on and reproduces this epistemic hierarchy. Only when speech expectations are directed toward powerful actors – those presumed to be "in-the-know" – do layers of omissions become interpreted as secrecy. This framing recreates the exclusionary dynamic discussed above, reaffirming the perception that meaningful knowledge is centralised within state apparatuses. The result is a persistent difficulty in recognising and articulating what is already known, including the substantial body of evidence compiled by NGOs, journalists, academics and international organisations. This reaffirms a subject position of exclusion and the sense that "public opinion, political elites and civil society in the country remain barely acquainted with the legal and ethical dimension of the armed drones program".[97]

Secrecy, then, is often invoked to account for the absence of public debate and widespread opposition to military state violence: "The lack of attention paid to the legal concerns and civilian casualties surrounding the CIA's drone program underlies the indifference of the American public toward drone warfare [...]. These strikes occur away from American eyes."[98] Secrecy, in this context, produces ignorance and lack of opposition to state violence and oppression. As Bijl has argued in the context of Dutch colonial violence, even when abundant evidence about such violence exists, it may still be framed as hidden or yet to be recovered. He suggests that constructing atrocities as secret serves a dual function; it enables critics to position themselves as moral arbiters with privileged insights, and it allows broader publics to maintain a posture of innocence, "having lived in blissful ignorance of the awful deeds committed by others".[99] In this way, secrecy becomes a cultural construct that enables strategic ignorance and helps render public indifference toward violence and oppression more intelligible – and potentially more socially acceptable.

However, this reading of secrecy is predicated on selective inattention to sources and information. It operates by disregarding the extensive documentation produced by NGOs, academics, journalists and international organisations. It persists through speech expectations which remain narrowly focused on imperial state actors as legitimate producers of truth who are necessary in order to know about warfare. In this way, the messy layers of silences and revelations are interpreted as secrecy not merely because of what is concealed but because of regimes of (not) listening that continually confirm the epistemic centrality of those presumed to be in control. Secrecy, then, is not merely a state instrument but a cultural and political process that organises how knowledge is produced, recognised and ignored.

Hearing secrecy

This chapter has argued that silence interpreted as secrecy plays important political functions in enabling military violence. I first looked at the role secrecy plays as a shield that protects state actors from public scrutiny. Due to its transnational character and its reliance on intelligence services and new weapon technologies, drone warfare has been particularly characterised by secrecy. This secrecy is maintained through institutional processes inscribed into the parliamentary and legal frameworks of Western states. Often criticised for obstructing democratic accountability, these mechanisms have prompted repeated calls for greater governmental transparency and disclosure.

Yet, as I have argued in this chapter, positioning transparency as a liberal panacea for curbing state violence is problematic. While often framed as directly opposed to secrecy, transparency creates its own hierarchies of exclusion. Transparency measures function as a veneer of legitimacy that may distract from or even legitimise violence and oppression. Efforts to oppose secrecy about state violence may thus paradoxically reinforce the violent practices they seek to challenge by casting the acts of violence themselves as problematic only insofar as they are hidden. Calls for more information in order to understand what is going on risk obscuring the extent to which secrecy has been important in *defining* what is going on. Secrecy is not just an obstacle to understanding these acts of state violence but is integral to its construction and normalisation as "secret, unaccountable, borderless wars".[100]

This is not to suggest that secrecy is a pregiven or fixed entity; rather, it is continually constituted through layered interactions of information and omission – including leaks, rumours, revelations, delays and classifications. Secrecy emerges only when these layers are heard and organised in particular ways. Situated within a global economy of silence, secrecy derives its meaning not in isolation but through practices of listening and not listening – practices that determine what is heard, what is ignored and how interpretations take place. For example, the detailed and often more reliable body of knowledge gathered by local communities, journalists, academics and NGOs about drone warfare is often dismissed. Instead, silence continues to be interpreted as secrecy – understood as an epistemic void or impossibility of knowing – as it emanates from state institutions. This reinforces a prevailing assumption that only powerful state actors hold legitimate knowledge. In this way, the performative spectacle of secrecy is perpetuated by entrenched expectations of speech focused on those presumed to be in control.

Once interpreted through these frameworks, secrecy reproduces the image of a powerful, omniscient targeting regime and an epistemically marginalised public. It generates a zone of doubt regarding what can be known about this violence, thereby destabilising the grounds upon which critique or objection might be formulated and leaving publics unsure of how, or even whether, to respond. In this way, secrecy politically enables state violence by producing a subject position of exclusion – a public that is denied the epistemic authority to know and speak. Simultaneously, this not speaking is framed as acquiescence and tacit consent, since "the public largely accepts and supports the program, despite the informational black hole that surrounds it".[101] It is through these layered processes of perception and interpretation that an apparent contradiction emerges. Because drone warfare has "a peculiar kind of public visibility"[102] the public can be understood as unable to know and speak about the war while at the same time this not-speaking gains meaning as tacit consent to the war. The next chapter explores this paradox further by examining the role of acquiescence in enabling and sustaining military violence.

Notes

All URLs were last accessed on October 30, 2025.

1 Simone Chambers, "Behind Closed Doors: Publicity, Secrecy, and the Quality of Deliberation," *Journal of Political Philosophy* 12, no. 4 (2004): 389–410, https://doi.org/10.1111/j.1467-9760.2004.00206.x; Oxford Research Group, *All Quiet on the ISIS Front? British Secret Warfare in an Information Age* (Knowles, Watson, Remote Control, 2017), www.academia.edu/34051576/ALL_QUIET_ON_THE_ISIS_FRONT_British_secret_warfare_in_an_information_age; Timothy Melley, *The Covert Sphere: Secrecy, Fiction, and the National Security State*, in *The Covert Sphere* (Cornell University Press, 2012), https://doi.org/10.7591/9780801465918

2 Satia, *Spies in Arabia*, 292.

3 Eva Horn, "Logics of Political Secrecy," *Theory, Culture & Society* 28, nos. 7–8 (2011): 103–22, https://doi.org/10.1177/0263276411424583

4 Amnesty International, "*Will I Be Next?*".
5 Austin Carson, "Facing Off and Saving Face: Covert Intervention and Escalation Management in the Korean War," *International Organization* 70, no. 1 (2016): 105, https://doi.org/10.1017/S0020818315000284
6 Chambers, "Behind Closed Doors."
7 Michael Poznansky, "Revisiting Plausible Deniability," *Journal of Strategic Studies*, March 2, 2020, 1–23, https://doi.org/10.1080/01402390.2020.1734570
8 Melley, *The Covert Sphere*.
9 Clare Birchall, "Introduction to 'Secrecy and Transparency': The Politics of Opacity and Openness," *Theory, Culture & Society* 28, nos. 7–8 (2011): 7–25, https://doi.org/10.1177/0263276411427744
10 S. Besson, "Sovereignty, International Law and Democracy," *European Journal of International Law* 22, no. 2 (2011): 386, https://doi.org/10.1093/ejil/chr029; Robert McCorquodale, "Defining the International Rule of Law: Defying Gravity?" *International and Comparative Law Quarterly* 65, no. 2 (2016): 293, https://doi.org/10.1017/S0020589316000026
11 Chambers, "Behind Closed Doors."
12 UK House of Commons. *HC Debates*, June 18, 2019, Vol 662, Westminster Hall, International Humanitarian Law: Protecting Civilians in Conflict, Cc28WH–47WH. 2019.
13 Drone Wars UK, *Falling Short: An Analysis of the Reporting of UK Drone Strikes by the MOD, Brookman-Byrne, Drone Wars UK*, 2018, https://dronewars.net/2018/07/09/falling-short/
14 Amnesty International, *The Hidden US War in Somalia: Civilian Casualties from Air Strikes in Lower Shabelle*, 2019, www.amnesty.org/en/documents/afr52/9952/2019/en/
15 Drone Wars UK, *Falling Short*.
16 ECCHR, *Litigating Drone Strikes*.
17 UN Doc A/HRC/28/38, *Summary of the Human Rights Council Interactive Panel Discussion of Experts on the Use of Remotely Piloted Aircraft or Armed Drones in Compliance with International Law; Report of the Office of the United Nations High Commissioner for Human Rights*, 2014.
18 UN Doc A/HRC/28/38, *Summary of the Human Rights Council Interactive Panel Discussion of Experts on the Use of Remotely Piloted Aircraft ....*
19 Airwars, *Limited Accountability*.
20 Amnesty International, *The Hidden US War in Somalia*. Emphasis added.

21 Center for Civilians in Conflict and Columbia Law School, *The Civilian Impact of Drones.*
22 ECCHR, *Litigating Drone Strikes.*
23 UK House of Commons, *HC Debates*, November 6, 2012, Vol. 552, Westminster Hall, Unmanned Aerial Vehicles, Cc197WH–204WH.
24 Oxford Research Group, *All Quiet on the ISIS Front?*
25 Oxford Research Group, *All Quiet on the ISIS Front?*
26 APPG, *All Party Parliamentary Group on Drones Inquiry Report.*
27 UK House of Commons, *HC Debates*, December 1, 2015, Vol. 603, Westminster Hall, Armed Drones, Cc50WH–72WH.
28 UK House of Commons, *HC Debates*, December 1, 2015, Vol. 603, Westminster Hall, Armed Drones, Cc50WH–72WH.
29 Müller and Böller, "The Tug-of-War over Drone Strike Oversight," 15.
30 Oona A. Hathaway et al., "Congressional Oversight of Modern Warfare: History, Pathologies, and Proposals for Reform," *William & Mary Law Review* 63, no. 1 (2021): 137–218.
31 US Congress, *Congressional Record*, Vol. 160 (95), House of Representatives, June 18, 2014, H5429–54, 2014, H5441.
32 US Congress, *Congressional Record*, Vol. 159 (32), Senate, March 6, 2013, S1181–226, H1189.
33 Müller and Böller, "The Tug-of-War over Drone Strike Oversight," 17.
34 US Congress, *Congressional Record*, Vol. 159 (85), Extensions of Remarks, June 14, 2013, E861, 2013.
35 Müller and Böller, "The Tug-of-War over Drone Strike Oversight," 2.
36 Public Technologies, "Representatives Lee & Burgess Introduce Drone Reform Act to Ensure Accountability in Military Drone Strikes," Press Release, September 18, 2023, www.publicnow.com/view/BEAAE4E73AF6BF42B3AC677D0104D72823990CEC
37 UN Doc A/HRC/28/38, *Summary of the Human Rights Council Interactive Panel Discussion of Experts on the Use of Remotely Piloted Aircraft …*, 25.
38 ECCHR, *Litigating Drone Strikes.*
39 UN Doc A/HRC/20/22/Add.3, *Report of the Special Rapporteur on Extrajudicial, Summary or Arbitrary Executions, Christof Heyns; Addendum, Follow-up to Country Recommendations – United States of America*, 2012, 3; UNIDIR, *Increasing Transparency, Oversight and Accountability.*
40 UN Doc A/HRC/RES/25/22, *Human Rights Council Resolution: "Ensuring Use of Remotely Piloted Aircraft or Armed Drones in*

Counter-Terrorism and Military Operations in Accordance with International Law, Including International Human Rights and Humanitarian Law," 2014.

41 Birchall, "Introduction to 'Secrecy and Transparency,'" 13.
42 White House, "Open Government Directive: M10-06," 2009, https://obamawhitehouse.archives.gov/open/documents/open-government-directive
43 Satia, *Spies in Arabia*, 292.
44 Satia, *Spies in Arabia*, 301.
45 Satia, *Spies in Arabia*, 302; see also 299.
46 UK House of Commons, *HC Debates*, June 23, 1938, Vol. 337, Bombing, North-West Frontier, Cc1255–56, 1938.
47 *The Times*, for example demanded public disclosure and transparency about police bombing while supporting the practice itself; in Satia, *Spies in Arabia*, 295.
48 UK House of Commons, *HC Debates*, July 3, 1924, Vol. 175, Bombing Operations, Iraq, Cc1490–92.
49 Birchall, "Introduction to 'Secrecy and Transparency,'" 13.
50 Satia, *Spies in Arabia*, 288.
51 Satia, *Spies in Arabia*, 292.
52 Satia, *Spies in Arabia*, 288.
53 Spencer Ackerman and Ed Pilkington, "Obama's War on Whistleblowers Leaves Administration Insiders Unscathed," US News, *The Guardian*, March 16, 2015, www.theguardian.com/us-news/2015/mar/16/whistleblowers-double-standard-obama-david-petraeus-chelsea-manning.
54 Owen David Thomas, "Security in the Balance: How Britain Tried to Keep Its Iraq War Secrets," *Security Dialogue* 51, no. 1 (2020): 78, https://doi.org/10.1177/0967010619839544
55 Orna Ben-Naftali and Roy Peled, "How Much Secrecy Does Warfare Need?" in *Transparency in International Law*, ed. Andrea Bianchi and Anne Peters (Cambridge University Press, 2013), 321.
56 ECCHR, *Litigating Drone Strikes.*
57 Robert Dover and Richard J. Aldrich, "Cryptography and the Global South: Secrecy, Signals and Information Imperialism," *Third World Quarterly*, August 3, 2020, 1–18, https://doi.org/10.1080/01436597.2020.1793665
58 UK House of Commons, *HC Debates*, July 3, 2018, Vol. 644, Counter-Daesh Update, Cc192–201, 2018.
59 Gary Hall, "We Can Know It for You: The Secret Life of Metadata," *MSOR Connections*, Sigma Network, 2010, https://pureportal.coven

try.ac.uk/en/publications/we-can-know-it-for-you-the-secret-life-of-metadata-2.

60 Center for Civilians in Conflict and Columbia Law School, *The Civilian Impact of Drones*, 60.

61 Andrea Bianchi and Anne Peters, *Transparency in International Law* (Cambridge University Press, 2013), 2.

62 Elisabeth Schweiger, "Fighting Silence: Covert Warfare and the Uphill Battle against the Unsaid," *European Journal of International Relations*, October 24, 2021, 135406612110538, https://doi.org/10.1177/13540661211053830

63 UK House of Commons, *HC Debates*, December 1, 2015, Vol. 603, Westminster Hall, Armed Drones, Cc50WH–72WH.

64 Oliver Kearns, "State Secrecy, Public Assent, and Representational Practices of US Covert Action," *Critical Studies on Security* 4, no. 3 (2016): 276–90.

65 Krasmann, "Targeted Killing and Its Law"; see also Matthew Windsor, "Narrative Kill or Capture: Unreliable Narration in International Law," *Leiden Journal of International Law* 28, no. 4 (2015): 764, https://doi.org/10.1017/S0922156515000412

66 Sandra Blakely, "Toward an Archaeology of Secrecy: Power, Paradox, and the Great Gods of Samothrace," *Archaeological Papers of the American Anthropological Association*, 2012; Horn, "Logics of Political Secrecy."

67 David E. Pozen, "Deep Secrecy," *Stanford Law Review*, no. 2 (2010): 260.

68 Blakely, "Toward an Archaeology of Secrecy," 49.

69 Shohei Sato, "'Operation Legacy': Britain's Destruction and Concealment of Colonial Records Worldwide," *The Journal of Imperial and Commonwealth History* 45, no. 4 (2017): 698, https://doi.org/10.1080/03086534.2017.1294256

70 Sato, "'Operation Legacy,'" 706.

71 Walters, "Everyday Secrecy," 64.

72 Walters, "Everyday Secrecy," 68.

73 See for a discussion of this Birchall, "Introduction to 'Secrecy and Transparency,'" 14.

74 Rory Cormac and Richard J. Aldrich, "Grey Is the New Black: Covert Action and Implausible Deniability," *International Affairs* 94, no. 3 (2018): 477–94, https://doi.org/10.1093/ia/iiy067

75 Michael F. Joseph and Michael Poznansky, "Media Technology, Covert Action, and the Politics of Exposure," *Journal of Peace Research* 55, no. 3 (2018): 320–35, https://doi.org/10.1177/0022343317731508

76 US Congress, *Congressional Record*, Vol. 159 (32), Senate, March 6, 2013, S1181–226, S1189.
77 Giuseppe Zappalà, "Killing by Metadata: Europe and the Surveillance-Targeted Killing Nexus," *Global Affairs*, The European Union and Armed Drones, vol. 1, no. 3 (2015): 251–58, https://doi.org/10.1080/23340460.2015.1080035; ECCHR, *Litigating Drone Strikes*.
78 Center for Civilians in Conflict and Columbia Law School, *The Civilian Impact of Drones*.
79 Timothy Melley, "Covert Spectacles and the Contradictions of the Democratic Security State," *Storyworlds: A Journal of Narrative Studies* 6, no. 1 (2014): 63, https://doi.org/10.5250/storyworlds.6.1.0061
80 Cormac and Aldrich, "Grey Is the New Black," 489.
81 WILPF, *The Humanitarian Impact of Drones*.
82 UN Doc A/HRC/14/24/Add.6, *Report of the Special Rapporteur on Extrajudicial, Summary or Arbitrary Executions, Philip Alston, Addendum, Study on Targeted Killings*, 2010, at 88.
83 UN Doc A/HRC/24/34, *Situation of Human Rights in Yemen; Report of the United Nations High Commissioner for Human Rights**, 2013, at 17.
84 US Congress, *Congressional Record*, Vol. 159 (85), Extensions of Remarks, June 14, 2013, E861.
85 APPG, *All Party Parliamentary Group on Drones Inquiry Report*.
86 Schweiger, "Fighting Silence."
87 Airwars, *Limited Accountability*.
88 See, for example, UN Doc A/HRC/31/57/Add.1, *Report of the Special Rapporteur on Torture and Other Cruel, Inhuman, or Degrading Treatment of Punishment: Observations on Communications Transmitted to Governments and Replies Received*, 2016, 642.
89 Airwars, *Limited Accountability*.
90 Airwars, *Limited Accountability*.
91 UN Doc A/HRC/28/38, *Summary of the Human Rights Council Interactive Panel Discussion of Experts on the Use of Remotely Piloted Aircraft ...*, 8.
92 Drone Wars UK, *Falling Short*.
93 Amnesty International, *The Hidden US War in Somalia*.
94 See, for example, Amnesty International, *The Hidden US War in Somalia*; WILPF, *The Humanitarian Impact of Drones*; Center for Civilians in Conflict and Columbia Law School, *The Civilian Impact of Drones*.

95 UN Doc A/HRC/43/61, *Situation of Human Rights in the Islamic Republic of Iran; Report of the Special Rapporteur on the Situation of Human Rights in the Islamic Republic of Iran*, 2020, at 29.
96 Amnesty International, *The Hidden US War in Somalia.*
97 Open Society Foundations, *Armed Drones in Europe*, Open Society, European Policy Institute, 2019, www.opensocietyfoundations.org/publications/armed-drones-in-europe
98 WILPF, *The Humanitarian Impact of Drones.*
99 Bijl, "Colonial Memory and Forgetting in the Netherlands and Indonesia," 447.
100 ECCHR, *Litigating Drone Strikes.*
101 Center for Civilians in Conflict and Columbia Law School, *The Civilian Impact of Drones.*
102 Center for Civilians in Conflict and Columbia Law School, *The Civilian Impact of Drones.*

5

Acquiescence

The previous chapter discussed the importance of secrecy in producing a subject position of exclusion – one from which it becomes epistemically and politically difficult to know and speak about state violence. This position not only encompasses the general public but also includes NGOs, courts, parliaments, the media and even state governments outside of the transnational targeting regime. From this subject position of exclusion, the capacity to engage with or contest warfare is severely constrained. Global audiences are constructed as external to the covert targeting machinery, lacking both access to information on attacks by the global superpower and the agency to intervene. Public disengagement is thus often interpreted as the result of information deprivation: there is no debate on the topic because there is no data on which to base discussion.

Similarly, the capacity – and perceived responsibility – of other states to react is unclear in the absence of verifiable information. As the International Centre for Counter-Terrorism concluded in its report on the European position on armed drones, "the public silence on the issue of drone use by other states" may be read as "a lack of precise knowledge of a specific attack".[1] Yet, this silence is still noticed, tracked and problematised, for example when "at last year's meeting of First Committee, only ten states spoke on the subject of drones".[2] Loud silences are captured in official settings, for example when "few States have yet expressed their views officially on the kinds of challenges of armed UAV use like those outlined above".[3] They are documented through requests for information and refusals to engage, such as when UN High Commissioner Emmerson asks for clarifications from states in the

UN General Assembly on legal issues in connection with armed drone attacks, urging "all States to respond as comprehensively as possible",[4] noting four years later that "no formal answers have been received to date".[5]

Within international law discourses, this silence has been interpreted as normatively consequential through its potential function as acquiescence to new legal frameworks, for example, around the right to self-defence.[6] Some legal scholars have invoked the "muted reaction [...] in regard to the U.S. drone campaign",[7] which leads them to the conclusion that "most other states seem to be willing to acquiesce in this reinterpretation of the customary law of self-defense".[8] Human rights advocates have expressed concern about public and state silences, warning that absence of opposition might function as de facto endorsement. They call on states to publicly formulate legal opposition to avoid "supporting a dangerous precedent set by other countries that have used armed drones in ways that undermine international law".[9]

Similarly, concerns have been voiced about the silence of the public. While understood to be shaped by systemic exclusion from information, this silence is also interpreted as a form of assent: "Secrecy, framed as preservation of national security, further diminishes the public's interest in exerting pressure on the government to justify lethal operations. However, as drone strikes become increasingly prominent and viewed as a successful tactic, they risk becoming 'the norm.'"[10] Silence-as-acquiescence is thus understood as politically significant for enabling state violence. Some scholars have indeed argued that contemporary warfare is less dependent on active public support or traditional forms of war propaganda and more fundamentally reliant on public acquiescence. Engaging with state rhetorics, Engels and Saas argue that discourses enabling contemporary warfare cannot be understood through conventional paradigms of war propaganda: "To be 'for' or 'against' war has today become a rather inconsequential distinction, fodder for bumper stickers and empty campaign promises. Overriding the for/against distinction is a general feeling of acquiescence in relation to war."[11]

As this chapter will demonstrate, acquiescence has long played an important role in liberal politics, from social contract theories to foundational myths underpinning the international system. Within this tradition, silence becomes imbued with meaning through underlying assumptions rooted in liberalism's close association of individual agency with voice. As such, silence becomes audible as acquiescence and thus a source of legitimacy for institutions and practices. Political theorists and legal scholars have attempted to delineate the conditions under which silence can be interpreted as consent. These conditions, I argue, often overlook the power relations that structure the very possibilities for speaking and being heard.

Like secrecy, acquiescence is a loud, expressive silence that relies not merely on a particular interpretation of silence but also on broader processes of not listening through which silence itself comes to be perceived. This chapter investigates the power relations that have historically excluded certain actors from possessing a recognised voice, focusing in particular on colonial relations of power that have denied the non-European world a legally recognised or authoritative voice. Speech expectations – through which silence becomes intelligible and loud – often persist irrespective of power asymmetries that inhibit the actual capacity of actors to speak or be heard. These dynamics are entrenched in regimes of not listening in international law that shape who is recognised as a valid producer of knowledge and which sources are acknowledged or dismissed.

Interpreting silence as acquiescence, without attending to the deep-rooted power asymmetries that shape possibilities of speaking and being heard, risks reinforcing epistemic injustice. It imposes the meaning of assent upon actors whose silence may stem from structural conditions of voicelessness – those who are unable to speak, denied recognition when they do speak or are not listened to. The interpretive move of silence-as-acquiescence also risks reproducing injustice towards those who bear the brunt of the violence being acquiesced to, often racialised and marginalised communities subjected to imperial violence and oppression. Understanding the political work of silence-as-acquiescence requires foregrounding these conditions of exclusion. The meaning and force of acquiescence derive not in spite of but through the power relations that structure global hierarchies of voice and recognition. This is why acquiescence born from unequal conditions does not necessarily function as consent to a new, general rule – such as a reinterpretation of the right to self-defence – but, rather, as tacit endorsement of imperial regimes and the systemic violence inflicted on non-white people in "outlying regions" of the world.

(Neo)liberal imaginings

Rooted in the primacy of individual agency, liberalism not only relies on acquiescence but imbues it with an added layer of legitimacy. Within liberal political imaginings, individual agency – closely associated with voice – is both presumed and idealised as a political foundation. Silence, therefore, does not merely register because expectations of speech are disappointed but is further imbued with political significance. This section sketches the foundational role of acquiescence within liberal political imaginings, tracing its function from classical contract theories to the constitution of international organisations and international law frameworks. I argue that these liberal imaginaries of acquiescence play a central role in enabling contemporary warfare – even though the legitimacy which is extracted from acquiescence masks the power relations in which state violence is embedded.

Acquiescence exposes an inner contradiction within liberalism. On the one hand, liberalism values the primacy of individual agency; on the other hand, this subjectivity is already bound by liberal rules. Acquiescence can thus be understood as a conceptual mechanism to reconcile this tension. As Simmons observes, "it is on this leg that consent theory must lean most heavily".[12] Individuals are supposed to be free, and bound only by voluntary consent, and yet it is quite apparent that the foundations of liberal political regimes are not made contingent on everyone's explicitly ascertained consent. As Simmons notes, "the paucity of express consenters is painfully apparent; most of us have never been faced with a situation where express consent to a government's authority was even appropriate, let alone actually performed such an act".[13]

Tacit and presumed consent thus functions – constitutionally and in daily political life – as a way of legitimising political decisions that have not in fact been accepted by everyone – or even by most.

Technical procedures and rules, like majority decision making, cannot themselves solve the conundrum, as they in turn rely on the presumption that everyone has in some form consented to being bound by them.[14] As Michael Freeden has argued, "tacit consent in Locke's version, then, is implicitly not merely held to be the consent to obey any number of laws and rules within a government's domain, but involves a preceding tacit consent to allow others to judge actions on behalf of any silent individual".[15]

Within the tradition of contract theories, as articulated in the works of Hobbes and Locke, the notion of tacit consent plays a key legitimising role. These theories explain the authority and legitimacy of liberal governance through a foundational narrative in which free individuals – or, rather, "men" – voluntarily transition from a pre-political "state of nature" into organised political communities. This transition must in some form be grounded in mutual agreement, as Locke put, it by "agreeing together mutually to enter into one Community, and make one body Politick".[16] However, balancing the ideal of individual freedom with the historical and empirical reality of political and legal structures presents a theoretical challenge. Liberalism is premised on the sovereignty of the individual, yet political authority must be – and historically has been – established even in the absence of express consent. It is precisely in this space that acquiescence functions as a conceptual bridge. Tacit consent is construed through a range of non-verbal acts and omissions, such as the absence of protest, the use of state infrastructure, participation in elections or simply residing within the territorial bounds of a state.[17] By allowing for the deduction of political will without explicit articulation, acquiescence sustains the appearance of legitimacy when no express agreement has been made.

Social contract theories have been described as "the most famous and influential political story of modern times"[18] and have profoundly shaped Western political thought, extending well beyond national foundation myths. A parallel justificatory logic can be found in the constitutional narrative of the international legal system. Just as individuals in contract theories are imagined to be bound only by laws to which they have consented, so too are states bound only by international laws they have agreed to. Yet the international legal regime has not been founded upon the explicit consent of all – or even most – states. Acquiescence, in this context, functions analogously to its role in social contract theories as a conceptual bridge to resolve this tension. Legal scholars often understand acquiescence as a mechanism for reconciling the factual state of the global order, on the one hand, and the legitimacy that is conventionally understood to derive from consent by at least the majority of states, on the other hand.[19] Some commentators adopt a more "realist" position, viewing acquiescence as a means to align international law with the political "reality", where "trends must then be tested against the requirements of world public order".[20] Within more voluntarist – or we might say liberal – strands of international legal thought, acquiescence serves to confirm that international law, even when not explicitly endorsed, ultimately emanates from the will of states as sovereign, law-generating actors.[21]

The invocation of acquiescence as a source of legitimacy for political orders has not gone unchallenged. Scholars have raised concerns regarding both the actual and the hypothetical intentionality underlying interpreted silences. In terms of hypothetical intentionality, it has been argued that silence can be understood to indicate tacit consent only under the condition that "the consequences of dissent cannot be extremely detrimental to the potential consenter".[22] For instance, the expectation that individuals demonstrate dissent by physically exiting the jurisdiction of a state has been criticised on the grounds that such requirements impose untenably high costs.[23] With respect to actual intentionality, critics note that even where the hypothetical conditions for tacit consent may be satisfied, this does not provide evidence that silence was, in fact, intended to express agreement.[24] On this basis, the idea of tacit consent as a legitimate foundation for political obligation has been dismissed as a legal and philosophical fiction. As one critic argues, "fictional consent is an absurdity because it violates the condition of intentionality".[25]

Despite such objections, however, acquiescence continues to exert considerable influence within liberal political thought – not only in foundational narratives but also in the routine functioning of political and legal systems. In the international sphere, acquiescence plays a pivotal role in the formation and interpretation of international laws because it does not depend on explicit consent.[26] The majority of customary international laws are based on silence interpreted as acquiescence.[27] As the draft conclusions of the International Law Commission put it, "Failure to react over time to a practice may serve as evidence of acceptance as law (*opinio juris*)".[28] To safeguard the effectiveness of the international legal system, some legal theorists argue that silence must be interpreted as acquiescence irrespective of the presumed intent of the silent state: "Normative effectivity and certainty can only be ensured in such constellations if a state's omission to react and the mere opportunity to articulate opinio juris is endowed with legal effects."[29] Particularly in contested areas, customary international law offers a distinct procedural advantage: unlike treaty law, it does not require the formal signature or express consent of state representatives. Instead it relies on evidence of *opinio juris* – the belief that a practice is accepted as law – alongside state practice. Crucially, this is assessed and interpreted by legal actors such as courts, scholars and international organisations, rather than being directly articulated by states. As a result, a practice that initially contravenes existing laws may gradually acquire legal validity if other states are understood to fail to register timely and effective objections.[30] In this way, silence-as-acquiescence can play a constitutive role in the legitimisation of otherwise unlawful practices.

Acquiescence gains traction because of the underlying taken-for-granted assumption of individual agency expressed through the subject's presumed ability to speak: "Just as silence can have communicative content in conventional conversations, it is possible for it to yield legal effects within the discursive process of law formation and evolution."[31] Through the expectation of speech, silence can garner meaning as a deliberate political or legal act, conferring legitimacy when interpreted as acquiescence. As the following sections will demonstrate, the presumption of individual agency and capacity for speech underlying such interpretations is more problematic than it may initially appear. Nonetheless, it functions as a foundational myth that sustains political and legal orders predicated on the ideal of individual sovereignty even as they impose rules that have never been expressly agreed to. As Michael Freeden argues, "government, needy of the legitimization that its subjects' silence cannot provide, deploys an imaginative – and very possibly spurious – ideological move. Harnessing the interpretation of tacitness as compliance assuages any doubts that may apply to the rulers' claim to legitimacy and consolidates the belief in the rightfulness of their authority."[32]

This dynamic also manifests in more functional terms within the routine operations of law and politics, through top-down decision-making processes that still pay rhetorical homage to individual autonomy through actual, manufactured or presumed acquiescence. The largely unquestioned role of tacit consent in foundational narratives of liberal political systems resonates with broader assumptions embedded in everyday social and political life. As Michael Freeden observes, the slight contradiction of the concept "tacit consent" as a compound noun is frequently overlooked, "so closely is it assumed to correspond both to political and social practices and to a plausible variation on signalling democratic legitimation".[33] The implications of this are evident in mundane institutional practices – in workplaces, organisations, hospitals, schools – where hierarchical structures prevail, yet decisions often derive a veneer of legitimacy through mechanisms of tacit consent. These may include gestures towards consultation (e.g. a chair asking if there are any objections or conducting perfunctory surveys) or the retrospective attribution of acquiescence through the absence of objections (e.g. "if you disagreed you should have said so"). In such contexts, silence can be strategically invoked and manufactured to legitimise institutions and practices.

This role of acquiescence has provoked some unease of commentators who have particularly focused on situations in which silence is misinterpreted as tacit consent. This discomfort is apparent in heated debates surrounding whether consent can ever be given without verbal communication in legal and ethical discussions concerning doctor–patient interactions and sexual relationships. Here, the stakes are heightened by the legal implications of acquiescence. Consent has been compared to promises, in that both "alter the rights that we hold against each other" and are thus "morally valid only with communication".[34] Theorists who argue that acquiescence can still be a valid form of obtaining consent tend to appeal to inferential frameworks that rely on non-behavioural facts understood as contextual cues that indicate an individual's mental state and serve the establishment of common knowledge.[35]

I argue that these attempts to ascertain the validity of acquiescence do not sufficiently address the underlying power relations within which the very existence and interpretation of loud silence is embedded. Silence is not encountered out there, independent of the interpreters' expectations. I argue that we need to reflect on the global economy of silence which underlies the ability to speak, who and what is listened to and how utterances and silences are interpreted as acquiescence. Because the political work of acquiescence is so fundamental, so commonplace and at the same time so prone to rely on and reinforce violent relations of power, it needs to be analysed within a wider political and historical context. In the case of remote warfare, this particularly requires us to think about coloniality and racialised relations of power.

Imperialism and the constitution of voice

The example often used to illustrate the legitimacy of tacit consent is, tellingly, a mundane, everyday example which can easily be visualised – the example of the boardroom. As Simmons describes it:

> Chairman Jones stands at the close of the company's board meeting and announces, "There will be a meeting of the board at which attendance will be mandatory next Tuesday at 8:00, rather than at our usual Thursday time. Any objections?" The board members remain silent. In remaining silent and inactive, they have all tacitly consented to the chairman's proposal to make a schedule change (assuming of course, that none of the members is asleep or has failed to hear).[36]

On the basis of this example, Simmons develops several contextual conditions for when silence can be presumed to communicate tacit consent, including that "the situation must be such that it is perfectly clear that consent is appropriate and that the individual is aware of what is happening"[37] and "that there must be a definite period of reasonable duration when objections or expressions of dissent are invited or clearly appropriate".[38] Simmons's boardroom image exemplifies a common framework through which tacit consent is conceptualised in understandings of acquiescence, from institutional practices to international law. Conditions for acquiescence in international law thus lean heavily on "facts" about the context and the act which has not been objected to. As the International Court of Justice (ICJ) argues in *Malaysia/Singapore*: "[t]he absence of reaction may well amount to acquiescence [...] [t]hat is to say, silence may also speak, but only if the conduct of the other State calls for a response".[39] State silence may thus be interpreted as acquiescence subject to certain contextual conditions, for example that the practice which "calls for a response" was "open and public".[40] The practice has to be made known in a way in which other States would have, or ought to have, knowledge of it.[41]

By focusing primarily on the circumstances of the practice, these prevailing accounts of tacit consent overlook the power relations that shape and constrain the capacity for voice. They often fail to engage with fundamental questions about the *possibilities for speech*. Which actors are excluded from entering the proverbial boardroom in the first place and thus from the processes through which consent is presumed to be given? Which actors might be there but are not recognised as speaking subjects (for example, catering staff)? As feminist and critical race theorists have pointed out, the construction of consent within liberal foundation myths overlooks patriarchal and racialised power relations as the basis of contracts between free, white "men" from which women and people of colour are *a priori* excluded as speaking subjects.[42]

From a postcolonial perspective, the very foundations of the state system were built on imperial relations which excluded colonial subjects from being recognised as actors at all. This is evident in regard to "new states", political entities which were granted state sovereignty after long struggles against imperialism. Their very recognition as sovereign states – and thus the creation of their subjectivity with a voice in the international system – was contingent on their tacit acceptance of pre-existing laws and customs.[43] In international relations and international law, the ability to speak resides with sovereign states. This framework (has) excluded the non-European world not only from claiming certain rights and privileges but also from having a recognisable subjectivity.[44] This was

suggest that the map [...] was in any way inaccurate."[52] The ICJ argued that the Siamese authorities could have objected to the French because they had knowledge of the map which the French cartographers had produced. The Court recites a long list of opportunities in which "it would have been natural for Thailand to raise the matter".[53]

However, the power asymmetries of the relationship were not analysed in the judgment and "the fact of French colonialism was completely ignored".[54] With few exceptions, even the dissenting opinions of the judgment focused on circumstantial matters, such as the question of whether the map called for a response, or whether the Siamese authorities had knowledge of the claim – for example, it is not clear whether the map clearly depicts the temple as lying outside of Siamese territory – rather than whether the political circumstances would have allowed for the Siamese authorities to speak against French colonial authorities. Yet, as Siamese Princess Phun Phitsamai Disku argued, "It was generally known at the time that we only give the French an excuse to seize more territory by protesting. Things had been like that since they came into the river Chao Phya with their gunboats and their seizure of Chanthaburi."[55]

Whether an actor is perceived to have had the capacity to raise their voice is implicitly shaped by how the surrounding context is interpreted, and by deeper ontological and epistemological assumptions. These include foundational beliefs about the nature of political authority – such as state sovereignty – as well as contingent understandings of what constitutes "voice". In the case of *Preah Vihear*, for example, significant weight was placed on a map as the central piece of evidence, rather than on the broader contextual or circumstantial factors.[56] Notably, the map in question had been produced by a French cartographer and the judgment itself acknowledged that Siam lacked the means to generate such cartographic documentation themselves.[57] The reliance on the map depends on the broader colonial epistemology underpinning the representation of land. The very notion of territory as a demarcated space defined by precise borders has served as a colonial device. As scholars have noted, mapping has historically functioned as an imperial tool, entailing "the labour of (im)material erasure, of violently projecting lands and peoples as empty, blank slates, not or under-used, there for the taking and the filling".[58] Through this epistemological framing, practices of extraction and dispossession were justified, appealing to particular conceptions of property, territoriality and rightful occupation.[59] The silence of Siam can only appear as acquiescence on the basis of such ontological and epistemological presumptions underlying the knowledge system of international law.

In liberal political thought, silence-as-acquiescence derives much of its normative force from the primacy accorded to voice and the accompanying expectation that subjects will speak out. This expectation, in turn, rests on the presumption that liberal regimes afford their subjects the capacity to do so. Silence acquires meaning as acquiescence only when high expectations of speech are maintained – often in disregard of the asymmetrical power relations which inhibit actors from raising their voice. By maintaining high expectations of speech, silence is noted as loud, expressive silence. In international law, such liberal political imaginings are projected onto states as sovereign actors, which by virtue of being states are presumed to have the ability and responsibility to speak. As one international law scholar puts it: "The argument sometimes raised that the omission of any protest may be due to a reason other than the tacit acceptance of the practice is unconvincing. Whatever the reason for such an omission, nowadays a State does this at its own risk."[60]

Such assumptions reproduce a liberal ideal of a "free speech" situation in interstate relations, ignoring the persistent and systemic asymmetries that define global power relations. The legacies of imperialism, as well as ongoing forms of economic and political dependency, constrain the ability of many governments in the Global South to contest the actions of more powerful states. These governments are often deeply entangled with and reliant upon Western powers, particularly the US, and, as some scholars argue, are "almost never in a position to credibly challenge states that use force in their territory illegally".[61] Even governments of relatively powerful states are embedded within networks of structural inequality that limit their scope for dissent. Thus, the liberal speech expectations that underpin interpretations of silence as acquiescence in international law are sharply misaligned with the dominance of the US in interstate relations after the end of the Cold War.

Nowhere is this clearer than in forums such as the UN Security Council, where the geopolitical power of the US profoundly shapes the possibilities for speech. This dynamic becomes apparent when examining the historical trajectory of UN Security Council debates by comparing reactions to US counterterrorism practices immediately before and after the end of the Cold War. In 1986, the US Air Force launched an armed attack in Libya which the US representative justified as targeted counterterrorism use of force "in exercise of the inherent right to self-defence [...] against terrorist-related targets".[62] The attacks "met with substantial and immediate criticism by the world community"[63] and delegations at the Security Council voiced critique of the "brutal, barbaric attack", the "unlawful, inhuman military raids" and "aggressive armed attacks" in no uncertain terms and condemned the bombing as a "form of State terrorism".[64] The General Assembly passed a resolution in November which condemned the US intervention.[65]

In stark contrast, in 1993 the US government carried out a counterterrorism intervention "designed to damage the terrorist infrastructure of the Iraqi regime",[66] as the American spokeswoman put it. A Security Council debate took place but the language at this debate was notably different to the language in 1986. The French representative argued that it "fully understands the reaction of the United States".[67] Representatives were reluctant to condemn the use of force and only went so far as to observe that "the alarming situation characterized by the information conveyed to this Council is an extraordinarily serious one".[68] The League of Arab States protested against the intervention outside the framework of the United Nations, but no serious opposition emerged within the Security Council.[69] The political context of the 1993 intervention in Iraq differed significantly from the 1986 intervention in Libya, not least because of the Gulf War in 1991. Yet, a comparable pattern is observable after the 1998 US missile strikes at sites in Afghanistan and Sudan, which were justified as acts of self-defence.[70] Even though the Non-Aligned Movement, China and several Arab states voiced objections to the strikes, these protests again occurred outside of the Security Council framework and "the Security Council did not meet publicly to evaluate the US military action".[71]

This pattern of silence has been interpreted by some scholars as evidence "that the international community has become more accepting of forceful responses to state-sponsored terrorism"[72] and, more broadly, of counterterrorism use of force from the 1990s onwards.[73] Such interpretations of silence-as-acquiescence have, in turn, been invoked to legitimise practices such as armed drone attacks: "In other words, it is important not to see the US on this point as some solitary outlier from other states."[74] However, this line of reasoning relies on high speech expectations – expectations that fail to account for the power relations within which the possibilities for speech are embedded and constrained. While the US has occupied a dominant global position – arguably the sole superpower in the post-Cold War era – this structural power asymmetry is often overlooked in legal and political interpretations of silence as acquiescence to US drone warfare.

Silence works as consent through the disappointed expectation of speech, through being an absence of protest when "the conduct of the other State calls for a response".[75] Protest is regarded as the expected move for states, and it is against this importance of objections that silence is framed as acquiescence.[76] Some international legal scholars have thus connected the silence surrounding drone warfare to a broader pattern of silences, suggesting that "the dominant trend in contemporary interstate relations seems to favor the view that States accept or at least tolerate acts of self-defense against a non-State actor".[77] I argue that such invocations of silence-as-acquiescence are deeply problematic because they ignore the expectations of speech and contextual assumptions through which silence becomes audible as loud silence. The next section focuses on the invocation of silence-as-acquiescence in international law and argues that not only the interpretation of silence-as-acquiescence but the very perception of silence depends on a regime of not listening, ranging from banal methodological choices to deeply embedded assumptions and expectations of speech that are based on Western-centric views of the world.

I hear no objections

Silence-as-acquiescence tends to be cited by international lawyers as "first, a fact and a verbal omission".[78] Such references are based on the assumption that the idea of tacit consent "is derived from facts – perceivable conduct – as they present themselves to an objective observer".[79] Indeed, the idea of silence as acquiescence is perceived as so self-evident that it is often merely invoked in half-sentences.[80] Based on the understanding that customary international law is a set of rules detected from the observation of state acts, the main question revolves around whether a given silence is "legally qualified silence"[81] and can be counted as acquiescence. Yet, this ignores not only the steep power asymmetries which structure the possibilities for speech but also the regimes of not listening through which silence becomes perceived as silence. These processes of not listening rely on taken-for-granted assumptions which are fundamentally Western-centric and reproduce steep power asymmetries.

Not only the interpretation of silence as acquiescence, but the assumption that a lack of protest exists, is based on exclusionary regimes of (not) listening. In the context of drone warfare and "targeted killing" practices, the perception of silence is possible only when protest in response to comparable acts is selectively ignored. As I have demonstrated elsewhere, while explicit condemnation of US practices has been relatively muted within the Security Council since the end of the Cold War, comparable justifications of counterterrorism uses of force by other states – such as Israel – have been consistently met with strong objections.[82] Such practices have been condemned in strong terms as "a patent violation of international law",[83] "armed aggression",[84] and a "violation of the sovereignty of a neighbouring State".[85]

When silence is invoked as acquiescence, the legal relevance of the act is often inferred directly from the justification offered by the state perpetrating the armed intervention.[86] This interpretive move serves to amplify the legal authority of a powerful state's unilateral claims, effectively magnifying the legitimacy of violent state behaviour. As a result, analytical focus shifts disproportionally towards the practices and legal reasoning of militarily dominant states. The provocative nature of practices, such as US "targeted killing" strikes, has led to a concentration of legal scholarship on such practices and the reaction – or lack of reaction – to them.[87] This focus is based on unspoken assumptions regarding the importance of the US and other powerful state actors and further reinforces this perceived centrality. Paradoxically, while the centrality of powerful states is implicitly assumed through this attention, the structural power relations that render certain forms of protest impossible or inaudible are often ignored in interpretations of silence as acquiescence.

The very invocation of silence as acquiescence depends on entrenched regimes of not listening, embedded in dominant epistemologies and legal practices that are rarely explicated. Much like the unspoken assumption that US practices merit particular attention, international law scholars and practitioners often take for granted that the UN – especially the UN Security Council – is the primary forum in which objections must be registered in order to be heard. This belief persists despite the fact that these institutions are marked by profound Western-centric power asymmetries that shape what can be said and by whom.

Although explicit protest against US counterterrorism operations, such as drone warfare, has been limited within the Security Council, it has continued outside of it. In 2014, for example, the UN Human Rights Council held an "interactive panel discussion on the use of remotely piloted aircraft or armed drones in compliance with international law"[88] and adopted Resolution 25/22 "Ensuring the use of remotely piloted aircraft or armed drones in counter-terrorism and military operations in accordance with international law, including international human rights and humanitarian law".[89] The resolution was adopted by a vote of twenty-nine state representatives in favour and six against.[90] The first sentence of the resolution refers to the prohibition of the interstate use of force, with particular reference to Article 2(4) of the UN Charter.[91]

Loud silence can thus emerge only through processes of not listening, for example, when speech expectations are directed at the UN Security Council, ignoring protest voiced at other forums. When silence is invoked simply as "a fact",[92] the underlying regimes of not listening which have created this "fact" are obscured. These regimes of not listening are embedded within material power relations and are frequently naturalised as taken-for-granted choices, inscribed into disciplinary standards. For example, the routine focus on debates at the UN Security Council reflects not only methodological norms but also deeper epistemological commitments to particular sites of authority and legitimacy. Such choices are perceived as standard practice precisely because they align with dominant understandings of the international order which has been shaped by asymmetries of power. As a result, loud silence stemming from regimes of not listening is presented as neutral and objective, rather than as contingent on specific configurations of power.

A similar basic assumption which is engrained within our regimes of not listening is the focus on state actors as "the predominant interpreters of treaties and creators of CIL [Customary International Law] within the international community".[93] As argued above, the presumption of legitimate voice residing with state actors is deeply problematic, given the intersecting power relations that have systematically excluded large segments of the population from being heard or adequately represented by their so-called "own" state. In former colonial contexts, this problem is further compounded by the fact that the territorial construction of many nation-states is based on colonial cartographies. These boundaries have often been drawn arbitrarily or strategically by colonial powers to entrench patterns of marginalisation, leave entire areas and minority groups politically disenfranchised and structurally excluded from state representation and international voice. This aspect is particularly relevant to consider for contemporary bombing practices since "UAVs have been limited to uses outside typical high-intensity military battlefields, often for clandestine purposes, and frequently with the acquiescence of the States whose territory they overfly".[94]

Despite these limitations, states continue to be presumed as the central and authoritative voices in international politics. Within the field of international law, it remains institutionally difficult to move beyond those state-centric parameters and incorporate voices from non-state actors. This exclusion is not typically maintained through overt forms of censorship, but, as discussed in Chapter 1, through more subtle mechanisms: the selection through which papers and reports are published, the allocation of research funding and the informal norms that determine who gains and retains professional legitimacy within the field. This is not to suggest that individuals within these fields are driven solely by instrumental motives. Rather, the argument is that structural conditions make it difficult to establish and sustain alternative modes of listening, thereby reinforcing a global economy of silence.

When non-state actors are included in international political and legal discussions, they are typically representatives of Western NGOs and human rights organisations that already possess institutional legitimacy within UN frameworks. For example, during the 2014 UN Human Rights Council's "Interactive Panel Discussion of Experts on the Use of Remotely Piloted Aircraft or Armed Drones", the panel featured legal experts, such as the UN Deputy High Commissioner for Human Rights, state representatives and NGOs, such as Amnesty International or the American Civil Liberties Union. Notably absent, however, were voices from communities directly affected by drone warfare.[95] This selective inclusion reflects assumptions regarding who is expected to speak which are based on what I have described as an economy of silence. Within this economy, market structures of intersecting professional fields and material possibilities for representation reproduce regimes of not listening and assign legal and political value to loud silences, such as perceived acquiescence.

These epistemic and institutional regimes are closely linked to methodological practices that shape what counts as valid knowledge and constrain the possibilities for alternative modes of listening. For example, while international law scholars might supplement UN records with alternative sources – such as media coverage or press releases – such sources tend to be overwhelmingly anglophone and Western. This is in part due to the institutional location of most international lawyers in Western academic and political settings, which reflects the broader material inequalities that structure access to education, research and funding. Additionally, limitations in language proficiency constrain the ability of many scholars to engage with alternative sources. Such biases are also sustained by prevailing norms about the credibility of sources, which commonly class anglophone and Western media outlets as reputable.

These media outlets are themselves embedded in regimes of (not) listening, shaped by the structures of exclusion within the field of journalism and assumptions about what counts as relevant and credible. In this way, Western-centric legal scholarship, journalism and institutional practices at international organisations reinforce one another, collectively sustaining a global economy of silence. The very perception of silence as loud, expressive silence thus fundamentally depends on regimes of not listening which influence who can be understood as a valid knowledge producer, where speech expectations are directed and which sources are – and are not – taken into account. Interpreting silence as acquiescence without accounting for the power asymmetries that shape the conditions of speech risks reinforcing structural injustice. It is to the detriment of those whose silence is interpreted as acquiescence when they have no voice, when they cannot speak or when they are systematically ignored.

An obligation to speak

The preceding analysis of the power structures that preclude actors from speaking and being heard, calls into question the interpretation of silence as acquiescence. However, this critique does not diminish the political significance of acquiescence as a functional mechanism for enabling and legitimising state violence. As demonstrated above, silence can be invoked and mobilised as acquiescence even in contexts where no genuine opportunity for speech exists – or indeed even where there was no silence to begin with. To understand the peculiar role acquiescence plays in the context of imperial warfare, it is necessary to investigate how silence is produced and interpreted not just in spite of, but through, asymmetrical power relations. Even in the context of asymmetric power structures, silence framed as acquiescence can serve to confer a veneer of democratic legitimacy to a practice by implying there is broad support for a practice. This representation, in turn, renders protest more difficult by relegating dissent to the margins, framing it as exceptional and unreasonable. The legitimacy constructed through presumed acquiescence can thereby contribute to the emergence of new legal or moral norms regarding acceptable conduct, or foster a sense of ambiguity around what counts as lawful or appropriate conduct.

Acquiescence has often been discussed in the context of oppressive domestic regimes – for example, the Nazi regime in Germany and its "rule of silence, indifference, toleration, and support",[96] the silence that sustains racialised violence in the United States,[97] or the patriarchal structures that perpetuate violence against women.[98] Yet, the political function of silence-as-acquiescence is often overlooked in analyses of military violence and warfare. This may be due, in part, to the enduring influence of a more traditional propaganda model which assumes that governments actively shape public opinion through rhetorical tactics designed to justify military violence, while suppressing dissent through direct censorship or control of information. As discussed in Chapter 3, however, this model overlooks more decentralised silences and silencings that characterise imperial warfare. These silences are not always imposed from above but are linked to what Stoler calls colonial aphasia and reinforced by entrenched regimes of not listening.

Investigating the role of acquiescence in warfare more closely is thus particularly important for imperial and remote warfare practices, such as drone warfare. These practices are often structured in ways that minimise the need for active public support – indeed they may function because such support is neither required nor actively sought. For example, drone warfare does not involve "boots on the ground", is portrayed as casualty free – for the aggressor – and avoids reliance on conscription or broader forms of noticeable sacrifice from the general public. These characteristics have played a significant role in the justification of drone strikes. Rather than relying on more traditional models of war propaganda – where governments seek to mobilise populations and generate active public assent – it could be argued that contemporary warfare is sustained through the systematic preclusion of dissent. As Engels and Saas argue in the context of War on Terror rhetorics by US administrations, "This war rhetoric aims to turn civic attention away from war and toward consumption; and when citizens must encounter war, this rhetoric aims to disempower the demos and thereby preclude dissent. This rhetoric does not aim for assent – it desires acquiescence."[99]

The important role of silence-as-acquiescence – the lack of protest to state violence – has been recognised by activists. In the context of drone warfare, human rights actors, like Amnesty International, have called on the public as well as state actors to break the silence and "oppose unlawful US policies and practices on the deliberate use of lethal force against terrorism suspects".[100] Such protest is seen as important in the context of evolving legal and ethical frameworks, since "after over a decade of inaction, and as more states acquire drone technologies, international action is urgently needed to address harm already caused, and to prevent unacceptable patterns of harm in the future".[101] Silence by states as well as by the public is here often cast through the legal and political effects of acquiescence: "In the absence of an outcry – indeed, with broad public and political support – drone strikes have become the policy norm and displaced alternative approaches."[102]

The call for protest and clarification of legal frameworks in response to state violence presupposes the existence of silence and casts it as the binary opposite of protest. In this reading, silence is interpreted as "lack of objections" – a reading that already positions it as potential acquiescence. As a result, silence acquires negative connotations, since a conflation of silence with lack of objections associates silence with complicity in violence and oppression. This reading raises fundamental questions not only about the capacity but also about the perceived *obligation* of subjects to speak. To frame silence as acquiescence is, therefore, to engage with deeper normative assumptions about political agency, responsibility and legitimacy. This tension has been explored by political theorists such as Rawls, who argues that "acquiescence in, or even consent to, clearly unjust institutions does not give rise to obligations".[103] This argument has been countered by Simmons, who argues that if the nature of the institution does not "unduly" influence the consenter, acquiescence can still be given.[104]

The interpretation of silence as acquiescence is grounded in liberal understandings of political communication, where, "circling around values like transparency, accountability and participation, we understand the political as a domain of the expression of the vox populi, i.e. in terms of the rights, as well as the duties, to partake in a communicative process pointed toward the negotiation of collectively binding decisions".[105] Within this ideological framework, it appears logical to assume that citizens have not only the capacity but also the moral obligation to protest against violent or unjust practices carried out by their democratically elected governments and funded through their taxes. Indeed, such logic was invoked by Mohammad Sidique Khan in his justification of the 7/7 bombing in London, explicitly referencing the responsibility of British citizens for their government's foreign policy.[106]

Yet, even – or perhaps especially – within the domestic politics of liberal democratic states, the expectation that all subjects can speak and be heard is deeply problematic. As Medina has argued, such expectations rest on "the naive assumption that protesting is an easy thing to do in Western liberal democracies, that when freedoms of assembly and expression are formally conferred by law, everyone can enter the public sphere to protest and everyone is ready and willing to listen to their protest".[107] As discussed in Chapter 4, speech and protest are frequently silenced within neoliberal political regimes. Media outlets, academic institutions and political bodies, such as courts or parliaments, are routinely hindered in their ability to scrutinise and expose acts of state violence. Perhaps more importantly, the unspoken assumptions underlying imperial warfare often render such violence irrelevant within dominant public discourses – even in the presence of available information and active protest. This marginalisation does not simply suppress speech, it configures what counts as intelligible or worthy of discussion.

This is not to deny that there is political responsibility to protest – Chapter 6 will return to this question in greater depth. As Gloria Wekker has noted, "the claim of innocence ... is a double-edged sword: it contains not-knowing but also not wanting to know".[108] My argument here, however, is that the conflation of silence with acquiescence is problematic, not only because it presumes a universal ability to speak but also because it neglects the regimes of not listening through which protest is ignored and silence is both perceived and imbued with meaning as acquiescence. Silence-as-acquiescence does not exist in a simple binary opposite to speech; rather, it acquires functions through text and context. The invocation of silence-as-acquiescence – even when intended critically – can itself contribute to the consolidation of that interpretation and entrench silence as an expression of consent, a dynamic I will return to in Chapter 6.

Sometimes silence is invoked as acquiescence in full awareness of its dubious origins, as a way of provoking a reaction or indeed clarifying the situation by superimposing a particular meaning in an attempt at "replacing silence's ostensible emptiness with meaningful activity".[109] International lawyers have argued that without the possibility of imbuing state silence with meaning as acquiescence, there would be a risk of increased legal ambiguity and "normative volatility".[110] Yet, the political effects of acquiescence are more complex than it appears at first glance. I argue that silence-as-acquiescence, while often invoked without reference to the power relations that shape the conditions of speaking and listening, cannot fully extricate itself from this heritage. In the case of drone warfare, the secrecy that surrounds such practices – producing a subject-position of exclusion – as well as the various forms of exclusion and silencing discussed earlier, remain an inescapable part of the political legacy of silence-as-acquiescence. Far from contributing to a clarification of legal and ethical frameworks, the invocation of silence-as-acquiescence tends to reaffirm the power relations from which it emerges. Because there remains at least a latent awareness of the asymmetries at play, acquiescence in this context may not function as clear endorsement of a new legal or moral standard. Instead, it may work as a more ambivalent, uneasy assent, a tacit tolerance of violence and injustice carried out by imperial elites in unruly, distant places. As Lobel observed it in the case of the 1998 US counterterrorist strikes, such silence is perhaps better understood as "acquiescence to the power of the world's sole remaining superpower".[111]

Assenting to violence

This chapter has examined the foundational role of tacit consent within liberal political imaginaries – from the mythical origins of contract theories and the international state system to the mundane operations of institutional decision making, democratic governance and international law. Tacit and presumed consent operates as a mechanism of legitimisation, authorising political decisions that have not, in fact, been accepted by everyone – or even by most. Whether in treaty formation, policy making or mundane institutional procedures, liberal regimes routinely rely on acquiescence to legitimise top-down decision making which still pays homage to individual autonomy.

Theorists and international lawyers have developed criteria under which silence may be interpreted as acquiescence, such as the requirement that the relevant act must be known to the silent party. Yet, as I have argued, such frameworks fail to address the deeper power relations that shape not only the interpretation of silence but its very existence. These include colonial, racialised, gendered and classed power structures that have historically constrained who is recognised as a speaking subject, whose voices are acknowledged and which utterances are heard as politically or legally meaningful. The exclusion of non-European actors from having a voice in international relations, and the legitimisation of colonial practices through their supposed acquiescence, illustrates the foundational violence on which many of these interpretive frameworks rest.

In order to critically assess the political and legal functions of silence-as-acquiescence, we must situate it within what I have called a global economy of silence – a system of material and institutional practices that shapes who is heard, who is ignored and how utterances and silences are interpreted. Because the political work of acquiescence is so central to the maintenance of legal and political orders – and because it so often reinforces violent relations of power – it needs to be analysed within this wider context. This is particularly pressing for discussions of imperial warfare, where state-centric assumptions persist even as global power asymmetries – especially postcolonial power relations – continue to structure what can be said, and by whom, in forums such as the UN Security Council.

When silence is invoked as acquiescence, this interpretation often ignores the power relations which exclude actors from having a voice, from raising their voice and from being heard. As my analysis of counterterrorism use of force in international law has shown, the interpretation of silence as acquiescence depends on entrenched regimes of (not) listening. These regimes operate through seemingly banal methodological choices – such as source selection, language proficiency or institutional location – but also through deeper, Western-centric, epistemic and ontological assumptions. The failure to hear what has in fact been said – albeit not in the expected format, voice or venue – and the interpretation of silence as acquiescence sustains the legitimisation and normalisation of violence and unjust practices.

Acquiescence functions through liberal myths about voice, the idea that every subject has the capacity and obligation to speak. Within this framework silence becomes conflated with "lack of protest" and interpreted as tacit consent to acts, even in cases where speaking and being heard was materially impossible, where access to information on acts was restricted and where dissent has been systematically silenced or rendered unintelligible. Silence is born and interpreted through these power structures and can gain political and legal functions as acquiescence despite and through their legacy. In such contexts, silence-as-acquiescence may not work as the clear endorsement of a new legal or moral standard but as ambiguous, uneasy assent to violence and injustice by the Empire. This brings us to a critical juncture: how can this dynamic of silent wars be resisted? The question demands not only an ethical response but also a rethinking of the epistemological structures through which silence emerges. The following chapter will take up this challenge by exploring the possibilities – and limits – of resistance to silent war.

Notes

All URLs were last accessed on October 30, 2025.

1 ICCT, "Towards a European Position on the Use of Armed Drones; International Centre for Counter-Terrorism, The Hague," 55.

2 Article 36, *Drones in the Use of Force: A Way Forward*, 2018, https://article36.org/wp-content/uploads/2020/12/A36-drones-use-of-force-way-forward-1.pdf

3 UNIDIR, *Increasing Transparency, Oversight and Accountability.*

4 UN Doc A/68/389, *Promotion and Protection of Human Rights and Fundamental Freedoms While Countering Terrorism : Note / by the Secretary-General*, 2013, para 79.

5 UN Doc A/HRC/34/61, *Report of the Special Rapporteur on the Promotion and Protection of Human Rights and Fundamental Freedoms While Countering Terrorism*, 2017, para 25.
6 Reinold, "State Weakness, Irregular Warfare, and the Right to Self-Defense Post-9/11"; Starski, "Silence within the Process of Normative Change"; Plaw and Reis, "The Contemporary Practice of Self-Defense"; Kenneth Anderson, *Targeted Killing in U.S. Counterterrorism Strategy and Law*, SSRN Scholarly Paper ID 1415070 (Social Science Research Network, 2009), https://papers.ssrn.com/sol3/papers.cfm?abstract_id=1415070; Chris Downes, "'Targeted Killings' in an Age of Terror: The Legality of the Yemen Strike," *Journal of Conflict and Security Law* 9, no. 2 (2004): 292, https://doi.org/10.1093/jcsl/9.2.277
7 Plaw and Reis, "The Contemporary Practice of Self-Defense," 243.
8 Plaw and Reis, "The Contemporary Practice of Self-Defense," 246.
9 PAX, *Military Drones and the EU; The Role of Unmanned Systems in the European Union's Defence Developments*, 2019, https://paxforpeace.nl/wp-content/uploads/sites/2/2025/03/pax-report-military-drones-and-the-eu.pdf
10 Center for Civilians in Conflict and Columbia Law School, *The Civilian Impact of Drones.*
11 Jeremy Engels and William Saas, "On Acquiescence and Ends-Less War: An Inquiry into the New War Rhetoric," *Quarterly Journal of Speech* 99, no. 2 (2013): 226.
12 A. John Simmons, "Tacit Consent and Political Obligation," *Philosophy & Public Affairs* 5, no. 3 (1976): 278.
13 Simmons, "Tacit Consent and Political Obligation," 278.
14 C. W. Cassinelli, "The 'Consent' of the Governed," *The Western Political Quarterly*, 1959.
15 Freeden, *Concealed Silences*, 184.
16 John Locke, *Second Treatise of Government*, section 14.
17 This is the contested argument Locke makes, but one that has also been picked up by other theorists, see, for example, J. M. Porter, "JP Plamenatz, Consent, Freedom and Political Obligation, Oxford: Oxford University Press, 1968, Pp. 182," *Canadian Journal of Political Science/Revue Canadienne de Science Politique* 2, no. 3 (1969): 168–71.
18 Carole Pateman, *The Sexual Contract* (Polity, 1997), 1.
19 See Olivier Corten, "The Controversies over the Customary Prohibition on the Use of Force: A Methodological Debate," *European Journal of International Law*, 16.5 (2005), 803–22; K. Wolfke, "Some Persistent Controversies Regarding Customary International

Law," *Netherlands Yearbook of International Law*, 24 (1993), 1–16, https://doi.org/10.1017/S0167676800000027; Maurice Mendelson, "The Subjective Element in Customary International Law," *British Yearbook of International Law*, 66.1 (1996), 177–208; Mark Eugen Villiger, *Customary International Law and Treaties: A Study of Their Interactions and Interrelations, with Special Consideration of the 1969 Vienna Convention on the Law of Treaties* (Matthias Nijhoff Publishers, 1985), vii; Niels Petersen, "Customary Law without Custom-Rules, Principles, and the Role of State Practice in International Norm Creation," *American University International Law Review*, 23 (2007), 275.

20 W. Michael Reisman, "International Legal Responses to Terrorism Symposium: Legal Responses to International Terrorism," *Houston Journal of International Law*, 22 (1999), 3–62; Andrew T. Guzman, "Against Consent," *Virginia Journal of International Law*, 52 (2011), 747–90.

21 Anthony A. D'Amato, *The Concept of Custom in International Law* (Cornell University Press, 1971); Mendelson, "The Subjective Element in Customary International Law"; Christine Gray, *International Law and the Use of Force* (Oxford University Press, 2008).

22 Simmons, "Tacit Consent and Political Obligation," 280.

23 Cassinelli, "The 'Consent' of the Governed," 398.

24 As Furner has argued "The gap separating a free act from an act of consent cannot be breached by any kind of awareness. It can only be breached by an intention to alter one's obligations. In the absence of such an intention, a fiction will need to be invoked, whereby the 'awareness' of consequence of an act is taken as if it were an intention to incur it." See James Furner, "Tacit Consent Without Political Obligation," *Theoria* 57, no. 124 (2010): 74, https://doi.org/10.3167/th.2010.5712403

25 Furner, "Tacit Consent Without Political Obligation," 80.

26 Curtis A. Bradley and Mitu Gulati, "Withdrawing from International Custom," *The Yale Law Journal*, 2010, 202–75, 209.

27 Villiger, *Customary International Law and Treaties*, vol. 7; Michael Byers, *Custom, Power, and the Power of Rules: International Relations and Customary International Law* (Cambridge University Press, 1999); Mendelson, "The Subjective Element in Customary International Law."

28 UN Doc A/CN.4/L.872, *International Law Commission. Identification of Customary International Law. Text of the Draft Conclusions Provisionally Adopted by the Drafting Committee*, 2016, 3.

29 Starski, "Silence within the Process of Normative Change," 30.
30 International Court of Justice, "Fisheries Case (United Kingdom vs. Norway)," 1951, 139.
31 Starski, "Silence within the Process of Normative Change," 15.
32 Freeden, *Concealed Silences*, 190.
33 Freeden, *Concealed Silences*, 181.
34 Tom Dougherty, "'Yes Means Yes': Consent as Communication," *Philosophy & Public Affairs* 43, no. 3 (2015): 224–53, 228.
35 Mollie Gerver, "Inferring Consent without Communication," *Social Theory and Practice* 46, no. 1 (2020): 39.
36 Simmons, "Tacit Consent and Political Obligation," 279.
37 Simmons, "Tacit Consent and Political Obligation," 279.
38 Simmons, "Tacit Consent and Political Obligation," 279.
39 International Court of Justice, *Sovereignty over Pedra Branca/Palau Batu Puteh, Middle Rocks and South Ledge (Malaysia/Singapore), Jurisdiction and Admissibility, Judgement of May 23, 2008 [2008] ICJ Rep. 14, at 51*, 2008.
40 International Arbitral Awards, *Island of Palmas Case (Netherlands v. USA)*, Judgment of April 4, 1928 [1928], UN Reports of International Arbitral Awards, 831, 1928.
41 International Court of Justice, *Fisheries Case (United Kingdom v. Norway)*, Judgment of December 18, 1951, [1951] ICJ Rep. 116, 1951.
42 Carole Pateman, *The Sexual Contract*, 5.
43 Brigitte Stern, "Custom at the Heart of International Law," *Duke Journal of Comparative & International Law*, 11.1 (2000), 89–108, 98.
44 Anghie, "Finding the Peripheries," 3.
45 UK House of Commons, *HC Debates*, March 18, 1930, Vol. 236, Mr. Montague's Statement, Cc1925–2006.
46 UK House of Commons, *HC Debates*, July 22, 1935, Vol. 304, Number of Royal Air Force, Cc1563–630.
47 UK House of Commons, *HC Debates*, July 5, 1933, Vol. 280, Foreign Office, Cc339–457.
48 I. C. MacGibbon, "The Scope of Acquiescence in International Law," *British Yearbook of International Law* 31 (1954): 143–86, 167; Anghie, "Finding the Peripheries," 3.
49 MacGibbon, "The Scope of Acquiescence," 168.
50 Amnesty International, "*Will I Be Next?*".
51 Simmons, "Tacit Consent and Political Obligation," 280.
52 International Court of Justice, *Case concerning the Temple of Preah Vihear (Cambodia v. Thailand)*, Judgment of June 15, 1962, ICJ Rep. 6, para 22.

53 International Court of Justice, *Case concerning the Temple of Preah Vihear (Cambodia v. Thailand)*, Judgment of June 15, 1962, ICJ Rep. 6, para 26; see also SallyTyler, "Of Temples and Territory: The ICJ's Preah Vihear Decision and Implications for Regional Dispute Resolution," *University of the District of Columbia David Clarke School of Law Law Review* 19 (2016): 133.
54 Phil C. W. Chan, "Acquiescence/Estoppel in International Boundaries: *Temple of Preah Vihear* Revisited," *Chinese Journal of International Law* 3, no. 2 (2004): 421–39, 433.
55 Disku, quoted in Dissenting Opinion of Judge Koo, International Court of Justice, *Case concerning the Temple of Preah Vihear (Cambodia v. Thailand)*, Judgment of June 15, 1962, ICJ Rep. 6, 91.
56 Evidence, such as Siam building roads to the mount of the temple or the prince visiting the temple without French protest; see in Chan, "Acquiescence/Estoppel in International Boundaries," 427.
57 International Court of Justice, *Case concerning the Temple of Preah Vihear (Cambodia v. Thailand)*, Judgment of June 15, 1962, ICJ Rep. 6, para 20.
58 Rutazibwa, "Hidden in Plain Sight," 231.
59 Brenna Bhandar, *Colonial Lives of Property: Law, Land, and Racial Regimes of Ownership* (Duke University Press, 2018), 3.
60 Wolfke, "Some Persistent Controversies Regarding Customary International Law," 9.
61 Dawood I. Ahmed, *Defending Weak States Against the 'Unwilling or Unable' Doctrine of Self-Defense* (Social Science Research Network, March 26, 2013), 18, https://papers.ssrn.com/abstract=2239817; Jutta Brunnée and Stephen J. Toope, *Legitimacy and Legality in International Law: An Interactional Account*, Cambridge Studies in International and Comparative Law, 67 (Cambridge University Press, 2010), 74.
62 UN Doc S/PV.2674, *United Nations Security Council Debate (2674th Meeting)*, 1986.
63 Gregory Francis Intoccia, "American Bombing of Libya: An International Legal Analysis," *Case Western Reserve Journal of International Law*, 19 (1987): 177.
64 UN Doc S/PV.2675, *United Nations Security Council Debate (2675th Meeting)*.
65 UN Doc A/RES/41/38, *UN General Assembly Resolution, Declaration of the Assembly of Heads of State and Government of the Organization of African Unity on the Aerial and Naval Military Attack against the Socialist People's Libyan Arab Jamahiriya by the Present United States Administration in April 1986*, 1986.

66 UN Doc S/PV.3245, *United Nations Security Council Debate (3245th Meeting)*, 1993.
67 UN Doc S/PV.3245, *United Nations Security Council Debate (3245th Meeting)*.
68 UN Doc S/PV.3245, *United Nations Security Council Debate (3245th Meeting)*.
69 Alan D. Surchin, "Terror and the Law: The Unilateral Use of Force and the June 1993 Bombing of Baghdad Notes," *Duke Journal of Comparative & International Law* 5, no. 2 (1994): 457–98.
70 UN Doc S/1998/780, *Letter dated August 20, 1998 from the Permanent Representative of the United States of America to the United Nations addressed to the President of the Security Council*, 1998.
71 Jules Lobel, "The Use of Force to Respond to Terrorist Attacks: The Bombing of Sudan and Afghanistan," *Yale Journal of International Law* 24 (1999): 537.
72 Surchin, "Terror and the Law," 486.
73 C. J. Tams, "The Use of Force against Terrorists," *European Journal of International Law* 20, no. 2 (2009): 359–97, https://doi.org/10.1093/ejil/chp031
74 Anderson, *Targeted Killing in U.S. Counterterrorism Strategy and Law*, 21; see also Murphy, "The International Legality of US Military Cross-Border Operations," 34.
75 International Court of Justice, "Sovereignty over Pedra Branca/Palau Batu Puteh, Middle Rocks and South Ledge (Malaysia/Singapore), Jurisdiction and Admissibility, Judgement of May 23, 2008 [2008] ICJ Rep. 14, at 51," 2008 para 121.
76 Mendelson, "The Subjective Element in Customary International Law," 193.
77 Murphy, "The International Legality of US Military Cross-Border Operations," 126.
78 Starski, "Silence within the Process of Normative Change," 22.
79 Starski, "Silence within the Process of Normative Change," 28.
80 Tams, "The Use of Force against Terrorists," 378; Reinold, "State Weakness, Irregular Warfare, and the Right to Self-Defense Post-9/11," 257.
81 Villiger, *Customary International Law and Treaties*, 7:39.
82 Schweiger, "'Targeted Killing' and the Lack of Acquiescence."
83 By the Spanish representative, see UN Doc S/PV.4836, *United Nations Security Council Debate (4836th Meeting)*, 2003.
84 By the Chinese representative, see UN Doc S/PV.5489, *United Nations Security Council Debate (5489th Meeting)*, 2006.

85 By the German representative, see UN Doc S/PV.4836.
86 As Reinold argues in the case of the Turkish intervention in Iraq: "International acquiescence in that intervention largely reflected Turkey's efforts to demonstrate that its campaign avoided excessive collateral damage to civilians and non-PKK infrastructure. In a note verbale to the Human Rights Council, Turkey emphasized that it 'targeted solely the PKK/KONGRA-Gel terrorist presence.'" See Reinold, "State Weakness, Irregular Warfare, and the Right to Self-Defense Post-9/11," 271; see also Andre De Hoogh, "Restrictivist Reasoning on the Ratione Personae Dimension of Armed Attacks in the Post 9/11 World," *Leiden Journal of International Law* 29, no. 1 (2016): 37.
87 Gray, *International Law and the Use of Force*, 117.
88 UN Doc A/HRC/28/38, *Summary of the Human Rights Council Interactive Panel Discussion of Experts on the Use of Remotely Piloted Aircraft ....*
89 UN Doc A/69/53, *Resolution Ensuring Use of Remotely Piloted Aircraft or Armed Drones in Counter-Terrorism and Military Operations in Accordance with International Law, Including International Human Rights and Humanitarian Law*, 2014.
90 Perhaps unsurprisingly the USA, UK, Japan, France, Republic of Korea and the former Yugoslav Republic of Macedonia.
91 UN Doc A/69/53, *Resolution Ensuring Use of Remotely Piloted Aircraft or Armed Drones ... in Accordance with International Law.*
92 Starski, "Silence within the Process of Normative Change," 22.
93 Starski, "Silence within the Process of Normative Change," 28.
94 UNIDIR, *Armed UAVs in Conflict Escalation and Inter-State Crisis*, United Nations Institute for Disarmament Research, George Woodhams and John Borrie, 2018, https://unidir.org/wp-content/uploads/2023/05/armed-uav-in-conflict-escalation-and-inter-state-crisis-en-747.pdf
95 UN Doc A/HRC/28/38, *Summary of the Human Rights Council Interactive Panel Discussion of Experts on the Use of Remotely Piloted Aircraft ....*
96 Robert Gellately, *Backing Hitler: Consent and Coercion in Nazi Germany* (Oxford University Press, 2002), 105.
97 Rasul A. Mowatt, "Black Lives as Snuff: The Silent Complicity in Viewing Black Death," *Biography* 41, no. 4 (2018): 777–806, https://doi.org/10.1353/bio.2018.0079
98 Caitlin E. Hasser, review of *Review of Silence and Complicity: Violence Against Women in Peruvian Public Health Facilities*, by The Center for Reproductive Law and Policy (CRLP) and The Latin

American and Caribbean Committee for the Defense of Women's Rights (CLADEM), *Women's Studies Quarterly* 31, no. 1/2 (2003): 264–67.

99 Engels and Saas, "On Acquiescence and Ends-Less War," 227.

100 Amnesty International, "*Will I Be Next?*".

101 Article 36, *Drones in the Use of Force: A Way Forward.*

102 Center for Civilians in Conflict and Columbia Law School, *The Civilian Impact of Drones.*

103 John Rawls, *A Theory of Justice: Original Edition* (Harvard University Press, 1971), 343, https://doi.org/10.2307/j.ctvjf9z6v

104 Simmons, "Tacit Consent and Political Obligation," 278. Simmons does add that it might be possible that "the harm done by supporting an unjust institution and our duty to fight injustice outweigh any obligation we may have to respect its authority (deriving from our consent to it)."

105 Brito Vieira et al., "The Nature of Silence," 425.

106 Vikram Dodd and Richard Norton-Taylor, "Video of 7/7 Ringleader Blames Foreign Policy," *The Guardian*, September 2, 2005, www.theguardian.com/uk/2005/sep/02/alqaida.politics

107 José Medina, "Introduction: Coming to Protest and Listening to Protest under Conditions of Oppression," in *The Epistemology of Protest: Silencing, Epistemic Activism, and the Communicative Life of Resistance*, ed. José Medina (Oxford University Press, 2023), 1.

108 Gloria Wekker, *White Innocence: Paradoxes of Colonialism and Race* (Duke University Press, 2016), 17.

109 Freeden, *Concealed Silences*, 190.

110 Starski, "Silence within the Process of Normative Change," 29.

111 Lobel, "The Use of Force to Respond to Terrorist Attacks," 540.

6

Resistance

I have argued throughout this book that the unspoken machinations of silence enable military violence through different and interconnected modalities. The previous chapter examined how the logic of acquiescence can confer democratic legitimacy onto contested practices – even in the absence of substantive support – thereby shifting normative and legal boundaries or generating ambiguity around existing norms. It can do so despite the prevailing secrecy around such practices, discussed in Chapter 4, that makes it difficult for audiences to know and speak about the war. I analysed the role of secrecy as both a shield that obstructs access to information and a spectacle of power that produces epistemic hierarchies, relegating all those outside the core of the targeting regime to a subject position of exclusion. In Chapter 3, I traced how key aspects of military violence – such as the impact it has on targeted communities – have been systematically ignored, omitted or backgrounded. I argued that these deep silences of neglect function not merely as absences but have performative effects, delineating what is to be deemed irrelevant and presenting a sanitised understanding of war. These silences of neglect are rooted in implicit, orientalist assumptions that I explored in Chapter 2. Unspoken assumptions – such as the unquestioned notion that humans categorised as guilty or aggressive ought to be killed – are discursively effective precisely because they remain unspoken and are thus presented as self-evident and beyond debate.

Despite the important political effects of these silences, it is important not to represent either silence or power as monolithic. I have already discussed various instances of speech, debate and protest which persist against and besides the silences around imperial warfare. Silence and speech are not binary opposites; rather, they are entangled with each other and constructed in relation to each other. This means that more words are not necessarily better or have more ethical effects. Some ways of speaking can reinforce the silences crucial to enabling military violence. For example, the focus on "innocent" civilian casualties reinforces the unspoken assumptions that those framed as "guilty" terrorists can or even should be killed. Similarly, the demand for speech from powerful state actors inadvertently reaffirms them as central knowledge producers and epistemic authorities. And the well-intentioned representation of the marginalised risks further essentialising and silencing them.

Instead of directly opposing or breaking silence, it is worth exploring the fractures and inconsistencies in hegemonic discursive constellations that open up space for critical engagement. This chapter discusses different ways of resisting imperial violence with, through and against silence. I highlight the limitations of some of the more obvious or straightforward responses to silence – namely the impulse to break silence or oppose it. Rather than treating silence solely as a problem or deficit, I suggest engaging its critical potential. Silence presents both a lens through which to interrogate entrenched regimes of not listening and a generative space for alternative forms of knowledge and resistance. Because silence is contingent upon practices of listening and interpretation, it carries an inherent ambiguity that can be mobilised politically for resistance. In what follows, I will examine a range of tactics employed by those who have resisted silent wars. These include strategies of consciously shifting out of dominant linguistic frames, tactics of reinterpreting silence itself – such as reading US silence on drone warfare not as strategic mastery but as bureaucratic incapacity – and efforts to consciously reconfigure who are recognised as speakers and what constitutes valid expertise.

Silence itself can be a communicative move which resists hegemonic discursive regimes, a way of evading linguistic domination or disrupting hegemonic speech expectations. Montoya has suggested to understand silence as both a centripetal force – in that silences can support status-quo power relations – and a centrifugal force which can undermine, challenge and destabilise power.[1]

Silence holds the potential for discursive effects that surpass possibilities of verbal expressions and may, in specific contexts, function as a powerful mode of protest and resistance. As Athanasiou has argued in her work on agonistic mourning, silent protest "disrupts the equation of visibility with the presence of a voice; an equation so operative in the ways in which political action is perceived in the discursive order of liberal representation and recognition".[2] Silent protest can serve as a powerful means of exposing and transcending the constraints of dominant discursive registers – those that delineate what is sayable – thereby inviting audiences to imagine alternative modes of expression, understanding and political realities.

None of these strategies fully escape the dilemmas inherent in moving within, and thus remaining entangled with, violent relations of power and hegemonic discursive formations. Indeed, it is arguable that such transcendence is not possible – at least not within dominant horizons of political imagination. Yet, the recognition of one's own complicity does not, I believe, justify a retreat into cynicism, indifference or a posture of supposed neutrality. Such withdrawal would merely deepen complicity by passively reproducing the dominant discursive modes enabling violence. Instead, I build on postcolonial, feminist and other critical traditions that have interrogated these tensions while reaffirming what has been called "the decolonial strategy of desilencing"[3] as both generative and necessary.[4] In this spirit, and in dialogue with the dilemmas surrounding efforts to break silence, demand speech and represent the marginalised, I turn to acts of resistance by grassroots movements, civil rights organisations, journalists, activists and NGOs – not as a purist escape from complicity, but as a situated practice that reimagines the possibilities for voice.

Breaking silence

Chapter 5 on acquiescence critically examined the presumed obligation within liberal political imaginaries for subjects to speak out against wrongs – a normative expectation whereby the failure to protest, or failure to be heard protesting – is often construed as acquiescence. I have demonstrated how the conditions for protesting are unequally distributed and constrained across different platforms. Even when voices do resound, they may be absorbed into dominant linguistic registers, rendered inaudible or denied uptake – thus stripped of their illocutionary and perlocutionary force.[5] Yet, these constraints do not render protest futile. On the contrary, I argue that there remains a moral and political responsibility to speak out and take a principled stance against violence, oppression and injustice; responsibility understood in the sense of what Athanasiou has termed response-ability.[6] Equally important – though less often discussed – is the responsibility to listen to protest, to take seriously the voices that have taken a stance and to "give proper uptake to legitimate protests".[7]

It is important to emphasise this point, because my focus thus far has been on mapping silences and processes of silencing, arguing that these are constitutive of military violence. However, these silences exist alongside, next to and entangled with speech. Indeed, within specific discursive spaces – such as academia or the NGO sector – drone warfare has in fact received considerable attention. It has been the subject of extensive debate, critique and documentation. Public demonstrations and acts of protest against drone warfare by a broad network of peace organisations have signalled vocal opposition. The Drone Campaign Network, for example, brought together more than thirty local grassroots and national organisations to coordinate protests against drone warfare in the UK, most notably at the RAF station at Waddington, the operating base for the Reaper drone.[8] In the US, groups like the Center for Civilians in Conflict, Human Rights Watch, Reprieve and the Interfaith Drone Network have challenged various aspects of drone warfare. For example, at the start of Joe Biden's presidency in 2021, a coalition of over a hundred civil society, peace and human rights organisations wrote to the US government arguing that drone warfare "has exacted an appalling toll on Muslim, Brown, and Black communities in multiple parts of the world".[9]

Similarly, in the context of colonial police bombing, numerous groups and institutions spoke up against the practice. While such opposition mainly emerged during the time period of the European Disarmament Conference, when the police bombing exception came under scrutiny, it nevertheless encompassed substantive protest and critique of the practice. The Humane Education Society positioned itself against all air bombing,[10] and branches of the League of Nations Union[11] as well as the National Peace Council spoke out against retaining police bombing as an exception to disarmament.[12] There were large protests, for example, in Birmingham in the Bull Ring outside Birmingham parish church in June 1933.[13] The Quakers – or Society of Friends – also took a principled stance against police bombing as part of their wider effort towards peace and disarmament.[14]

Such instances of speaking up are significant not only for their potential effects on dominant discourses and institutional practices but also for the ways in which they can bring together and transform those who engage in protest. Drawing on Medina's epistemology of protest, the act of speaking out can contribute to the formation of the "protesting public"[15] – a collective political subject constituted through shared acts of resistance. Protest in this view is not merely reactive or instrumental; it is a generative political activity through which new subjectivities, perspectives and visions of the world are created. Moreover, protesting can create new audiences and reconfigure existing ones. As Medina argues, such practices have the potential to produce "communicative or epistemic versions of ourselves that are different from the way we are currently constituted as hearers and knowers and the way we are prepared (or unprepared) to listen. In short, protest has the power to change available forms of communicative receptivity and to generate new forms of sensibility."[16]

Instances of speaking up serve not only to raise an issue as worthy of public attention but also pay tribute to lives lost and suffering endured – forms of violence which are otherwise rendered ungrieveable within dominant discourses. In doing so, such invocations render perceptible the deep silences that persist around such expressions, or in other spaces and discourses. Silence, relational and contingent as it is, carries a certain fragility; even a single voice can crack the seeming self-evidence of presuppositions, challenge entrenched taboos and disrupt assumptions of irrelevance. There is a cumulative dimension to protest. Successive acts of speaking out can gather momentum, as was seen in the global reverberations of movements such as Black Lives Matter and #MeToo.

However, framing protest as the "breaking" of silence risks reifying the idea of silence as void and neglects to recognise its entanglements with speech. Silences often persist alongside and within acts of protest, manifesting differently across discursive spaces. As Wendy Brown has argued, silences "do not shatter the moment their strategic function has been exposed, but must be assaulted repeatedly with stories, histories, theories, and discourses in alternate registers until the silence itself is rendered routinely intelligible as a historically injurious force".[17]

The effects of protest do not only depend on the locution itself, the sheer act of speaking or even the possibility of being heard, but also on how hearing takes place – with the potentials for speech itself being complicit in or becoming co-opted by violent relations of power. In these conditions, words are not in and of themselves normatively "good", and indeed, speaking out can become part of oppression and silencing. Wendy Brown has pointed to this paradox:

> While the silences in discourses of domination are a site for insurrectionary noise, while they are the corridors to be filled with explosive counter tales, it is also possible to make a fetish of breaking silence. It is possible as well that this ostensible tool of emancipation carries its own techniques of subjugation – that it converges with unemancipatory tendencies in contemporary culture, establishes regulatory norms, coincides with the disciplinary power of ubiquitous confessional practices; in short, it may feed the powers it meant to starve.[18]

Silence is not the binary opposite to utterances but works in messy layers with and through speech and text. Attempts to break the silence can inadvertently reinforce silences and dominant relations of violent power, depending on the registers through which they take place. As Mignolo has warned, "opposing and being 'critical' of the content without delinking from the enunciation keeps you trapped in the enunciation of the CMP [colonial matrix of power]".[19] Speaking out does not necessarily constitute resistance to dominant registers of speech and silence – and may indeed reproduce them. For example, if protest is focused on civilian casualties in drone strikes, this further backgrounds the wider effects of bombing campaigns on people living in areas subjected to surveillance and bombing, including the harm to economic and social structures, the fragmenting of community life and the creation of isolation, psychological harm and self-policing behaviours. As Edney-Browne has argued, drone warfare constitutes a form of "psychological colonization" which not only affects individuals but also changes the social and political fabric of communities.[20]

Protest that centres on civilian death risks reinforcing the binary logic inherent in a framework of war – namely the division between civilians on the one hand and combatants or terrorists on the other hand. This dichotomy underpins the legal and operational architecture of targeting practices and assumes the existence of innocent civilians who should be spared, while simultaneously producing the category of the guilty, whose killing is perceived permissible or even desirable. As discussed in Chapter 2, this distinction is deeply racialised and reproduces orientalist imaginaries that ultimately render entire regions targetable. Protest that centres on civilian casualties thus inadvertently reaffirms the unspoken assumption that the "terrorist" can – and perhaps should – be killed. Yet, the categories of "terrorist" and "combatant" are far from stable; they are constantly reconstituted through legal and political epistemological regimes. The practice of so-called "signature strikes", for instance – where individuals are targeted not based on identity or status but on behavioural patterns or social connections – illustrates the fluid and expansive nature of such classifications.[21] In some instances, the label of "combatant" is stretched to encompass all military-aged males.

Even critical engagements with drone warfare that focus on targeting procedures often remain within the operational logic of military violence, addressing the question of *how* killing is conducted, thus backgrounding the question *whether* such violence should occur at all. Debates frequently centre on the technology of armed drones – and, more recently, fully autonomous weapons and AI-assisted weapon systems. This mirrors earlier techno-fixation, such as the 1920s fascination with aerial warfare (see Chapter 2), and reveals a persistent fetishisation of military technology – not only in the justificatory narratives of state actors but also within critiques of military state practices. Framed within a militarised logic of force and capability, this technological gaze reinforces the "rhetoric of modernity" and sustains the image of the West as technologically advanced and superior – even if that Western self is critiqued in its technological awe-fulness. Such discourses unwittingly perpetuate colonial hierarchies, while obscuring the long history of colonial violence that has historically relied on other technological means for domination.

Speaking out while remaining within dominant discursive registers can inadvertently reproduce the very silences and forms of silencing most central to enabling military violence. This is not to suggest that working within hegemonic discourses is necessarily ethically wrong – indeed, it can be a tactical choice to gain traction or legitimacy or to reach particular audiences. However, such engagement reinforces the dynamics of what this book has identified as "silent war", in which a kaleidoscope of silences sustain and legitimise war practices. To shift away from these dynamics requires moving beyond the prevailing discursive focus on civilian casualties, targeting procedures or the technological apparatus for destruction – frames that remain tethered to the logic of military necessity and operational ethics.

What might it mean, then, to break from these dominant frames and their associated silences? It would involve reorientating the conversation away from technical, procedural debates, toward a deeper interrogation of the structural and historical conditions that make imperial violence possible and palatable. This might include foregrounding histories of oppression and centring the epistemologies and lived experiences of those most affected by imperial violence. For instance, Fly Kites Not Drones is a joint campaign, based on the initiative by Afghan Peace Volunteers,[22] with UK peace organisations.[23] The campaign has adopted the symbol of the kite in public protests and demonstrations, deploying its visual and affective registers as a powerful counter to drone warfare. The colourful, ephemeral image of the kite – associated with childhood, freedom and play – stands in stark contrast to the ominous presence of armed drones overhead. The demand to "Fly Kites Not Drones" deliberately shifts discourse away from a military-operational frame – which centres on the *how* of drone warfare – and instead rejects the use of military violence as such. As a symbolic invocation, it invites a different mode of political engagement, foregrounding the everyday realities of life under the threat of aerial bombardment. It opens up an alternative horizon – one shaped by play, vulnerability and joy – against the normalisation of violence from above. In so doing, it creates an affective register that unsettles the rationalising narratives of security that so often dominate discussions of imperial violence.

Demanding speech

In June 2013, a group of activists dubbed the Waddington 6, cut through the fence at RAF Waddington as an act to "symbolically penetrate the wall of secrecy which surrounds UK's killer drones".[24] This protest came within the context of long-standing critiques of state secrecy by NGOs, activists and journalists. These actors have highlighted the difficulties of holding members of the transnational targeting regime accountable, given the pervasive secrecy that shrouds drone attacks. These groups have demanded greater transparency and have sought to expose the harm produced not only from drone violence itself but by the silence and obfuscation surrounding it. As Reprieve powerfully articulated in its submission to the US Senate Judiciary hearing in 2022: "there has been one overarching similarity that has bound the communities that have been impacted by US strikes – the complete silence with which their pleas for transparency and accountability have been met".[25] As discussed in previous chapters, there have been consistent calls on state actors to break this silence – whether by acknowledging their own roles in the covert targeting programme or by publicly objecting to the "targeted killing" practices of powerful states like the US.

Yet, such attempts to oppose silence and demand speech of states carry inherent risks. They may inadvertently reinforce the very silences they seek to challenge – or conjure silence and imbue it with meaning. For example, within international law, the call for states to object against "targeted killing" presupposes that drone warfare constitutes a novel and legally relevant practice, thereby solidifying "targeted killing" as a legal category.[26] It also presumes an absence of protest that can be interpreted as acquiescence, ignoring expressions of protest that have taken place across different platforms and registers (as discussed in Chapter 5). Furthermore, such demands fail to reckon with the political conditions of imperial violence, where structural conditions shape who can speak, who is heard and what is registered as a legitimate form of protest. Within such asymmetries, the demand to speak or object may paradoxically generate the very appearance of acquiescence it aims to prevent.

Similarly, as discussed in Chapter 4, demands for more transparency and for states to reveal more information can (re)create secrecy as a spectacle of power by those who are cast to be in-the-know. Demands for more information from state actors and intelligence services risk reaffirming these institutions as the primary epistemic authorities on drone warfare – those from whom we must await disclosure in order to "know" the war. This reinforces a hierarchy of knowledge in which access to truth appears to be reserved for those within the opaque corridors of the top-secret, transnational targeting regime. Everyone else – general publics, parliaments, courts, NGOs, journalists, academics – is implicitly cast in a subject position of exclusion. Such a framing marginalises alternative sites of knowledge production and devalues the extensive body of information and analysis that already exists on drone warfare.

Silence does not exist independently of the listeners and "remains subject to the interpretations of the receiver to whom its message is addressed".[27] This also means that perceiving silence can open a critical space, an invitation to reflect on what has not been heard and a generative site of interpretation. Silence need not be understood solely through dominant modalities such as secrecy or acquiescence. Instead, silence offers possibilities for creative resistance that challenge and move beyond entrenched assumptions and speech expectations. For example, some human rights actors have chosen to interpret state silence on "targeted killing" practices as confirmation of the practice's dubious legitimacy:

> There is a stigma attached to targeted killing – especially given its controversial use by the US during the war on terror. It is therefore unsurprising that no politician would like to put their name to such a public "targeted killing" policy. Add this to the fact that the legality

> of such actions has been questioned by a number of human rights groups and international actors and the government's reticence to release more information is understandable.[28]

Rather than treating state silence as an obstacle or void – an unexpected absence that creates legal uncertainty or reshapes norms through acquiescence – it is possible to shift discursive power through the very act of listening and interpreting. This involves reaffirming the solidity of norms on the basis that "the existing legal framework was sufficient and did not need to be adapted to the use of drones, rather, it was the use of armed drones that must comply with international law".[29] This approach avoids ambiguity and acquiescence being conjured into existence through the act of listening and interpreting. It also reconfigures the epistemic hierarchy by challenging the assumptions that state officials are the authoritative interpreters of the laws and norms of military violence. As a US representative put it in Congress: "In fact, we should not be asking him for drone memos, we should be giving him drone memos. We should not be asking him how is he going to run the drone program, we should be telling him how he is to run the drone program. That is our authority. We have abdicated our authority."[30]

Similarly, instead of interpreting the silence by military agencies solely as a strategic use of secrecy by powerful actors, it can be read as a sign of incompetence and institutional incapacity – an inability rather than a powerful move. Amnesty International has thus highlighted the limitations of USAFRICOM's understanding of strikes, since "in practice, intelligence assets are limited, and often rely on a single source. As General Bolduc confirmed [...] 'the only assessment we [AFRICOM] have is we continue to fly over the objective post-strike to get a sense of the environment from the air.'"[31] Taking the knowledge and expertise of non-state actors as a starting point, some human rights advocates have reversed the positionality of exclusion typically reinforced by appeals to greater state transparency. Rather than asking government agencies for more information, they have instead offered them assistance in investigating attacks since, as Airwars have argued "the MoD's monitoring capabilities may not at present be fit for purpose".[32]

The extensive body of information provided by whistleblowers, investigative journalism and the analytical work of civil society groups means that even specific actors and institutions can, in fact, be held accountable. For example, the Menwith Hill Accountability Campaign has built on such documentation to show how "according to documents leaked by Edward Snowden and reported by 'The Intercept', in 2016 Menwith Hill was used to aid 'a significant number of capture-kill operations'".[33] This has enabled the campaign to bring informed resistance against drone warfare right to the doorsteps of the US military base at Menwith Hill in Yorkshire, holding regular vigils and peace protests as well as exerting political pressure in local and regional politics. Rather than confronting silence by dominant actors through demands for disclosure or speech, such strategies move beyond a subject-position of exclusion and thus subvert dominant epistemic hierarchies.

To question and subvert entrenched regimes of (not) listening, it is necessary to consciously shift towards other modes of listening and "redefin[e] expertise".[34] In the sections above, I suggest subtle shifts – such as centring the knowledge produced by human rights advocates, rather than maintaining speech expectations directed primarily at state actors. In some cases, even parliamentary representatives have drawn on leaked documentation, since, "as we know, leaked war logs reveal that coalition forces have tried to cover up the fact that they have killed hundreds of civilians in unreported incidents".[35] These shifts remain modest in their attempts to listen differently and barely begin to challenge the entrenched hegemonic regimes of not listening that sustain imperial violence.

Ultimately, any meaningful attempt to redefine expertise requires a sustained and deliberate engagement with radically different theories, epistemologies and experiences. Scholars such as Ahmad have argued that sources from anticolonial movements need to be taken seriously in order to grasp colonial oppression and decolonise knowledge production.[36] Questioning what and who is listened to requires abandoning narrow assumptions about what constitutes "expertise" and "authority" – including which styles and modes of speaking are taken seriously – and instead embracing a plurality of voices and ways of knowing. Even so, as Ahmad himself discusses, such attempts at redefining expertise are problematic because they themselves carry risks of extracting knowledge outside of their political context.[37] They raise the challenge of how to move "towards centring them in a way that does not reproduce a desire for colonising hierarchies".[38] There are significant risks involved in reclaiming, extracting and representing the expertise of those who have traditionally been silenced.

Representing the silenced

Confronted with the systematic exclusion of marginalised voices and perspectives, it is tempting to call for an emancipatory programme to open up space for silenced perspectives – to 'give[] voice to the marginalised, silenced 'other'"[39] and "demand [...] that the unseen and the unacknowledged be made visible and heard".[40] Some human rights actors have taken up this call by attempting to amplify the experiences of "victims of drone strikes",[41] striving to make their voices audible. As Amnesty International has noted, the process of investigating and documenting the consequences of imperial violence can make a meaningful difference to those affected: "As Liban, a resident of Darussalam village told Amnesty International about the death of three young farmers in a US air strike in November 2017: 'We have been waiting for someone to come ask us about this. We lost these boys, and no one is talking about it. It seared into our flesh. We came [here] to tell the truth, because of the boys we lost, we have to tell the world.'"[42]

Representing those muted within dominant discourses and amplifying their voices holds the potential to disrupt the erasure and silencing of the suffering of the "other", thereby challenging the abstraction and sanitisation of inflicted violence. However, attempts to speak on behalf of others are inherently fraught with risks, including the possibility of misrepresentation, essentialisation and reinforcement of existing power structures. When speaking for and speaking about others, "I am engaging in the act of representing the other's needs, goals, situation, and in fact, who they are. I am representing them as such and such, or in post-structuralist terms, I am participating in the construction of their subject-positions".[43] Speaking for "victims of drone strikes" and representing the suffering of the subaltern entails significant risks, including the potential reproduction of a subjectivity characterised by mute victimhood. As Gayatri Spivak famously argued in her critique of Western intellectual complicity, the construction of the subaltern subject "will, in the long run, cohere with the work of imperialist subject-constitution".[44] This challenge extends beyond the manner of representation, to the fundamental question of whether representation should occur at all. Edward Said similarly contended that the representation of the other reinforces their muteness, since it "is always governed by some version of the truism that if the Orient could represent itself, it would; since it cannot, the representation does the job, for the West, and faute de mieux, for the poor Orient".[45]

This, then, raises a fundamental dilemma at the heart of representation. As Athanasiou has observed, it compels us to confront the question of "how to acknowledge unjust disposability and loss without reducing affected subjects and communities to essentialised objects of representation".[46] The imperative to bear witness to suffering is complicated by the risks of speaking for others. In light of these concerns, silence can appear as a more ethical or "safer" response. Yet, as Linda Alcoff has persuasively argued, political action often depends on speaking for others, since "both collective action and coalitions would seem to require the possibility of speaking for".[47] What Alcoff terms the "retreat response" – the refusal to speak for others out of concerns for misrepresentation or epistemic violence –not only risks a loss of political effectiveness as a passive stance, but it is in itself a positive act, "since it allows the continued dominance of current discourses and acts by omission to reinforce their dominance".[48]

In the context of imperial warfare, the choice of not speaking about the experience of those who are harmed by military violence has discursive effects – it further discursively enacts their suffering to be irrelevant and sanitises the appearance of military "operations" as ethically clean and risk free (see Chapter 3). Indeed, Alcoff further contends that understanding the "retreat response" as a neutral or self-effacing stance is rooted in (neo)liberal imaginaries of voice and the autonomous individual. The position is based on "an illusion, well-supported in the individualist ideology of the West, that a self is not constituted by multiple intersecting discourses but consists in a unified whole capable of autonomy from others".[49] From within this illusionary framework, silence can be misapprehended as a disengaged or even generous act – an ostensibly neutral gesture that gives space to the oppressed to speak for themselves. Yet, such a stance falsely assumes that choosing not to speak exists outside of power.

Abstaining from speech on the grounds that the oppressed can and should speak for themselves does little to transform the discursive registers of their oppression; on the contrary, it may inadvertently reinforce the exclusive structures it seeks to oppose. As Maggio puts it, "the Western approach to the subaltern is either to speak for or to silently let them speak for themselves. Both strategies silence the subaltern because they ignore the positional relations of the dominant to the subaltern."[50] The expectation that the subaltern should speak for themselves from a position of their own autonomous self-hood rests on an already essentialised construction of the "other" as both radically different and disconnected from the "self" – as an elusive subjectivity presumed to exist outside of the speaker's own discursive and political entanglements and responsibilities. This returns us to the fundamental tension within acts of representation, which Athanasiou poignantly describes as a dilemma "whereby the presumption of intimacy with the other's pain risks confirming narcissistic moral claims to know or feel the other's pain, whereas the invocation of distance and inevitable ungraspability risks dissipating the need, or the obligation, to take responsibility and action for justice".[51]

The inherent tension between the dangers of speaking for others and the risks of remaining silent in the face of discursive complicity cannot be reduced to a simple binary. Rather, it underlies a spectrum of possibilities – each embedded within the specificities of the context and positionality of both the speakers and the listeners. Yet, as Alcoff argues, while speaking for others may be a necessary pragmatic response to specific conditions, it cannot be the ultimate horizon of political responsibility. The more fundamental task, she argues, is to transform the discursive conditions themselves – so it becomes possible to speak *to* rather than *for* the other.[52] This shift demands reconfiguring discursive structures and regimes of (not) listening. It raises fundamental questions about the political possibilities of representing the silenced: "what kind of intersubjective event in language might be activism of/for those forced outside language? What kinds of performative contradiction would it mobilise but also what modes of complicity with the violences of belonging would it risk?"[53]

Rutazibwa's suggestion of redefining expertise is powerful in this context, as it foregrounds the need to interrogate how voice is constructed within regimes of not listening. It invites us to critically examine how expertise is conferred or denied – depending on the content of what is said, who is speaking, from what body and positionality, with what accent, tone and style. Yet, even as such interventions attempt to transform the conditions of speaking, they remain enmeshed in the underlying dilemmas of representation. For example, human rights actors have attempted to create space for the subaltern to speak as experts on drone warfare, such as when "PAX and the British NGO Reprieve invited two Pakistani victims of drone strikes, Kareem Khan and Noor Behram, to the Netherlands where they spoke to Dutch politicians (including Van Bommel) and journalists about the lack of accountability and transparency of U.S. drones strikes".[54] Changing discursive conditions – such as inviting speakers from communities most affected by drone warfare to speak as experts – can create more pluralised forms of knowledge. However, such efforts do not resolve the deeper tensions inherent in the representation of the subaltern. They risk essentialising the "Other" as mute and passive "victims of drone strikes", co-opting and absorbing their voices into dominant Western epistemological frameworks. These voices may become instrumentalised in the service of particular agendas – such as the struggle for greater state transparency. In this context, the very construction of the subaltern as the subaltern for whom to speak – or for whom space is created to speak – is itself disempowering, hence Gayatri Spivak's famous argument that the subaltern cannot speak.[55]

Even the act of creating conditions for speaking *to and with* the other can be fraught with risk. In their influential essay on cultural imperialism and the demand for the woman's voice, Lugones and Spelman critically reflect on the power asymmetry between white and Black and Hispanic women regarding knowledge of situated experiences.[56] They employ the analogy of an individual entering a conversation without familiarity with a key text that underpins the conversation: "That person is either left out or will impose herself on us and either try to engage in the discussion or try to change the subject. Women of color are put in these situations by white/Anglo women and men constantly."[57] Lugones and Spelman illuminate the imperative to acknowledge the inherent difficulties and potential harms involved in speaking *to* the other when the conditions of speaking are steeped in entrenched epistemic power imbalances: "The first thing to recognize and accept is that you disturb our own dialogues by putting yourself in the left-out position and not leaving us in some meaningful sense to ourselves."[58]

There is no escaping, transcending or simply leaving behind the discursive complicity and the fraught tensions that characterise the dilemma between speaking for the oppressed, speaking to them or remaining silent. For acts of solidarity, this predicament cannot be resolved, since "solidarity implies attempts to build coalitions between asymmetrically and unequally situated subjects".[59] The objective, then, should not be to resolve or erase these inner contradictions, nor to feign their absence, but, rather, to navigate them care-fully – alert to their dangers and open to critique. As Rutazibwa asserts, such engagement "requires from those of us at the hegemonic centre a willingness to a dislocation of power; an openness to (have others) redefine expertise and rigour, and to discomfort in the face of new knowledges".[60] This resonates with the appeal from Lugones and Spelman:

> So you need to learn to become unintrusive, unimportant, patient to the point of tears, while at the same time open to learning any possible lessons. You will also have to come to terms with the sense of alienation, of not belonging, of having your world thoroughly disrupted, having it criticized and scrutinized from the point of view of those who have been harmed by it, having important concepts central to it dismissed, being viewed with mistrust, being seen as of no consequence except as an object of mistrust.[61]

When we speak *for* the other, or even when we create space for the other to speak or speak *to* the other, we risk reaffirming our own centrality and the presumed authority of the "dominant" discourses into which marginalised voices and perspectives must be brought. This assumption – that certain discourses are so paramount that the silenced voice must be incorporated – warrants critical interrogation. To whom is this discourse important? For whom does the silence of the oppressed constitute a problem? What underlying assumptions about voice, political action and silence is this imperative based on? While silence by marginalised actors may be an outcome of exclusion, the ubiquitous conflation of their silence with voicelessness risks erasing their agency. Silence may also represent a strategic disengagement or disdain for discursive spaces and their parameters – a political act in its own right.

Silent protest

Silence, as Wendy Brown has argued, can be "a political value, a means of preserving certain practices and dimensions of existence from regulatory power, from normative violence, as well as from the scorching rays of public exposure".[62] Against the imperatives of "compulsory discursivity",[63] silence can function as a means to preserve autonomy. As José Ciro Martínez has shown in his ethnographic work with communities living in hashish-trafficking hubs in Spain and Morocco, it is insightful to analyse the "attempted (and often successful) obfuscations of state-imposed legibility".[64] He investigates strategies frequently dismissed as merely delinquent or criminal – such as contraband trade, banking abroad, throwing stones at police cars, tax evasion, informal labour. While these practices are integral to the economic survival and financial viability of communities, they also function to generate alternative spaces and safeguard them through deliberate opacity. Martínez here reveals silent forms of resistance beyond liberal imaginings. As he argues, "the pursuit of opacity rarely takes on recognisable vernaculars of protest or resistance. It is always the expression of a specific situation, the necessary creation of communities amidst the forms of capture they come up against."[65]

States and imperial authorities engaged in governmentality seek to render the lives of those to be governed visible, audible and legible. Resistance to such regimes of legibility entails a deliberate pushback against being made transparent and often manifests through covert and hidden channels. For those most subjected to or actively contesting imperial, state and military power, secrecy becomes a necessary condition of survival and resistance. This is why, as Ahmad puts it, "much critical intellection under conditions of violence had to be collective, underground, on-the-run and anonymous, in non-European languages, and in forms that can escape capture and destruction by states".[66] Such resistance entails everyday tactics of secrecy and opacity to evade imperial authority – and its eyes and ears.

However, understanding silence by marginalised actors only as reactive protection from legibility risks to overlook the vectors of power and resistance which can operate through them, because "even as silence is a response to domination, it is not enforced from above but rather deployed from below: refusing to speak is a method of refusing colonization, of refusing complicity in injurious interpellations or in subjection through regulation".[67] While silence is often grasped through its centripetal effects of stabilising relations of power, Montoya has argued that silence is also uniquely positioned as a centrifugal force because "silence can disturb and disrupt the linguistic hegemony that is inherent in and coalesces the power relations".[68] If moving within discursive registers that oppress, control and co-opt ways of speaking, silence can be a centrifugal strategy to subvert and resist.

Within institutional and discursive structures, silence disrupts logocentric expectations "precisely because the ideal of transparent speech is the presumed mode of participation, in our cultural practices, a standard to which silence is not reducible".[69] It is because of these expectations that exit-based decisions often become politically salient in liberal democracies, such as voting abstentions, political disengagement or "voting with the feet" by leaving organisations or jurisdictions.[70] Non-responses to calls for participation can undermine the functioning and authority of powerful regimes. While the ambiguity of such exit-based silences means that they are often not classed as "genuine" protest, we can also understand that very ambiguity as part of its subversive force: "Silence as non-participation is threatening to institutional forces in that silence resists whatever demands are made without necessarily opposing."[71]

Silence is not merely a safer or less risky alternative to direct confrontation; rather, it can produce communicative effects that transcend those achievable through overt utterances. For example, silence can work to communicate utter dissent and disregard, the ultimate form of dismissal precisely because no response is made whatsoever. When a politically incorrect remark by a family member at a gathering is met with stony silence, this silence might not just be a diplomatic non-response, but can, depending on the context, function as the most effective way of communicating profound disdain and disregard. Perlocutionary silencing – when propositions are not taken up and there are no communicative effects to an utterance – can thus not only function to silence oppressed perspectives but can also be mobilised in subversive ways.

The specific discursive effects of silence also play a role when silence is used in performative resistance to violence and injustice, for example in silent vigils. Silence as a form of performative protest can invoke layers of meaning and affective responses which transcend the possibilities of linguistic forms of resistance. When the Women in Black, "a world-wide network of women committed to peace with justice",[72] organise silent vigils dressed in black, the silence of their protest performs a political act in ways that subvert the dominant grid of what can be said and heard. As Athanasiou has argued, the silent vigil "enacts – rather than claims to retrieve – what was hitherto unheard of, that is, what was eclipsed by the common languages of political or judicial speech. It seeks, in other words, to do justice to unspeakability; as if this were possible".[73]

Standing in solidarity – and complicity – with deaths that are framed as ungrievable, these silent vigils do not attempt to speak about the other or re-present them but instead invoke ambiguous, affective registers of grief, penance, admonishment. In Athanasiou's words, silence as a form of resistance responds to injustices that "demand witness when nothing is left to be said and when the pains of injustice cannot be fully reducible to the available idioms of language and representation. At the same time, it is meant to echo what has gone unsaid and what remains to be said in light of the historic voicelessness of the gendered and racialised others of discursivity."[74] While not retreating from the responsibility of opposing violence and injustice, these protests simultaneously resist the impulse to break silence, instead inhabiting an uncomfortably physical presence, alongside the complicity and grief which these injustices entail. In doing so, they performatively transcend the lines of dominant discourses, drawing attention to that which is unsayable.

Other forms of protest have sought to transcend dominant discursive registers by employing artistic and creative modes that engage audiences at an emotive level, including through poetry, theatre, art, photography and music. Similar to the silent vigils which Athanasiou analyses, such protest "lays claim to the political imagination by attending to narratives yet-to-be heard. It is a way to reclaim the testimonial performative power of inaudible and disqualified voices beyond the authoritative premises of speech, or, at least, beside them."[75] For example, Pakistani photojournalist Noor Behram, a resident of Waziristan, spent years photographing and evidencing the impact of drone warfare. His work has been exhibited in a gallery in London and has received coverage by *The Wire* and other media outlets. A selection of photos, accompanied by impressions Behram recalls from the particular location he visited, this exhibition relates the suffering of living under drones through, but also beyond, the gruesome violence of dead bodies. For example, a photo titled "Datta Khel, Oct. 18, 2010" shows the picture of an injured child at Mirin Shah hospital, who died an hour after Behram took the picture.[76] Another picture, titled "Datta Khel, Oct. 28, 2010", depicts the lone figure of a man searching in the rubble of his house. His family, who he had lived with, all died in the strike. A group of neighbours gathered when they saw Behram taking pictures of the man but Behram recalls that they were not in a mood to talk.[77]

Walters, who has analysed Behram's work as what he calls parrhesiastic exposure, or truth-telling to power, hints at the ways in which this work differs from other journalistic attempts at counting the dead: "Behram's reporting is, in contrast, much more situated, personal and embodied. His disclosure is an act in its own right, a relatively undetached account of what he saw and felt as he arrived at each scene. Behram is a subject in this war: he speaks in part as a resident living in its midst."[78] Because Behram's work centres on his experiences, incorporating both the photographs he captured and the vivid impressions of suffering he witnessed, it holds the potential to move beyond the dominant linguistic registers typically used to represent drone warfare.

The project #NotABugSplat, launched by an international collective of Pakistani, American and French artists with the support of the NGO Reprieve, also relies on images as a non-verbal form of protest. The giant art installation features a photo of a child whose parents died in a drone strike. The name of the project derives from the military slang used by drone pilots to describe those who died as "bug splats". The scale of the installation allows it to be captured by satellites, thereby rendering it a permanent feature on online mapping sites and visible through a drone camera. It thus reconfigures the relationship between the view from below and the pilot's aerial perspective so that "what an operator sees on his screen is not an anonymous dot on the landscape, but an innocent child victim's face".[79] The photo of the child laid out on the landscape zooms in on their features as if trying to recentre the human who is living under drones, thus relating to audiences in an emotive mode that transcends linguistic registers.

Music and protest songs offer another means to move beyond discursive structures. The act of singing, as opposed to protesting through demands, slogans or rational arguments, transforms the nature and affective quality of protest. Drawing on Sanger's analysis of the Civil Rights movement, activists perceived the act of singing freedom songs as providing "specific rhetorical possibilities for them that they perceived to be less attainable through other outlets".[80] Singing becomes a mode of cultivating courage and hope, particularly when speech proves inadequate to express – and redress – the horrors of a situation. Singing engages different audiences than verbal protest, conveying and evoking emotions that can transform the audiences who pause to listen.[81] Protest songs often employ lyrics that are less steeped in dominant linguistic structures, instead channelling moral, spiritual and emotional registers. For example, Protest in Harmony, an Edinburgh-based protest choir, has performed a song by one of the song leaders, Penny Stone, written in response to the naming of the Israeli drone Heron:

The only Heron

The first flight of a great bird, take to the sky,
stretch out your long legs, wide wings they will carry you,
Guided by waterways, glide over land,
Wade in the water and catch.
The only heron I want to see flying
grows from a fledgeling into a bird,
The only heron I want to see flying
grows from a fledgeling into a bird.

Hearing otherwise

Words used for weapons, such as the "Predator" or "Reaper" drone, or the category of "MALE" (medium altitude long endurance) drones, reflect the hyper-masculine performativity of imperial self-representations. Asymmetry of military capacities is here frequently celebrated and/or taken for granted,[82] for example when the US Air Force has described its drone programme as projecting power without vulnerability. Such self-representation of the imperial self as a Goliath often conceals deep insecurities, weaknesses and anxieties. In a report aptly titled "MALE Performance Anxiety", the charity DroneWars has documented the fallibility of MALE drones, highlighting not only technical malfunctions but also the vulnerabilities of being brought down by non-state actors, such as the Houthi or Hezbollah.[83]

Tracing the web of silences sustaining military violence and oppression can similarly lead to a sense of the discursive omnipotence of the imperial core that overlooks the fractures, ambiguities and contingencies inherent in discursive formations. This chapter has drawn on acts of resistance to imperial warfare by a range of actors – including NGOs, human rights advocates, activists and journalists. Rather than treating silence primarily as a problem, the chapter engaged with its critical potential. Silence can thus serve as a lens through which to interrogate entrenched regimes of not listening and fundamentally question which voices and perspectives come to be heard. Silence also opens up a creative space for new forms of knowledge and resistance. Because silence is contingent upon processes of listening and interpretation, its ambiguity and relationality can be mobilised politically for resistance.

The chapter has examined a range of tactics employed by those who have resisted silent wars. I first engaged with attempts to break the silence and speak out against practices of imperial violence. Speaking out acknowledges an issue as relevant and politically salient. It not only raises awareness about the topic but is also a generative political activity through which new subjectivities, perspectives and visions of the world are created. However, speaking out is not a simple antithesis to silence, given that silence is constituted with and through text. Attempts to break the silence may thus inadvertently reinforce the very silences most central to sustaining warfare – when it remains within dominant discursive frames rooted in the logic of military necessity and operational ethics, such as the focus on civilian casualties, targeting procedures or military technology. I highlighted the importance of practices of resistance that consciously shift out of such dominant linguistic frames. For example, the campaign Fly Kites Not Drones invokes the symbol of the kite to foreground the everyday realities of life under the threat of aerial bombardment, thus creating an affective register against the normalisation of violence.

Resisting "silent wars" is not an easy task, given how fraught are any attempts at breaking silence, speaking out, demanding speech or speaking for others. The direct confrontation of loud silences – such as demands for state officials to speak – may thus inadvertently reinforce their effects. The chapter has discussed the tactic of reinterpreting silence, which is based on the recognition that silence need not be understood solely through dominant modalities such as secrecy or acquiescence. Instead, the inherent ambiguity and relationality of silence offers possibilities for creative resistance that challenge and move beyond entrenched assumptions and speech expectations. For example, instead of opposing the silence by state officials and interpreting it solely as a strategic use of secrecy, it can be read as a sign of incompetence and institutional incapacity – an inability rather than a spectacle of power. Such reinterpretations subtly shift the epistemic hierarchies reinforced by the loud silences discussed in this book. Rather than signalling the epistemic superiority of state officials by demanding speech from them, alternative sites and sources are reaffirmed as producing authoritative knowledge about imperial violence.

I have argued that any attempts to subvert entrenched regimes of (not) listening need to consciously shift towards new modes of listening, reconfigure who are recognised as speakers and what constitutes valid expertise. Such efforts necessitate particular attention to those voices and perspectives that have been marginalised, changing discursive conditions in ways that make it possible to hear and speak *to* the silenced. This strategy must confront the profound dilemma inherent in the participation in, and complicity with, unjust discursive structures. Speaking for the subaltern, or even creating space for the silenced to speak, risks further essentialising, instrumentalising and co-opting the silenced. Even the presumption that the silenced need to be brought into specific discourses reproduces presumptions of the importance of these discourses – and of the silence of the subaltern as oppression and voicelessness. Instead, silence can be a subversive force of disengagement with dominant linguistic structures and can be mobilised in resistance. Silence as a form of performative protest can invoke layers of meaning and affective responses which transcend the possibilities of linguistic forms of resistance. This includes silent vigils and non-linguistic forms of protest, such as photography, music and art. Such forms of resistance performatively exceed the limitations of dominant discursive registers, drawing critical attention to that which has remained unspoken and is – as yet – unsayable.

Notes

All URLs were last accessed on October 30, 2025.

1 Margaret E. Montoya, "Silence and Silencing: Their Centripetal and Centrifugal Forces in Legal Communication, Pedagogy and Discourse," *University of Michigan Journal of Law Reform* 33 (1999): 268.

2 Athena Athanasiou, *Agonistic Mourning: Political Dissidence and the Women in Black* (Edinburgh University Press, 2017) 231.

3 Rutazibwa, "Hidden in Plain Sight," 234.

4 Rutazibwa, "Hidden in Plain Sight," 234.

5 José Medina, *The Epistemology of Protest: Silencing, Epistemic Activism, and the Communicative Life of Resistance* (Oxford University Press, 2023), 106.
6 Athanasiou, *Agonistic Mourning*, 230.
7 Medina, "Introduction," 12.
8 Drone Campaign Network, at https://dronecampaignnetwork.wordpress.com/
9 Coalition Letter Calls for End of US Lethal Strikes Abroad, ACLU, at www.aclu.org/documents/coalition-letter-calls-end-us-lethal-strikes-abroad
10 *Manchester Guardian*, "Police bombing," August 28, 1933.
11 *Manchester Guardian*, "Disarmament: Britain and Police Bombing," June 26, 1933.
12 *Manchester Guardian*, "Disarmament: Letters to the Editor," June 26, 1933.
13 *Manchester Guardian*, "Right to Police Bombing: Effect in Wartime: Dr. Barne's Example: Birmingham Protest," June 19, 1933.
14 *Manchester Guardian*, "Disarmament: Britain and Police Bombing," June 26, 1933; see also Maureen Waugh, "Quakers, Peace and the League of Nations: The Role of Bertram Pickard," *Quaker Studies* 6, no. 1 (2002): 4; Peter Brock and Thomas P. Socknat, *Challenge to Mars: Pacifism from 1918 to 1945* (University of Toronto Press, 1999), 136.
15 Medina, "Introduction," 3.
16 Medina, "Introduction," 3–4.
17 Wendy Brown, *Edgework: Critical Essays on Knowledge and Politics* (Princeton University Press, 2009), 84, https://doi.org/10.1515/9781400826872
18 Brown, *Edgework*, 84.
19 Mignolo, *The Politics of Decolonial Investigations*, 14.
20 Alex Edney-Browne, "The Psychosocial Effects of Drone Violence: Social Isolation, Self-Objectification, and Depoliticization," *Political Psychology* 40, no. 6 (2019): 1341–56, https://doi.org/10.1111/pops.12629
21 Heller, "'One Hell of a Killing Machine.'"
22 Fly Kites Not Drones, at www.flykitesnotdrones.org/who-we-are
23 Voices for Creative Non-Violence UK, the Drone Campaign Network, Pax Christi UK and Quaker Peace & Social Witness.
24 Drone Campaign Network, Flyer on "Drones: The True Cost of War," at https://dronecampaignnetwork.wordpress.com/wp-content/uploads/2012/09/dronesside.jpg

25 Reprieve, "Statement of Reprieve on '"Targeted Killing" and the Rule of Law: The Legal and Human Costs of 20 Years of U.S. Drone Strikes' Before the Senate Judiciary Committee, February 9, 2022," 2022, 1, https://reprieve.org/us/2022/02/09/us-targeted-killing-programme/
26 Krasmann, "Targeted Killing and Its Law."
27 De Behar, *A Rhetoric of Silence*, 122:7.
28 Oxford Research Group, *All Quiet on the ISIS Front?*
29 UN Doc A/HRC/28/38, *Summary of the Human Rights Council Interactive Panel Discussion of Experts on the Use of Remotely Piloted Aircraft ...*, 56.
30 US Congress, *Congressional Record*, Vol. 159 (32), Senate, March 6, 2013, S1181–226, S1193.
31 Amnesty International, *The Hidden US War in Somalia.*
32 Airwars, *Limited Accountability.*
33 Pace and Menwith Hill Accountability Campaign and Yorkshire CND, "Menwith Hill in 3D," 22.
34 Rutazibwa, "Hidden in Plain Sight," 240.
35 UK House of Commons, *HC Debates*, November 7, 2012, Vol. 552, Westminster Hall, Combat Troop Withdrawal (Afghanistan), Cc224 WH–245WH.
36 Mahvish Ahmad, "Movement Texts as Anti-Colonial Theory," *Sociology* 57, no. 1 (2023): 54–71, https://doi.org/10.1177/00380385221098516
37 Ahmad, "Movement Texts as Anti-Colonial Theory," 62.
38 Rutazibwa, "Hidden in Plain Sight," 240.
39 Anna M. Agathangelou and L. H. M. Ling, "Postcolonial Dissidence within Dissident IR: Transforming Master Narratives of Sovereignty in Greco-Turkish Cyprus," *Studies in Political Economy* 54, no. 1 (1997): 9.
40 Róisín Ryan-Flood and Rosalind Gill, eds, *Secrecy and Silence in the Research Process: Feminist Reflections*, Transformations: Thinking through Feminism (Routledge, 2010), 1.
41 PAX, *Human Rights and Human Realities; Local Perspectives on Drone Strikes and International Law; Dvaladze, Jansen, Zwijnenburg, PAX for Peace*, 2018, https://paxforpeace.nl/publications/human-rights-and-human-realities/
42 Amnesty International, *The Hidden US War in Somalia.*
43 Alcoff, "The Problem of Speaking for Others," 9.
44 Spivak, "Can the Subaltern Speak?" 295.
45 Said, *Orientalism*, 21.
46 Athanasiou, *Agonistic Mourning*, 265.
47 Alcoff, "The Problem of Speaking for Others," 11.
48 Alcoff, "The Problem of Speaking for Others," 20.

49 Alcoff, "The Problem of Speaking for Others," 21.
50 Maggio, "Can the Subaltern Be Heard?" 422.
51 Athanasiou, *Agonistic Mourning*, 269.
52 Alcoff, "The Problem of Speaking for Others," 23.
53 Athanasiou, *Agonistic Mourning*, 253.
54 Open Society Foundations, *Armed Drones in Europe*, Open Society, European Policy Institute (2019), www.opensocietyfoundations.org/publications/armed-drones-in-europe
55 Spivak, "Can the Subaltern Speak?" 294.
56 Maria C. Lugones and Elizabeth V. Spelman, "Have We Got a Theory for You! Feminist Theory, Cultural Imperialism and the Demand for 'the Woman's Voice,'" in *Feminism and Philosophy* (Routledge, 2018).
57 Lugones and Spelman, "Have We Got a Theory for You!" 484.
58 Lugones and Spelman, "Have We Got a Theory for You!" 484.
59 Athanasiou, *Agonistic Mourning*, 269.
60 Rutazibwa, "Hidden in Plain Sight," 240.
61 Lugones and Spelman, "Have We Got a Theory for You!" 485.
62 Brown, *Edgework*, 85.
63 Brown, *Edgework*, 85.
64 José Ciro Martínez, "Pursuing Opacity: Geographies of Visibility in the Western Mediterranean," *Antipode* 56, no. 4 (2024): 1381, https://doi.org/10.1111/anti.13045
65 Martínez, "Pursuing Opacity," 1388.
66 Ahmad, "Movement Texts as Anti-Colonial Theory," 55.
67 Brown, *Edgework*, 97.
68 Montoya, "Silence and Silencing," 266.
69 Kennan Ferguson, "Silence: A Politics," *Contemporary Political Theory* 2, no. 1 (2003): 63.
70 Sebastien Bourdin and Jiwan Tail, "Abstentionist Voting – Between Disengagement and Protestation in Neglected Areas: A Spatial Analysis of The Paris Metropolis," *International Regional Science Review* 45, no. 3 (2022): 263–92, https://doi.org/10.1177/01600176211034131; Amanda Driscoll and Michael J. Nelson, "Ignorance or Opposition? Blank and Spoiled Votes in Low-Information, Highly Politicized Environments," *Political Research Quarterly* 67, no. 3 (2014): 547–61, https://doi.org/10.1177/1065912914524634; Mark E. Warren, "Voting with Your Feet: Exit-Based Empowerment in Democratic Theory," *American Political Science Review* 105, no. 4 (2011): 683–701, https://doi.org/10.1017/S0003055411000323; Nathan Hanna, "An Argument for Voting Abstention," *Public Affairs Quarterly* 23, no. 4 (2009): 275–86; Patrick Cunha Silva and Brian F Crisp, "Ballot Spoilage as a

Response to Limitations on Choice and Influence," *Party Politics* 28, no. 3 (2022): 521–27, https://doi.org/10.1177/1354068821990258; R. Michael Alvarez et al., "A Taxonomy of Protest Voting," *Annual Review of Political Science* 21 (2018): 135–54, https://doi.org/10.1146/annurev-polisci-050517-120425; Ilya Somin, "Foot Voting versus Ballot Box Voting: Why Voting with Your Feet Is Crucial to Political Freedom," *European Political Science* 18, no. 4 (2019): 587–602, https://doi.org/10.1057/s41304-018-0195-2; Won-Taek Kang, "Protest Voting and Abstention Under Plurality Rule Elections: An Alternative Public Choice Approach," *Journal of Theoretical Politics* 16, no. 1 (2004): 79–102, https://doi.org/10.1177/0951629804038903

71 Ferguson, "Silence," 56.

72 Women in Black, at https://womeninblack.org/about-women-in-black/

73 Athanasiou, *Agonistic Mourning*, 239.

74 Athanasiou, *Agonistic Mourning*, 230.

75 Athanasiou, *Agonistic Mourning*, 232.

76 "Datta Khel, Oct. 18, 2010" from the exhibition by Noor Behram published with the Wire, at www.wired.com/2011/12/photos-pakistan-drone-war/

77 "Datta Khel, Oct. 28, 2010" from the exhibition by Noor Behram published with the Wire, at www.wired.com/2011/12/photos-pakistan-drone-war/

78 William Walters, "Parrhēsia Today: Drone Strikes, Fearless Speech and the Contentious Politics of Security," in *Affective Economies, Neoliberalism, and Governmentality*, ed. Anne-Marie d'Aoust (Routledge, 2017), 290.

79 NotABugSplat, at https://notabugsplat.com/

80 Kerran L. Sanger, "Functions of Freedom Singing in the Civil Rights Movement: The Activists' Implicit Rhetorical Theory," *Howard Journal of Communications* 8, no. 2 (1997): 180, https://doi.org/10.1080/10646179709361752

81 Elizabeth Bloodgood and Shelley Deane, *Where Have All the Protest Songs Gone? Social Movements' Message and Their Voice in Politics*. Semantic Scholar, September 1, 2005, 5. www.semanticscholar.org/paper/Where-Have-All-the-Protest-Songs-Gone%3A-Protest-And-Bloodgood-Deane/3628bab0541442a3223ea12a460307bca48b2d11

82 *Royal Air Force Autonomous Collaborative Platform Strategy*, n.d.

83 Chris Cole, "MALE Performance Anxiety: Technical Problems and SAMs Bring Large Drones down to Earth," Drone Wars UK, June 24, 2024, https://dronewars.net/2024/06/24/male-performance-anxiety-technical-problems-and-sams-bring-large-drones-down-to-earth/

Conclusion

I write this conclusion in a moment marked by profound anxiety and global instability, as imperial powers continue to undermine international legal frameworks and inflict destruction and death upon marginalised regions of the world. Such military violence is both enabled by, and productive of, deeply entrenched material and institutional asymmetries in global politics. It is legitimised to domestic and international audiences through discursive strategies that invoke "national security" while portraying the "enemy" negatively. Yet, beyond the visible and audible logics of such overt propaganda, military violence also relies – in some cases primarily – on the hidden architecture of silence: on what is left unsaid, silenced, omitted and erased. This book has traced how interlinking functions of silence sustain imperial violence. I have investigated what I term *loud silences* – such as secrecy – that are noted and performative, and *deep silences* that influence the boundaries of linguistic registers. These silences, I argue, not only accompany violent oppression but actively shape the conditions of its possibility.

Deep silences operate through unspoken assumptions that render certain ideas unquestionable and beyond debate. As Chapter 2 demonstrated, both contemporary and colonial discourses on bombing campaigns are underpinned by an unquestioned assumption that "bad guys" – labelled "rebels" in colonial contexts or "terrorists" in the present – should be targets of lethal force. This presumption is entangled with implicit, orientalist representations of the places and people subjected to bombardment. It is further reinforced by implicatures that position the imperial power as morally superior and obligated to take control. Crucially, by operating through presupposition and implicature, rather than explicit argument, such assumptions elude critique and become further entrenched as taken-for-granted knowledge that is beyond debate.

Violence justified through such underlying assumptions becomes normalised and discursively backgrounded. This manifests in the structures of neglect and omission underlying discourses on imperial violence, where specific aspects are systematically backgrounded or erased. For example, UK parliamentary debates frequently centre on the psychological wellbeing of drone operators, contrasting sharply with the lack of attention paid to the experiences and suffering of those subjected to surveillance and aerial bombardment. Such asymmetries reflect and reproduce a racialised hierarchy of political relevance: they delineate what matters, whose lives are significant and whose suffering is rendered politically inconsequential. Crucially, these deep silences are not simply absences or discursive limits; they possess illocutionary and performative force in sustaining military violence. By remaining silent on the deaths of non-white people, their lives are further marginalised and framed as irrelevant. By neglecting to engage with the chaos, terror and destruction inflicted by military violence, it is normalised as rational, lawful and clean.

These deep silences are embedded within registers of racialised assumptions and operate through banal silencings – the everyday, often unnoticed, decisions of not speaking and ignoring which link to what Stoler has termed a condition of colonial aphasia.[1] Deep silences are also sustained by a wider economy of material and institutional power structures – including restrictions on congressional oversight, limitations on media access to sources and the institutionalisation of state secrecy. As explored in Chapter 4, secrecy here functions both as a barrier to public oversight and as a performative force in its own right. It actively constructs the image of a powerful, omniscient core and epistemically marginalised outsiders. In doing so, secrecy cultivates a zone of uncertainty about the knowability of state violence, thereby destabilising the foundations upon which critique or dissent might otherwise be articulated.

Conceiving of secrecy as a pregiven or static entity risks obscuring the ways in which it is continually constructed through layered practices of interpreting utterances and omissions – including leaks, rumours, revelations, delays and classifications. Secrecy emerges through the contingent organisation of these layers and becomes meaningful as a loud, expressive silence only when these layers are heard, ignored and interpreted in specific ways. Situated within the material and ideational power structures of the global economy of silence, secrecy gains significance not in isolation but through entrenched regimes of not listening. Within this economy, the extensive and reliable body of knowledge about drone warfare – collected by local communities, journalists, international organisations and NGOs – is frequently dismissed or marginalised. Instead, silence emanating from powerful state institutions is interpreted as secrecy, construed as an epistemic void about the war and a condition of unknowability. This interpretive framing reaffirms the assumption that legitimate knowledge is the prerogative of powerful state actors, while those on the outside remain epistemically excluded, unable to fully comprehend or speak about state violence.

At the same time, silence on the part of these "outsiders" is often read not as marginalisation but as acquiescence – as a lack of objections and tacit consent to military violence. In this way, silence by different publics is appropriated as acquiescence to legitimise violent and unjust practices. As Chapter 5 demonstrated, this dynamic is rooted in liberal myths of voice – the assumption that every subject possesses both the capacity and the obligation to speak. Within this framework, silence is collapsed into "lack of protest", interpreted as passive acceptance, even in contexts where speech is materially constrained, access to information is restricted and dissent is actively repressed or rendered unintelligible. Silence is interpreted through these power structures and can gain political and legal functions as acquiescence through their legacy. In such contexts, silence-as-acquiescence may not function as endorsement of a new legal standard but it may produce a more ambiguous, uneasy assent to imperial violence and injustice.

Silence, far from being a mere absence, actively shapes, enables and sustains military violence and systems of oppression. The logics of silence are multifaceted, encompassing both deep silences – such as implicit orientalist assumptions and structural forms of neglect – and loud silences, including instances of secrecy and acquiescence.

While these silences are interlinked, I do not mean to suggest that they form a coherent or monolithic whole. Rather, they are fractured, ambiguous, unstable and contingent. As I argued in Chapter 1, silences are constituted through entrenched regimes of (not) listening. When silence is invoked as acquiescence in international law, for instance, such readings rest on Western-centric assumptions and seemingly mundane methodological choices that obscure or ignore what has in fact been said elsewhere. In this way, the very perception and interpretation of silence is contingent upon specific practices of not listening and the selective organisation and interpretation of layers of utterances and silences.

The interpretive lines along which silence is organised are not neutral; rather, they frequently move "in accordance with racialized, gendered, sexed, ableist, and classed terms of (un)livability".[2] Silence is not the mere opposite of speech but is co-constituted with dominant linguistic registers. This means that more words may not necessarily lead to better or more ethical political outcomes. Indeed, some forms of speaking may reinforce the very silences that sustain imperial violence. For example, the focus on "innocent" civilian casualties risks reaffirming the implicit assumptions that those deemed "bad guys" are legitimate targets of violence. Similarly, demands for speech and greater transparency from powerful state actors can unintentionally affirm their epistemic centrality, dismissing other sources of information. Even well-meaning attempts to "give voice to the silenced" risk further essentialising them as mute, passive and dependent.[3]

Rather than attempting to directly oppose or "break" silence, I suggest attending to the fractures, dissonances and contradictions within the discursive constellations surrounding it – openings that make critical engagement possible. Precisely because silence is always mediated through listeners and their interpretive frameworks, there is potential to disrupt dominant modes of hearing and reinterpret loud silences in ways that challenge, rather than reinforce, hegemonic power. Silence itself can function as a powerful strategy of resistance, one that unsettles logocentric expectations of speech. It may communicate profound disdain or disregard – targeted at particular utterances or entire discursive situations. In some contexts, silence generates communicative effects that exceed those of overt expression. This is evident in performative protests, such as silent vigils, which evoke layers of meaning and hint towards that which cannot (yet) be spoken.[4]

Silence acquires meaning through processes of (not) listening – and within those processes lies a form of agency. While not all of us are in positions to speak, we are all implicated as listeners in shaping what is heard. In this light, I argue that silence should not be treated solely as a problem or deficit. Instead, silence offers a critical lens for interrogating regimes of not listening and it opens up generative space for alternative ways of knowing. Silence shifts our attention away from dominant voices and prevalent narratives, directing focus towards what remains unsaid or unheard. It compels us to interrogate our own habits of (not) listening. Precisely because of its intangibility, it invites deeper inquiry into how knowledge is produced within asymmetric power structures that fundamentally limit possibilities for voice. Silence urges us not only to speak out against violence and injustice but to transform the very structures of our hearing and work towards listening otherwise.

Notes

1 Stoler, "Colonial Archives and the Arts of Governance."
2 Athanasiou, "(Im)Possible Breathing," 95.
3 Spivak, "Can the Subaltern Speak?"; Maggio, "Can the Subaltern Be Heard?"; Alcoff, "The Problem of Speaking for Others."
4 Athanasiou, *Agonistic Mourning*.

Bibliography

Note: All URLs were last accessed on October 30, 2025.

Aalberts, Tanja. "Rethinking the Principle of (Sovereign) Equality as a Standard of Civilisation." *Millennium-Journal of International Studies* 42, no. 3 (2014): 767–89.

Ackerman, Spencer, and Ed Pilkington. "Obama's War on Whistleblowers Leaves Administration Insiders Unscathed." US News. *The Guardian*, March 16, 2015. www.theguardian.com/us-news/2015/mar/16/whistleblowers-double-standard-obama-david-petraeus-chelsea-manning

Afxentiou, Afxentis. "A History of Drones: Moral(e) Bombing and State Terrorism." *Critical Studies on Terrorism* 11, no. 2 (2018).

Agathangelou, Anna M., and L. H. M. Ling. "Postcolonial Dissidence within Dissident IR: Transforming Master Narratives of Sovereignty in Greco-Turkish Cyprus." *Studies in Political Economy* 54, no. 1 (1997): 7–38.

Åhäll, Linda. "The Dance of Militarisation: A Feminist Security Studies Take on 'the Political.'" *Critical Studies on Security* 4, no. 2 (2016): 154–68. https://doi.org/10.1080/21624887.2016.1153933

Ahmad, Mahmood. "The Legality of Unmanned Aerial Vehicles Outside the Combat Zone: A Case Study of the Federally Administered Tribal Areas of Pakistan." *Defense & Security Analysis*, www.tandfonline.com/doi/abs/10.1080/14751798.2014.921448

Ahmad, Mahvish. "Movement Texts as Anti-Colonial Theory." *Sociology* 57, no. 1 (2023): 54–71. https://doi.org/10.1177/00380385221098516

Ahmad, Muhammad Idrees. "The Magical Realism of Body Counts: How Media Credulity and Flawed Statistics Sustain a Controversial Policy." *Journalism* 17, no. 1 (2016): 18–34. https://doi.org/10.1177/1464884915593237

Ahmad, Nehaluddin, Faizah Rahim, and Nurulqayyimah Aziz. "Can International Humanitarian Law Regulate Recent Drone Strikes? A Case Study." *Journal of East Asia and International Law* 17 (2024): 159.

Airwars. "Civilian Casualties, Airwars Assessment, CS 1950, Idlib Syria." n.d. https://airwars.org/civilian-casualties/cs1950-october-15-2020/

Airwars. "Civilian Casualties, Airwars Assessment, USSOM274-C, Jilib Somalia." https://airwars.org/civilian-casualties/ussom274-c-february-2-2020/

Airwars. *Limited Accountability: A Transparency Audit of the Coalition Air War against So-Called Islamic State.* Remote Control, Oxford Research Group. 2016. https://airwars.org/wp-content/uploads/2016/12/Airwars-report_Web-FINAL1.compressed.pdf

Alakklouk, Bader, and Birol Gülnar. "The Impact of Citizen Journalism and Social Media in News Coverage of the Israeli Attacks on Gaza." *South Asian Journal of Social Sciences and Humanities* 4, no. 4 (2023): 76–100.

Alcoff, Linda. "The Problem of Speaking for Others." *Cultural Critique*, no. 20 (1991): 5–32. https://doi.org/10.2307/1354221

Alexander, Amanda. "The Genesis of the Civilian." *Leiden Journal of International Law* 20, no. 2 (2007): 359–76. https://doi.org/10.1017/S0922156506003347

Alexander, Amanda. "A Short History of International Humanitarian Law." *European Journal of International Law* 26, no. 1 (2015): 109–38. https://doi.org/10.1093/ejil/chv002

Alexander, Amanda. "The 'Good War': Preparations for a War against Civilians." *Law, Culture and the Humanities* 15, no. 1 (2019): 227–52. https://doi.org/10.1177/1743872116651224

Allen, Paula Gunn. *The Sacred Hoop: Recovering the Feminine in American Indian Traditions.* Beacon Press, 1992.

Altheide, David, and Jennifer Grimes. "War Programming: The Propaganda Project and the Iraq War." *The Sociological Quarterly* 46 (September 2005): 617–43. https://doi.org/10.1111/j.1533-8525.2005.00029.x

Alvarez, R. Michael, D. Roderick Kiewiet, and Lucas Núñez. "A Taxonomy of Protest Voting." *Annual Review of Political Science* 21 (2018): 135–54. https://doi.org/10.1146/annurev-polisci-050517-120425

Amnesty International. *"Will I Be Next?" US Drone Strikes in Pakistan.* 2013. www.amnestyusa.org/reports/will-i-be-next-us-drone-strikes-in-pakistan/

Amnesty International. *The Hidden US War in Somalia: Civilian Casualties from Air Strikes in Lower Shabelle.* 2019. www.amnesty.org/en/documents/afr52/9952/2019/en/

Amnesty International. *Somalia: Zero Accountability as Civilian Deaths Mount from US Air Strikes.* 2020. www.amnesty.org/en/latest/news/2020/04/somalia-zero-accountability-as-civilian-deaths-mount-from-us-air-strikes/

Anderson, Kenneth. *Targeted Killing in U.S. Counterterrorism Strategy and Law*. SSRN Scholarly Paper ID 1415070. Social Science Research Network, 2009. http://papers.ssrn.com/abstract=1415070

Anghie, Antony. "Colonialism and the Birth of International Institutions: Sovereignty, Economy, and the Mandate System of the League of Nations." *New York University Journal of International Law and Politics* 34 (2001): 513.

Anghie, Antony. "Finding the Peripheries: Sovereignty and Colonialism in Nineteenth-Century International Law." *Harvard International Law Journal* 40 (1999): 1.

Anghie, Antony. "The War on Terror and Iraq in Historical Perspective." *Osgoode Hall Law Journal* 43 (2005): 45.

Anthony, Scott. "The Future's in the Air: Imperial Airways and the British Documentary Film Movement." *Journal of British Cinema and Television* 8, no. 3 (2011): 301–21. https://doi.org/10.3366/jbctv.2011.0041

APPG. *All Party Parliamentary Group on Drones Inquiry Report: The UK's Use of Armed Drones: Working with Partners*. 2018. www.bsg.ox.ac.uk/sites/default/files/2018-07/INH_PG_Drones_AllInOne_v25.pdf

Arendt, Hannah, and Jens Kroh. *Eichmann in Jerusalem*. Viking Press, 1964.

Article 36. *Drones in the Use of Force: A Way Forward*. 2018. https://article36.org/wp-content/uploads/2020/12/A36-drones-use-of-force-way-forward-1.pdf

Athanasiou, Athena. *Agonistic Mourning: Political Dissidence and the Women in Black*. Edinburgh University Press, 2017.

Athanasiou, Athena. "(Im)Possible Breathing: On Courage and Criticality in the Ghostly Historical Present." *Redescriptions: Political Thought, Conceptual History and Feminist Theory* 23, no. 2 (2020): 92–106. https://doi.org/10.33134/rds.337

Basham, Victoria M. "Liberal Militarism as Insecurity, Desire and Ambivalence: Gender, Race and the Everyday Geopolitics of War." *Security Dialogue* 49, nos. 1–2 (2018): 32–43. https://doi.org/10.1177/0967010617744977

BBC News. "Al-Qaeda Leader Killed in US Drone Strike in Afghanistan." November 5, 2016. www.bbc.com/news/world-asia-37882010

Bell, P. M. H. "Censorship, Propaganda and Public Opinion: The Case of the Katyn Graves, 1943." *Transactions of the Royal Historical Society* 39 (December 1989): 63–83. https://doi.org/10.2307/3678978

Besson, S. "Sovereignty, International Law and Democracy." *European Journal of International Law* 22, no. 2 (2011): 373–87. https://doi.org/10.1093/ejil/chr029

Bhambra, Gurminder K. "Brexit, Trump, and 'Methodological Whiteness': On the Misrecognition of Race and Class." *The British Journal of*

Sociology 68, no. S1 (2017): S214–32. https://doi.org/10.1111/1468-4446.12317

Bhandar, Brenna. *Colonial Lives of Property: Law, Land, and Racial Regimes of Ownership*. Duke University Press, 2018.

Bianchi, Andrea, and Anne Peters. *Transparency in International Law*. Cambridge University Press, 2013.

Bijl, Paul. "Colonial Memory and Forgetting in the Netherlands and Indonesia." In *Colonial Counterinsurgency and Mass Violence*, edited by Bart Luttikhuis and A. Dirk Moses. Routledge, 2018.

Birchall, Clare. "Introduction to 'Secrecy and Transparency': The Politics of Opacity and Openness." *Theory, Culture & Society* 28, nos. 7–8 (2011): 7–25. https://doi.org/10.1177/0263276411427744

Birdsall, Andrea. "Drone Warfare in Counterterrorism and Normative Change: US Policy and the Politics of International Law." *Global Society*, 2018, 1–22.

Bjerre, Thomas Ærvold. "Unmanned? Military Masculinities in Filmic Representations of US Drone Operators." *Men and Masculinities* 26, no. 1 (2023): 24–43. https://doi.org/10.1177/1097184X221139820

Bjørkelo, Brita, Ståle Einarsen, Morten Birkeland Nielsen, and Stig Berge Matthiesen. *Silence Is Golden? Characteristics and Experiences of Self-Reported Whistleblowers*. Taylor & Francis, 2011.

Blakely, Sandra. "Toward an Archaeology of Secrecy: Power, Paradox, and the Great Gods of Samothrace." *Archaeological Papers of the American Anthropological Association*, 2012.

Blenkinsopp, John, and Marissa S. Edwards. "On Not Blowing the Whistle: Quiescent Silence as an Emotion Episode." In *Emotions, Ethics and Decision-Making*, vol. 4, edited by Wilfred J. Zerbe, Charmine E. J. Härtel, and Neal M. Ashkanasy. Emerald Group Publishing Limited, 2008.

Bloodgood, Elizabeth, and Shelley Deane. *Where Have All the Protest Songs Gone? Social Movements' Message and Their Voice in Politics*. Semantic Scholar, September 1, 2005. www.semanticscholar.org/paper/Where-Have-All-the-Protest-Songs-Gone%3A-Protest-And-Bloodgood-Deane/3628bab0541442a3223ea12a460307bca48b2d11

Bourdin, Sebastien, and Jiwan Tai1. "Abstentionist Voting – Between Disengagement and Protestation in Neglected Areas: A Spatial Analysis of the Paris Metropolis." *International Regional Science Review* 45, no. 3 (2022): 263–92. https://doi.org/10.1177/01600176211034131

Brito Vieira, Mónica, Theo Jung, Sean W. D. Gray, and Toby Rollo. "The Nature of Silence and Its Democratic Possibilities." *Contemporary Political Theory* 18, no. 3 (2019): 424–47. https://doi.org/10.1057/s41296-019-00330-2

Brock, Peter, and Thomas P. Socknat. *Challenge to Mars: Pacifism from 1918 To 1945*. University of Toronto Press, 1999.

Brown, Wendy. *Edgework: Critical Essays on Knowledge and Politics*. Princeton University Press, 2009. https://doi.org/10.1515/9781400826872

Butler, Judith. *Precarious Life: The Powers of Mourning and Violence*. Verso, 2004.

Byers, Michael. *Custom, Power, and the Power of Rules: International Relations and Customary International Law*. Cambridge University Press, 1999.

Carson, Austin. "Facing Off and Saving Face: Covert Intervention and Escalation Management in the Korean War." *International Organization* 70, no. 1 (2016): 103–31. https://doi.org/10.1017/S0020818315000284

Carston, Robyn, and Alison Hall. "3. Implicature and Explicature." In *Cognitive Pragmatics*, edited by Hans-Jörg Schmid. De Gruyter, 2012.

Cassinelli, C. W. "The 'Consent' of the Governed." *The Western Political Quarterly*, 1959.

Chambers, Simone. "Behind Closed Doors: Publicity, Secrecy, and the Quality of Deliberation." *Journal of Political Philosophy* 12, no. 4 (2004): 389–410. https://doi.org/10.1111/j.1467-9760.2004.00206.x

Chan, Phil C. W. Chan, "Acquiescence/Estoppel in International Boundaries: *Temple of Preah Vihear* Revisited," *Chinese Journal of International Law* 3, no. 2 (2004): 421–39.

Chimni, B. S. "Customary International Law: A Third World Perspective." *American Journal of International Law* 112, no. 1 (2018): 1–46. https://doi.org/10.1017/ajil.2018.12

Colby, Elbridge. "How to Fight Savage Tribes." *American Journal of International Law* 21, no. 2 (1927): 279–88.

Cole, Chris. "MALE Performance Anxiety: Technical Problems and SAMs Bring Large Drones down to Earth." Drone Wars UK, June 24, 2024. https://dronewars.net/2024/06/24/male-performance-anxiety-technical-problems-and-sams-bring-large-drones-down-to-earth/

Combined Joint Task Force – Operation Inherent Resolve. "Civilian Casualty Assessment." March 10, 2022. Release No. 20210310. CJTF-OIR CIVCAS Press release Mar 22.pdf

Cormac, Rory, and Richard J. Aldrich. "Grey Is the New Black: Covert Action and Implausible Deniability." *International Affairs* 94, no. 3 (2018): 477–94. https://doi.org/10.1093/ia/iiy067

Dada, Opeoluwa Dayo. "A Look at Media Subtle Act of Bias and Framing in Russia–Ukraine Crisis." SSRN Scholarly Paper 4277332. November 15, 2022. https://doi.org/10.2139/ssrn.4277332

Daily Herald. "Bombs for Natives." n.d.

Daily Mail. "5,000 Men." November 22, 1927.

Daily Mail. "Bombing for Taxes." February 24, 1923.

Daily Mail. "Bombing for Taxes." February 12, 1924.

Daily Mail. "British in Frontier Skirmish." July 28, 1933.

Daily Mail. "Mespot Waste." March 2, 1923.
Daily Mail. "Premier and Air Rights." November 14, 1933.
Daily Mail. "Secret of a Gorge." June 12, 1924.
Daily Mail. "Sir A. Cobham's Film 'Swoop.'" July 18, 1927.
Daily Mail. "Warplanes Disperse Massed Warriors." October 9, 1935.
Darcy, Oliver. "Trump Says Right-Wing Voices Are Being Censored. The Data Says Something Else | CNN Business." CNN, May 28, 2020. www.cnn.com/2020/05/28/media/trump-social-media-conservative-censorship/index.html
De Behar, Lisa Block. *A Rhetoric of Silence and Other Selected Writings*. Vol. 122. Walter de Gruyter, 1995.
De Hoogh, Andre. "Restrictivist Reasoning on the Ratione Personae Dimension of Armed Attacks in the Post 9/11 World." *Leiden Journal of International Law* 29, no. 1 (2016): 19–42.
Desoutter, Morgane. "War, Social Media and Gender: An Analysis of the Use of TikTok by Ukrainian Soldiers." *Critical Military Studies* 0, no. 0 (2025): 1–27. https://doi.org/10.1080/23337486.2025.2472100
Dingli, Sophia, and Thomas N. Cooke, eds. *Political Silence: Meanings, Functions and Ambiguity*. Interventions. Routledge, 2019.
Dodd, Julian. "What 4' 33" Is." *Australasian Journal of Philosophy*, 2017, 1–13.
Dodd, Vikram, and Richard Norton-Taylor. "Video of 7/7 Ringleader Blames Foreign Policy." UK News. *The Guardian*, September 2, 2005. www.theguardian.com/uk/2005/sep/02/alqaida.politics
Donadey, Anne. "Between Amnesia and Anamnesis: Re-Membering the Fractures of Colonial History." *Studies in 20th & 21st Century Literature* 23, no. 1 (1999). https://doi.org/10.4148/2334-4415.1457
Dougherty, Tom, "'Yes Means Yes': Consent as Communication," *Philosophy & Public Affairs* 43, no. 3 (2015): 224–53.
Dover, Robert, and Richard J. Aldrich. "Cryptography and the Global South: Secrecy, Signals and Information Imperialism." *Third World Quarterly*, August 3, 2020, 1–18. https://doi.org/10.1080/01436597.2020.1793665
Downes, Chris. "'Targeted Killings' in an Age of Terror: The Legality of the Yemen Strike." *Journal of Conflict and Security Law* 9, no. 2 (2004): 277–94. https://doi.org/10.1093/jcsl/9.2.277
Driscoll, Amanda, and Michael J. Nelson. "Ignorance or Opposition? Blank and Spoiled Votes in Low-Information, Highly Politicized Environments." *Political Research Quarterly* 67, no. 3 (2014): 547–61. https://doi.org/10.1177/1065912914524634
Drone Wars UK. *Falling Short: An Analysis of the Reporting of UK Drone Strikes by the MOD*, Brookman-Byrne, Drone Wars UK. 2018. https://dronewars.net/2018/07/09/falling-short/

"Drones and the War on Terror: When Can the US Target Alleged American Terrorists Overseas." Hearing before the Committee on the Judiciary House of Representatives, 113th Congress, Serial No. 113–2. 2013. www.congress.gov/event/113th-congress/house-event/LC646/text

ECCHR. *Litigating Drone Strikes: Challenging the Global Network of Remote Killing*. European Center for Constitutional and Human Rights. 2017. www.ecchr.eu/en/publication/litigating-drone-strikes-challenging-the-global-network-of-remote-killing/

Edney-Browne, Alex. "The Psychosocial Effects of Drone Violence: Social Isolation, Self-Objectification, and Depoliticization." *Political Psychology* 40, no. 6 (2019): 1341–56. https://doi.org/10.1111/pops.12629

Elkins, Caroline. *Britain's Gulag: The Brutal End of Empire in Kenya*. Random House, 2005.

Engels, Jeremy, and William Saas. "On Acquiescence and Ends-Less War: An Inquiry into the New War Rhetoric." *Quarterly Journal of Speech* 99, no. 2 (2013): 225–32.

Ferguson, Kennan. "Silence: A Politics." *Contemporary Political Theory* 2, no. 1 (2003): 49–65.

Fletcher, Robert. "The Art of Forgetting: Imperialist Amnesia and Public Secrecy." *Third World Quarterly* 33, no. 3 (2012): 423–39. https://doi.org/10.1080/01436597.2012.657476

Foucault, Michel. *The History of Sexuality: Volume I: An Introduction*. Pantheon Books, 1978.

Freeden, Michael. *Concealed Silences and Inaudible Voices in Political Thinking*. Oxford University Press, 2022.

Furner, James. "Tacit Consent Without Political Obligation." *Theoria* 57, no. 124 (2010). https://doi.org/10.3167/th.2010.5712403

Gaggioli, Gloria, and Pavle Kilibarda. "Counterterrorism and the Risk of Over-Classification of Situations of Violence." *International Review of the Red Cross* 103, nos. 916–17 (2021): 203–36. https://doi.org/10.1017/S1816383121000424

Gani, Jasmine K., and Rabea M. Khan. "Positionality Statements as a Function of Coloniality: Interrogating Reflexive Methodologies." *International Studies Quarterly* 68, no. 2 (2024): sqae038.

Gantt Shafer, Jessica. "Donald Trump's 'Political Incorrectness': Neoliberalism as Frontstage Racism on Social Media." *Social Media+Society* 3, no. 3 (2017): 2056305117733226

Garwood-Gowers, Andrew. "Israel's Airstrike on Syria's Al-Kibar Facility: A Test Case for the Doctrine of Pre-Emptive Self-Defence?" *Journal of Conflict and Security Law* 16, no. 2 (2011): 263–91.

Gellately, Robert. *Backing Hitler: Consent and Coercion in Nazi Germany*. Oxford University Press, 2002.

Gerver, Mollie. "Inferring Consent without Communication." *Social Theory and Practice* 46, no. 1 (2020): 27–53.

Graham-Harrison, Emma, and Joe Dyke. "Lives Torn Apart by British Airstrikes in Mosul Give Lie to UK's 'Perfect' Precision War." World News. *The Guardian*, March 21, 2023. www.theguardian.com/world/2023/mar/21/british-airstrikes-mosul-civilian-victims-iraq

Gray, Christine. *International Law and the Use of Force*. Oxford University Press, 2008.

Gregory, Thomas. "Drones, Targeted Killings, and the Limitations of International Law." *International Political Sociology* 9, no. 3 (2015): 197–212. https://doi.org/10.1111/ips.12093

Guriev, Sergei M., and Daniel Treisman. "How Modern Dictators Survive: Cooptation, Censorship, Propaganda, and Repression." *SSRN Electronic Journal*, ahead of print, 2015. https://doi.org/10.2139/ssrn.2571905

Hall, Gary. "We Can Know It for You: The Secret Life of Metadata." *MSOR Connections*, Sigma Network, 2010. https://pureportal.coventry.ac.uk/en/publications/we-can-know-it-for-you-the-secret-life-of-metadata-2

Hanna, Nathan. "An Argument for Voting Abstention." *Public Affairs Quarterly* 23, no. 4 (2009): 275–86.

Hasser, Caitlin E. Review of *Review of Silence and Complicity: Violence Against Women in Peruvian Public Health Facilities*, by The Center for Reproductive Law and Policy (CRLP) and The Latin American and Caribbean Committee for the Defense of Women's Rights (CLADEM). *Women's Studies Quarterly* 31, no. 1/2 (2003): 264–67.

Hathaway, Oona A., Tobias Kuehne, Randi Michel, and Nicole Ng. "Congressional Oversight of Modern Warfare: History, Pathologies, and Proposals for Reform." *William & Mary Law Review* 63, no. 1 (2021): 137–218.

Heller, K. J. "'One Hell of a Killing Machine': Signature Strikes and International Law." *Journal of International Criminal Justice* 11, no. 1 (2013): 89–119. https://doi.org/10.1093/jicj/mqs093

Herman, Edward S., and Noam Chomsky. *Manufacturing Consent: The Political Economy of the Mass Media*. Pantheon Books, 2002.

Heyns, Christof, Dapo Akande, Lawrence Hill-Cawthorne, and Thompson Chengeta. "The International Law Framework Regulating the Use of Armed Drones." *International & Comparative Law Quarterly* 65, no. 4 (2016): 791–827. https://doi.org/10.1017/S0020589316000385

Hiebert, Ray Eldon. "Public Relations and Propaganda in Framing the Iraq War: A Preliminary Review." *Public Relations Review* 29, no. 3 (2003): 243–55.

Hobson, John M. *The Eastern Origins of Western Civilisation [Electronic Resource] / John M. Hobson*. Cambridge University Press, 2004.

Hobson, John M. "Is Critical Theory Always for the White West and for Western Imperialism? Beyond Westphilian towards a Post-Racist Critical IR." *Review of International Studies* 33, no. S1 (2007): 91–116. https://doi.org/10.1017/S0260210507007413

Holman, Brett. "Spectre and Spectacle: Mock Air Raids as Aerial Theatre in Interwar Britain." In *Aviation in the Literature and Culture of Interwar Britain*, edited by Michael McCluskey and Luke Seaber. Springer International Publishing, 2020.

Horn, Eva. "Logics of Political Secrecy." *Theory, Culture & Society* 28, nos. 7–8 (2011): 103–22. https://doi.org/10.1177/0263276411424583

Howell, Alison. "Forget 'Militarization': Race, Disability and the 'Martial Politics' of the Police and of the University." *International Feminist Journal of Politics* 20, no. 2 (2018): 117–36. https://doi.org/10.1080/14616742.2018.1447310

Howley, Kevin. "Violence, Intimidation and Incarceration: America's War on Whistleblowers." *Communication & Theatre Faculty Publications*, August 1, 2020. https://scholarship.depauw.edu/commtheatre_facpubs/3

Human Rights Clinic and Center for Civilians in Conflict, and Columbia Law School. "The Civilian Impact of Drones: Unexamined Costs, Unanswered Questions." 2012. https://civiliansinconflict.org/publications/research/civilian-impact-drones-unexamined-costs-unanswered-questions/

Ikenberry, G. John. *Liberal Leviathan: The Origins, Crisis, and Transformation of the American World Order*. Princeton University Press, 2011.

International Arbitral Awards. *Island of Palmas Case (Netherlands v. USA)*, Judgment of April 4, 1928 [1928], UN Reports of International Arbitral Awards, 831. 1928.

International Court of Justice. *Fisheries Case (United Kingdom v. Norway)*, Judgment of December 18, 1951, [1951] ICJ Rep. 116. 1951.

International Court of Justice. *Case concerning the Temple of Preah Vihear (Cambodia v. Thailand)*, Judgment of June 15, 1962, ICJ Rep. 6. 1962.

International Court of Justice. *Sovereignty over Pedra Branca/Palau Batu Puteh, Middle Rocks and South Ledge (Malaysia/Singapore), Jurisdiction and Admissibility*, Judgment of May 23, 2008 [2008] ICJ Rep. 14, at 51. 2008.

Isharaza, Muganzi M. "Hierarchies of Editorial Power in International NGOs." *Journalism Studies* 20, no. 12 (2019): 1764–81. https://doi.org/10.1080/1461670X.2019.1638296

Joseph, Michael F., and Michael Poznansky. "Media Technology, Covert Action, and the Politics of Exposure." *Journal of Peace Research* 55, no. 3 (2018): 320–35. https://doi.org/10.1177/0022343317731508

Kang, Won-Taek. "Protest Voting and Abstention under Plurality Rule Elections: An Alternative Public Choice Approach." *Journal of*

Theoretical Politics 16, no. 1 (2004): 79–102. https://doi.org/10.1177/0951629804038903

Kania, Andrew. "Silent Music." *The Journal of Aesthetics and Art Criticism* 68, no. 4 (2010): 343–53.

Kauffman, David R. "The Theory of Silence." *Musical Offerings* 2, no. 1 (2011): 1.

Kaye, David. *Online Propaganda, Censorship and Human Rights in Russia's War against Reality*. Cambridge University Press, 2022.

Kearns, Oliver. "State Secrecy, Public Assent, and Representational Practices of US Covert Action." *Critical Studies on Security* 4, no. 3 (2016): 276–90.

Kearns, Oliver. "Secrecy and Absence in the Residue of Covert Drone Strikes." *Political Geography* 57 (2017): 13–23.

Kessler, Oliver, and Wouter Werner. "Extrajudicial Killing as Risk Management." *Security Dialogue* 39, nos. 2–3 (2008): 289–308.

Khan, Rabea M. "A Case for the Abolition of 'Terrorism' and Its Industry." *Critical Studies on Terrorism* 0, no. 0 (n.d.): 1–24. https://doi.org/10.1080/17539153.2024.2327727

Kieh, George Klay. "Neo-Colonialism: American Foreign Policy and the First Liberian Civil War." *The Journal of Pan African Studies* 5, no. 1 (2012): 164–84.

Kinsella, Helen M. "Discourses of Difference: Civilians, Combatants, and Compliance with the Laws of War." *Review of International Studies* 31, no. S1 (2005): 163–85. https://doi.org/10.1017/S0260210505006844

Kinsella, Helen. *The Image before the Weapon: A Critical History of the Distinction between Combatant and Civilian*. 1st ed. Cornell University Press, 2011.

Kopela, Sophia. "The Legal Value of Silence as State Conduct in the Jurisprudence of International Tribunals." *Australian Year Book of International Law* 29 (2010): 87–134.

Koskenniemi, Martti. "The Fate of Public International Law: Between Technique and Politics." *The Modern Law Review* 70, no. 1 (2007): 1–30.

Krasmann, Susanne. "Targeted Killing and Its Law: On a Mutually Constitutive Relationship." *Leiden Journal of International Law* 25, no. 3 (2012): 665–82. https://doi.org/10.1017/S0922156512000337

Kurzon, Dennis. "Towards a Typology of Silence." *Journal of Pragmatics* 39, no. 10 (2007): 1673–88.

Livsey, Tim. "Open Secrets: The British 'Migrated Archives', Colonial History, and Postcolonial History." *History Workshop Journal* 93, no. 1 (2022): 95–116. https://doi.org/10.1093/hwj/dbac002

Lobel, Jules. "The Use of Force to Respond to Terrorist Attacks: The Bombing of Sudan and Afghanistan." *Yale Journal of International Law* 24 (1999): 537.

Loomba, Ania. *Colonialism/Postcolonialism*. Routledge, 2005.

Lugones, María. "Heterosexualism and the Colonial/Modern Gender System." *Hypatia* 22, no. 1 (2007): 186–219. https://doi.org/10.1111/j.1527-2001.2007.tb01156.x

Lugones, Maria C., and Elizabeth V. Spelman. "Have We Got a Theory for You! Feminist Theory, Cultural Imperialism and the Demand for 'the Woman's Voice.'" In *Feminism and Philosophy*. Routledge, 2018.

Ma, Veronica. "Propaganda and Censorship: Adapting to the Modern Age." *Harvard International Review* 37, no. 2 (2016): 46–50.

MacGibbon, I. C. "The Scope of Acquiescence in International Law," *British Yearbook of International Law* 31 (1954): 143–86, p. 167.

Maggio, J. "'Can the Subaltern Be Heard?' Political Theory, Translation, Representation, and Gayatri Chakravorty Spivak." *Alternatives: Global, Local, Political* 32, no. 4 (2007): 419–43.

Maitland, Sara. *A Book of Silence*. Granta, 2009.

Manchanda, Nivi. "The Janus-Faced Nature of Militarization." *Critical Military Studies*, January 13, 2022, 1–5. https://doi.org/10.1080/23337486.2021.2022852

Manchester Guardian. "Britain and Police Bombing." June 26, 1933.

Manchester Guardian. "Letters to the Editor: Police Bombing: Does Use in India Mean Use in Europe?" August 16, 1933.

Manchester Guardian. "Police Bombing." May 29, 1933.

Manchester Guardian. "Police Bombing." August 28, 1933.

Manchester Guardian. "Right to Police Bombing: Effect in Wartime: Dr Barnes's Example: Birmingham Protest." June 19, 1933.

Martin, Thomas, Elisabeth Schweiger, and Nick Ritchie. "The Limits of National Security and Foreign Policy Orthodoxy: Labour's Challenge to UK Policy under Jeremy Corbyn." *Critical Studies on Security* (2025): 1–27. https://doi.org/10.1080/21624887.2025.2538361

Martínez, José Ciro. "Pursuing Opacity: Geographies of Visibility in the Western Mediterranean." *Antipode* 56, no. 4 (2024): 1378–98. https://doi.org/10.1111/anti.13045

Martini, Alice. "Making Women Terrorists into 'Jihadi Brides': An Analysis of Media Narratives on Women Joining ISIS." *Critical Studies on Terrorism* 11, no. 3 (2018): 458–77. https://doi.org/10.1080/17539153.2018.1448204

Mbembe, Achille. "Necropolitics." *Public Culture* 15, no. 1 (2003): 11–40. https://doi.org/10.1215/08992363-15-1-11

McCluskey, Michael, and Luke Seaber. *Aviation in the Literature and Culture of Interwar Britain*. Springer Nature, 2020.

McCorquodale, Robert. "Defining the International Rule of Law: Defying Gravity?" *International and Comparative Law Quarterly* 65, no. 2 (2016): 277–304. https://doi.org/10.1017/S0020589316000026

Medina, José. "Introduction: Coming to Protest and Listening to Protest under Conditions of Oppression." In *The Epistemology of Protest: Silencing, Epistemic Activism, and the Communicative Life of Resistance*, edited by José Medina. Oxford University Press, 2023.

Medina, José. *The Epistemology of Protest: Silencing, Epistemic Activism, and the Communicative Life of Resistance.* Oxford University Press, 2023.

Meerssche, Dimitri Van Den. "Global South Perspectives on Methodology and Critique in International Law." *Leiden Journal of International Law* 37, no. 4 (2024): 763–72. https://doi.org/10.1017/S0922156524000396

Melley, Timothy. *The Covert Sphere: Secrecy, Fiction, and the National Security State.* In *The Covert Sphere*. Cornell University Press, 2012.

Melley, Timothy. "Covert Spectacles and the Contradictions of the Democratic Security State." *Storyworlds: A Journal of Narrative Studies* 6, no. 1 (2014): 61–82. https://doi.org/10.5250/storyworlds.6.1.0061

Mendelson, Maurice. "The Subjective Element in Customary International Law." *British Yearbook of International Law* 66, no. 1 (1996): 177–208.

Mignolo, Walter D. *The Politics of Decolonial Investigations.* Duke University Press, 2021.

Montoya, Margaret E. "Silence and Silencing: Their Centripetal and Centrifugal Forces in Legal Communication, Pedagogy and Discourse." *University of Michigan Journal of Law Reform* 33 (1999): 263.

Mowatt, Rasul A. "Black Lives as Snuff: The Silent Complicity in Viewing Black Death." *Biography* 41, no. 4 (2018): 777–806. https://doi.org/10.1353/bio.2018.0079

Mukenge, Muadi. "Sensationalism at Work: Creating the Myth of the Mau Mau." *Ufahamu: A Journal of African Studies* 21, nos. 1–2 (1993). https://doi.org/10.5070/F7211-2016741

Müller, Marcus, and Florian Böller. "The Tug-of-War over Drone Strike Oversight: Congress and the Politics of Drone Warfare during the Obama Presidency." *Congress & the Presidency* 0, no. 0 (2022): 1–26. https://doi.org/10.1080/07343469.2022.2070298

Murphy, Sean D. "The International Legality of US Military Cross-Border Operations from Afghanistan into Pakistan" *International Law Studies* 85 (2009): 109–39.

Mutua, Makau W. "Critical Race Theory and International Law: The View of an Insider-Outsider." *Villanova Law Review* 45, no. 5 (2000).

O'Connell, Mary Ellen. "Combatants and the Combat Zone." *University of Richmond Law Review* 43 (2008): 845.

O'Connell, Mary Ellen. "Remarks: The Resort to Drones under International Law." *Denver Journal of International Law & Policy* 39 (2010): 585.

Okafor, Obiora Chinedu. "Newness, Imperialism, and International Legal Reform in Our Time: A TWAIL Perspective." *Osgoode Hall Law Journal* 43 (2005): 171.

Open Society Foundations. *Armed Drones in Europe*. Open Society, European Policy Institute. 2019. www.opensocietyfoundations.org/publications/armed-drones-in-europe

Orna Ben-Naftali and Roy Peled. "How Much Secrecy Does Warfare Need?" In *Transparency in International Law*, edited by Andrea Bianchi and Anne Peters, Anne. Cambridge University Press, 2013.

Overy, Richard. *The Morbid Age: Britain between the Wars*. London, 2009.

Oxford Research Group. *All Quiet on the ISIS Front? British Secret Warfare in an Information Age*. Knowles, Watson, Remote Control. 2017. www.academia.edu/34051576/ALL_QUIET_ON_THE_ISIS_FRONT_British_secret_warfare_in_an_information_age

Oyěwùmí, Oyèrónkẹ́. *The Invention of Women: Making an African Sense of Western Gender Discourses*. University of Minnesota Press, 1997.

Pace, Barnaby, and Menwith Hill Accountability Campaign and Yorkshire CND. "Menwith Hill in 3D: Domes, Data and Drone Strikes." 2021. www.themhac.uk/sites/default/files/2021-10/MHAC%20Domes%20Data%20and%20Drones%2003.08.21.pdf

Paris, Michael. *Warrior Nation: Images of War in British Popular Culture, 1850–2000*. Reaktion, 2000.

Parks, Lisa, and Caren Kaplan. *Life in the Age of Drone Warfare*. Duke University Press, 2020.

Pateman, Carole. *The Sexual Contract*. Polity, 1997.

PAX. *Human Rights and Human Realities; Local Perspectives on Drone Strikes and International Law*. Dvaladze, Jansen, Zwijnenburg, PAX for Peace. 2018. https://paxforpeace.nl/publications/human-rights-and-human-realities/

PAX. *Military Drones and the EU; The Role of Unmanned Systems in the European Union's Defence Developments*. 2019. https://paxforpeace.nl/wp-content/uploads/sites/2/2025/03/pax-report-military-drones-and-the-eu.pdf

Pirie, Gordon H. "Cinema and British Imperial Civil Aviation, 1919–1939." *Historical Journal of Film, Radio and Television* 23, no. 2 (2003): 117–31. https://doi.org/10.1080/0143968032000091068

Plaw, Avery, and Joao Franco Reis. "The Contemporary Practice of Self-Defense: Evolving Toward the Use of Preemptive or Preventive Force?" In *Preventive Force: Drones, Targeted Killing, and the Transformation of Contemporary Warfare*, edited by Kerstin Fisk and Jennifer M. Ramos. New York University Press, 2016.

Porter, J. M. "JP Plamenatz, Consent, Freedom and Political Obligation, Oxford: Oxford University Press, 1968, Pp. 182." *Canadian Journal of Political Science/Revue Canadienne de Science Politique* 2, no. 3 (1969): 391.

Pozen, David E. "Deep Secrecy." *Stanford Law Review*, no. 2 (2010): 257–340.

Poznansky, Michael. "Revisiting Plausible Deniability." *Journal of Strategic Studies*, March 2, 2020, 1–23. https://doi.org/10.1080/01402390.2020.1734570

Public Technologies. "Representatives Lee & Burgess Introduce Drone Reform Act to Ensure Accountability in Military Drone Strikes." Press Release. September 18, 2023. www.publicnow.com/view/BEAAE4E73AF6BF42B3AC677D0104D72823990CEC

Pugliese, Joseph. "Prosthetics of Law and the Anomic Violence of Drones." *Griffith Law Review* 20 (2011): 931.

Quijano, Anibal. "Coloniality of Power and Eurocentrism in Latin America." *International Sociology* 15, no. 2 (2000): 215–32.

Ranji, Banafsheh. "Traces of Orientalism in Media Studies." *Media, Culture & Society* 43, no. 6 (2021): 1136–46. https://doi.org/10.1177/01634437211022692

Rawls, John. *A Theory of Justice: Original Edition*. Harvard University Press, 1971. https://doi.org/10.2307/j.ctvjf9z6v

Reinold, Theresa. "State Weakness, Irregular Warfare, and the Right to Self-Defense Post-9/11." *The American Journal of International Law* 105, no. 2 (2011): 244–86. https://doi.org/10.5305/amerjintelaw.105.2.0244

Reprieve. "Statement of Reprieve on '"Targeted Killing" and the Rule of Law: The Legal and Human Costs of 20 Years of U.S. Drone Strikes' Before the Senate Judiciary Committee, February 9, 2022." 2022. https://reprieve.org/us/2022/02/09/us-targeted-killing-programme/

Rocha, Ester, and Brian H. Kleiner. "To Blow or Not to Blow the Whistle? That Is the Question." *Management Research News* 28, no. 11/12 (2005): 80–87.

Rothschild, Joyce, and Terance D. Miethe. "Whistle-Blower Disclosures and Management Retaliation: The Battle to Control Information about Organization Corruption." *Work and Occupations* 26, no. 1 (1999): 107–28.

Royal Air Force Autonomous Collaborative Platform Strategy. n.d.

Rutazibwa, Olivia. "The Decolonization of Our Storytelling," speech delivered at the International Baccalaureate (IB) Peterson Academic Symposium in The Hague, the Netherlands, July 5–6, 2012. https://oliviarutazibwa.wordpress.com/2012/07/05/the-decolonization-of-our-storytelling/?utm_source=chatgpt.com

Rutazibwa, Olivia U. "Hidden in Plain Sight: Coloniality, Capitalism and Race/Ism as Far as the Eye Can See." *Millennium: Journal of International*

Studies 48, no. 2 (2020): 221–41. https://doi.org/10.1177/0305829819889575

Ryan-Flood, Róisín, and Rosalind Gill, eds. *Secrecy and Silence in the Research Process: Feminist Reflections*. Transformations: Thinking through Feminism. Routledge, 2010.

Said, Edward W. *Orientalism: Western Conceptions of the Orient*. Reprinted with a new afterword. Penguin History. Penguin Books, 1995.

Sanger, Kerran L. "Functions of Freedom Singing in the Civil Rights Movement: The Activists' Implicit Rhetorical Theory." *Howard Journal of Communications* 8, no. 2 (1997): 179–95. https://doi.org/10.1080/10646179709361752

Satia, Priya. *Spies in Arabia: The Great War and the Cultural Foundations of Britain's Covert Empire in the Middle East*. Oxford University Press, 2008. http://hdl.handle.net/2027/heb08808

Satia, Priya. "Drones: A History from the British Middle East." *Humanity: An International Journal of Human Rights, Humanitarianism, and Development* 5, no. 1 (2014): 1–31. https://doi.org/10.1353/hum.2014.0002

Sato, Shohei. "'Operation Legacy': Britain's Destruction and Concealment of Colonial Records Worldwide." *The Journal of Imperial and Commonwealth History* 45, no. 4 (2017): 697–719. https://doi.org/10.1080/03086534.2017.1294256

Sbisà, Marina. "Presupposition and Implicature: Varieties of Implicit Meaning in Explicitation Practices." *Journal of Pragmatics* 182 (September 2021): 176–88. https://doi.org/10.1016/j.pragma.2021.05.027

Schmitt, Eric. "American Drone Strike in Libya Kills Top Qaeda Recruiter." *New York Times*, March 28, 2018. www.nytimes.com/2018/03/28/world/africa/us-drone-strike-libya-qaeda.html

Schröter, Melani. *Silence and Concealment in Political Discourse*. Discourse Approaches to Politics, Society and Culture (DAPSAC), v. 48. John Benjamins Publishing Company, 2013.

Schröter, Melani, and Charlotte Taylor. *Exploring Silence and Absence in Discourse: Empirical Approaches*. Springer, 2017.

Schweiger, Elisabeth. "Listen Closely: What Silence Can Tell Us about Legal Knowledge Production." *London Review of International Law* 6, no. 3 (2018): 391–411.

Schweiger, Elisabeth. "'Targeted Killing' and the Lack of Acquiescence." *Leiden Journal of International Law* 32, no. 4 (2019): 741–57. https://doi.org/10.1017/S0922156519000475

Schweiger, Elisabeth. "The Lure of Novelty: 'Targeted Killing' and Its Older Terminological Siblings." *International Political Sociology*, ahead of print, 2019. https://doi.org/10.1093/ips/olz006

Schweiger, Elisabeth. "Fighting Silence Covert Warfare and the Uphill Battle against the Unsaid." *European Journal of International Relations*, October 24, 2021. https://doi.org/10.1177/13540661211053830

Seaber, Luke. "From This New Culture of the Air We Finally See': 'Groundmindedness' in the 1930s." In *Aviation in the Literature and Culture of Interwar Britain*, edited by Michael McCluskey and Luke Seaber. Springer International Publishing, 2020.

Shaw, Tony. "Early Warnings of the Red Peril: A Pre-History of Cold War British Cinema, 1917–1939." *Film History* 14, no. 3/4 (2002): 354–68.

Silva, Patrick Cunha, and Brian F. Crisp. "Ballot Spoilage as a Response to Limitations on Choice and Influence." *Party Politics* 28, no. 3 (2022): 521–27. https://doi.org/10.1177/1354068821990258

Simmons, A. John. "Tacit Consent and Political Obligation." *Philosophy & Public Affairs* 5, no. 3 (1976): 274–91.

Smith, Leonard V. "Sovereignty under the League of Nations Mandates: The Jurists' Debates." *Journal of the History of International Law / Revue d'histoire Du Droit International* 21, no. 4 (2019): 563–87. https://doi.org/10.1163/15718050-12340133

Somin, Ilya. "Foot Voting versus Ballot Box Voting: Why Voting with Your Feet Is Crucial to Political Freedom." *European Political Science* 18, no. 4 (2019): 587–602. https://doi.org/10.1057/s41304-018-0195-2

Sparrow, Robert. "War without Virtue?" In *Killing by Remote Control*, by Jeff McMahan, edited by Bradley Jay Strawser. Oxford University Press, 2013. https://doi.org/10.1093/acprof:oso/9780199926121.003.0005

Spivak, Gayatri Chakravorty. "Can the Subaltern Speak?" In *Marxism and the Interpretation of Culture*, edited by Nelson Cary and Lawrence Grossberg. University of Illinois Press, 1988.

Starski, Paulina. "Silence within the Process of Normative Change and Evolution of the Prohibition on the Use of Force: Normative Volatility and Legislative Responsibility." *Journal on the Use of Force and International Law* 4, no. 1 (2017): 14–65.

Stern, Brigitte. "Custom at the Heart of International Law." *Duke Journal of Comparative & International Law* 11 (2001): 89.

Stoler, Ann Laura. "Colonial Archives and the Arts of Governance." *Archival Science* 2, no. 1 (2002): 87–109. https://doi.org/10.1007/BF02435632

Surchin, Alan D. "Terror and the Law: The Unilateral Use of Force and the June 1993 Bombing of Baghdad Notes." *Duke Journal of Comparative & International Law* 5, no. 2 (1994): 457–98.

Tams, C. J. "The Use of Force against Terrorists." *European Journal of International Law* 20, no. 2 (2009): 359–97. https://doi.org/10.1093/ejil/chp031

Tasseron, Michael, and Brendan T Lawson. "Legitimizing Military Action through Statistics and Discourse in the 2014 IDF Assault on Gaza." *Media, War & Conflict* 15, no. 2 (2022): 238–56. https://doi.org/10.1177/1750635220917692

The Times. "Police Bombing." May 30, 1933.

The Times. "Police Bombing." June 21, 1933.

Thomas, Owen David. "Security in the Balance: How Britain Tried to Keep Its Iraq War Secrets." *Security Dialogue* 51, no. 1 (2020): 77–95. https://doi.org/10.1177/0967010619839544

Tomlinson, Lucas. "US Drone Strike Kills 2 Senior Al Qaeda Operatives in Syria." *Fox News*, October 15, 2020. www.foxnews.com/world/us-drone-strike-kills-2-senior-al-qaeda-operatives-in-syria

Tyler, Sally. "Of Temples and Territory: The ICJ's Preah Vihear Decision and Implications for Regional Dispute Resolution." *University of the District of Columbia Law Review* 19 (2016).

UK House of Commons. *HC Debates*, July 3, 1924, Vol 175, Bombing Operations, Iraq, Cc1490–2. 1924.

UK House of Commons. *HC Debates*, March 18, 1930, Vol 236, Mr. Montague's Statement, Cc1925–2006. 1930.

UK House of Commons. *HC Debates*, May 26, 1930, Vol 239, India Office, Cc825–949. 1930.

UK House of Commons. *HC Debates*, April 29, 1932, Vol 265, India Office, Cc703–84. 1932.

UK House of Commons. *HC Debates*, March 14, 1933, Vol 275, Supply, Cc1795–896. 1933.

UK House of Commons. *HC Debates*, June 13, 1933, Vol 279, Foreign Office, Cc29–146. 1933.

UK House of Commons. *HC Debates*, June 26, 1933, Vol 279, Disarmament (Draft Convention), Cc1161–2. 1933.

UK House of Commons. *HC Debates*, July 5, 1933, Vol 280, Foreign Office, Cc339–457. 1933.

UK House of Commons. *HC Debates*, December 13, 1933, Vol 284, International Police Force, Cc445–502. 1933.

UK House of Commons. *HC Debates*, March 19, 1935, Vol 299, Air Estimates, Cc1015–117. 1935.

UK House of Commons. *HC Debates*, July 11, 1935, Vol 304, Foreign Office, Cc509–631. 1935.

UK House of Commons. *HC Debates*, July 22, 1935, Vol 304, Number of Royal Air Force, Cc1563–630. 1935.

UK House of Commons. *HC Debates*, June 16, 1938, Vol 337, Aerial Warfare, Cc395–7. 1938.

UK House of Commons. *HC Debates*, June 23, 1938, Vol 337, Bombing, North-West Frontier, Cc1255–6. 1938.

UK House of Commons. *HC Debates*, November 6, 2012, Vol 552, Westminster Hall, Unmanned Aerial Vehicles, cc197WH-204WH. 2012.

UK House of Commons. *HC Debates*, November 7, 2012, Vol 552, Westminster Hall, Combat Troop Withdrawal (Afghanistan), cc224WH-245WH. 2012.

UK House of Commons. *HC Debates*, December 11, 2012, Vol 555, Westminster Hall, Unmanned Aerial Vehicles, cc27WH-48WH. 2012.

UK House of Commons. *HC Debates*, October 13, 2015, Vol 600, Drones in Conflict, Cc288–94. 2015.

UK House of Commons. *HC Debates*, December 1, 2015, Vol 603, Westminster Hall, Armed Drones, cc50WH-72WH. 2015.

UK House of Commons. *HC Debates*, March 20, 2018, Public Bill Committees, Data Protection Bill [Lords] (Fifth Sitting), Cc161–94. 2018.

UK House of Commons. *HC Debates*, July 3, 2018, Vol 644, Counter-Daesh Update, Cc192–201. 2018.

UK House of Commons. *HC Debates*, June 18, 2019, Vol 662, Westminster Hall, International Humanitarian Law: Protecting Civilians in Conflict, cc28WH–47WH. 2019.

UK House of Commons. *HC Debates*, October 14, 2020, Public Bill Committees, Overseas Operations (Service Personnel and Veterans) Bill (Fifth Sitting), Cc131–62. 2020.

UK House of Commons. *HC Debates*, November 19, 2020, Vol 684, Integrated Review, Cc487–505. 2020.

UN Doc A/68/389. *Promotion and Protection of Human Rights and Fundamental Freedoms While Countering Terrorism : Note / by the Secretary-General*. 2013.

UN Doc A/69/53. *Resolution Ensuring Use of Remotely Piloted Aircraft or Armed Drones in Counter-Terrorism and Military Operations in Accordance with International Law, Including International Human Rights and Humanitarian Law*. 2014.

UN Doc A/CN.4/682. *International Law Commission, Report by Special Rapporteur Michael Wood, Third Report on Identification of Customary International Law*. 2015.

UN Doc A/CN.4/L.872. *International Law Commission. Identification of Customary International Law. Text of the Draft Conclusions Provisionally Adopted by the Drafting Committee*. 2016.

UN Doc A/HRC/14/24/Add.6. *Report of the Special Rapporteur on Extrajudicial, Summary or Arbitrary Executions, Philip Alston*. 2010.

UN Doc A/HRC/14/24/Add.6. *Report of the Special Rapporteur on Extrajudicial, Summary or Arbitrary Executions, Philip Alston, Addendum, Study on Targeted Killings*. 2010.

UN Doc A/HRC/20/22/Add.3. *Report of the Special Rapporteur on Extrajudicial, Summary or Arbitrary Executions, Christof Heyns; Addendum, Follow-up to Country Recommendations – United States of America*. 2012.

UN Doc A/HRC/24/34. *Situation of Human Rights in Yemen; Report of the United Nations High Commissioner for Human Rights**. 2013.

UN Doc A/HRC/28/38. *Summary of the Human Rights Council Interactive Panel Discussion of Experts on the Use of Remotely Piloted Aircraft or Armed Drones in Compliance with International Law: Report of the Office of the United Nations High Commissioner for Human Rights*. 2014.

UN Doc A/HRC/31/57/Add.1. *Report of the Special Rapporteur on Torture and Other Cruel, Inhuman, or Degrading Treatment of Punishment: Observations on Communications Transmitted to Governments and Replies Received*. 2016.

UN Doc A/HRC/34/61. *Report of the Special Rapporteur on the Promotion and Protection of Human Rights and Fundamental Freedoms While Countering Terrorism*. 2017.

UN Doc A/HRC/43/61. *Situation of Human Rights in the Islamic Republic of Iran; Report of the Special Rapporteur on the Situation of Human Rights in the Islamic Republic of Iran*. 2020.

UN Doc A/HRC/44/38. *Report of the Special Rapporteur on Extrajudicial, Summary or Arbitrary Executions*. 2020.

UN Doc A/HRC/RES/25/22. *Human Rights Council Resolution: "Ensuring Use of Remotely Piloted Aircraft or Armed Drones in Counter-Terrorism and Military Operations in Accordance with International Law, Including International Human Rights and Humanitarian Law."* 2014.

UN Doc A/RES/41/38. *UN General Assembly Resolution, Declaration of the Assembly of Heads of State and Government of the Organization of African Unity on the Aerial and Naval Military Attack against the Socialist People's Libyan Arab Jamahiriya by the Present United States Administration in April 1986*. 1986.

UN Doc S/1998/780, *Letter dated August 20, 1998 from the Permanent Representative of the United States of America to the United Nations addressed to the President of the Security Council*, 1998.

UN Doc S/PV.2674. *United Nations Security Council Debate (2674th Meeting)*. 1986.

UN Doc S/PV.2675. *United Nations Security Council Debate (2675th Meeting)*. 1986.

UN Doc S/PV.3245. *United Nations Security Council Debate (3245th Meeting)*. 1993.

UN Doc S/PV.4836. *United Nations Security Council Debate (4836th Meeting)*. 2003.

UN Doc S/PV.5489. *United Nations Security Council Debate (5489th Meeting)*. 2006.

UN Human Rights Office. *Media Statement: UN Human Rights Office Condemns Targeting Journalists and Attacks on Hospitals*. June 6, 2025. www.un.org/unispal/document/un-human-rights-office-condemns-targeting-journalists-and-attacks-on-hospitals/

UN, Office of the Regional Humanitarian Coordinator for the Syria Crisis. *Statement by Kevin Kennedy, Regional Humanitarian Coordinator for the Syria Crisis, on Violence Impacting Aid Workers in North-West Syria Amman*. October 18, 2020.

UNIDIR. *Increasing Transparency, Oversight and Accountability of Armed Unmanned Aerial Vehicles*, United Nations Institute for Disarmament Research. 2017. https://unidir.org/publication/increasing-transparency-oversight-and-accountability-of-armed-unmanned-aerial-vehicles/

UNIDIR. *Armed UAVs in Conflict Escalation and Inter-State Crisis*, United Nations Institute for Disarmament Research, George Woodhams and John Borrie. 2018. https://unidir.org/wp-content/uploads/2023/05/armed-uav-in-conflict-escalation-and-inter-state-crisis-en-747.pdf

US Africa Command. "Civilian Casualty Assessment Quarterly Report; 3rd Quarter, FY2020." 2020. www.africom.mil/what-we-do/airstrikes/civilian-harm-report/us-africa-command-civilian-casualty-assessment-quarterly-report-3rd-quarter-fy2020

US Africa Command. "Press Release on Twitter, 2nd February 2020." https://tinyurl.com/bd5kxjph

US Congress. *Congressional Record*, Vol 159 (32), Senate, March 6, 2013, S1181–226. 2013.

US Congress. *Congressional Record*, Vol 159 (85), Extensions of Remarks, June 14, 2013, E861. 2013.

US Congress. *Congressional Record*, Vol 160 (95), House of Representatives, June 18, 2014, H5429–54. 2014.

US Congress. *Congressional Record*, Vol 164 (68), House of Representatives, April 26, 2018, H3643–88. 2018.

US Congress. *Congressional Record*, Vol 165 (69), Senate, April 29, 2019, S2469–84. 2019.

US Congress. *Congressional Record*, Vol 166 (208), Senate, December 9, 2020, S7296–317. 2020.

Van Vleck, Jenifer. *Empire of the Air: Aviation and the American Ascendancy*. Harvard University Press, 2013.

Villiger, Mark Eugen. *Customary International Law and Treaties: A Study of Their Interactions and Interrelations, with Special Consideration of the 1969 Vienna Convention on the Law of Treaties*. Vol. 7. Matthias Nijhoff Publishers, 1985.

Walters, William. "Everyday Secrecy: Oral History and the Social Life of a Top-Secret Weapons Research Establishment during the Cold War." *Security Dialogue* 51, no. 1 (2020): 60–76. https://doi.org/10.1177/0967010619887850

Walters, William. "Parrhēsia Today: Drone Strikes, Fearless Speech and the Contentious Politics of Security." In *Affective Economies, Neoliberalism, and Governmentality*, edited by Anne-Marie d'Aoust. Routledge, 2017.

Warren, Mark E. "Voting with Your Feet: Exit-Based Empowerment in Democratic Theory." *American Political Science Review* 105, no. 4 (2011): 683–701. https://doi.org/10.1017/S0003055411000323

Waugh, Maureen. "Quakers, Peace and the League of Nations: The Role of Bertram Pickard." *Quaker Studies* 6, no. 1 (2002): 4.

Wekker, Gloria. *White Innocence: Paradoxes of Colonialism and Race*. Duke University Press, 2016.

White House. "Open Government Directive: M10-06." 2009. https://obamawhitehouse.archives.gov/open/documents/open-government-directive

Wilke, Christiane, and Helyeh Doutaghi. "Legal Technologies: Conceptualizing the Legacy of the 1923 Hague Rules of Aerial Warfare." *Leiden Journal of International Law* 37, no. 1 (2024): 88–110. https://doi.org/10.1017/S0922156523000493

WILPF. *The Humanitarian Impact of Drones*. Women's International League for Peace and Freedom. 2017. https://article36.org/wp-content/uploads/2017/10/Humanitarian-impact-of-drones.pdf.

Windsor, Matthew. "Narrative Kill or Capture: Unreliable Narration in International Law." *Leiden Journal of International Law* 28, no. 4 (2015): 743–69. https://doi.org/10.1017/S0922156515000412

Winseck, Dwayne. "Information Operations 'Blowback': Communication, Propaganda and Surveillance in the Global War on Terrorism." *International Communication Gazette* 70, no. 6 (2008): 419–41. https://doi.org/10.1177/1748048508096141

Wolfke, K. "Some Persistent Controversies Regarding Customary International Law." *Netherlands Yearbook of International Law* 24 (December 1993): 1–16. https://doi.org/10.1017/S0167676800000027

Zappalà, Giuseppe. "Killing by Metadata: Europe and the Surveillance-Targeted Killing Nexus." *Global Affairs*, The European Union and Armed Drones, vol. 1, no. 3 (2015): 251–58. https://doi.org/10.1080/23340460.2015.1080035

Index

EU authorised representative for GPSR:
Easy Access System Europe, Mustamäe tee 50,
10621 Tallinn, Estonia
gpsr.requests@easproject.com

www.ingramcontent.com/pod-product-compliance
Ingram Content Group UK Ltd.
Pitfield, Milton Keynes, MK11 3LW, UK
UKHW021833100926
8556IPUK00004B/325
* 9 7 8 1 5 2 6 1 6 9 5 3 2 *